OTHER BOOKS BY MORT ROSENBLUM

Olives

Secret Life of the Seine

Who Stole the News?

The Abortion Pill
(with Etienne-Emile Baulieu)

Moments of Revolution
(with David and Peter Turnley)

Back Home

Squandering Eden
(with Doug Williamson)

Mission to Civilize

Coups and Earthquakes

A Goose in Toulouse

A Goose in Toulouse

and Other Culinary Adventures
in France

Mort Rosenblum

HYPERION

New York

Library of Congress Cataloging-in-Publication Data
Rosenblum, Mort.
    A goose in Toulouse : and other culinary adventures in France /Mort
Rosenblum.
        p.   cm.
    Includes index.
    ISBN 0-7868-6465-6
        1. Gastronomy.   2. Toulouse (France)—Description and travel.
3. Toulouse (France)—Social life and customs.   I. Title.
TX637.R678   2000
641'.01'3—dc21   00-039656

Designed by Cassandra J. Pappas

FIRST EDITION

10 9 8 7 6 5 4 3 2 1

For Elise Rosenblum Light,
beloved sister,
who never stopped finding new ways to give.

Acknowledgments

A glance at the cascade of business cards, letters, and stained scraps of butcher paper beneath my desk suggests that I'll make a hash of these acknowledgments. Uncounted people have helped me put this book together, beginning with Raymond Thuilier, the old man in Les Baux who got me hooked on good French food half a lifetime ago.

But some specific debts are due, with particular gratitude. Molly O'Neill helped me shape the concept. Geri Thoma, my agent, believed in it; Leigh Haber, my editor, made it happen. Mary Scarvalone's drawings gave it flair and beauty. Bill Patrick lent me his highly skilled ear. Gretchen Hoff, Michèle Aulagnon, Debbie Seward, Nancy Harmon Jenkins, Claudia McQuillian, Dariane Pictet, Edward Behr, Hazel Young, Ari Weinzweig, Paul Theroux, Phil Cousineau, Chris Dickey, Pat Thompson, and Jim Bitterman peppered me with good ideas. And I owe much to research by Rebecca Prime, Linda White, Daphné Benoit, Paula Wasley, and *la famille* Baudin.

My sister and the family pie queen, Jane Kay, retained enthusiasm for the manuscript no matter how many times I cornered her and demanded: Read this.

For a reporter, this is one of those happy situations where just about all sources can be named. The thanks I owe, and offer, are evident in the text. French people, I've found, are often reluctant to be identified when making critical remarks. Not, however, where food is concerened.

The mother of all *mercis* belongs to my pal, Froggy, Jérôme Delay; to his parents, Jean-Pierre and Annie; to his cousins, Michèle and Françoise; and to the rest of the Delay clan. Also, to the Romanas of Ampus. In France, one learns nothing from the outside looking in. Because of generosity by the Delays and the Romanas, I was able to look outward from inside happy family circles.

And finally, my debt to Jeannette Hermann Rosenblum is so great that I won't attempt to characterize it. She held firm during endless hours of angst and never even got to taste Bernard Loiseau's truffle-scented Bresse chicken. Of course, she did try Georges Blanc's.

M. R.

Contents

A Goose in Toulouse

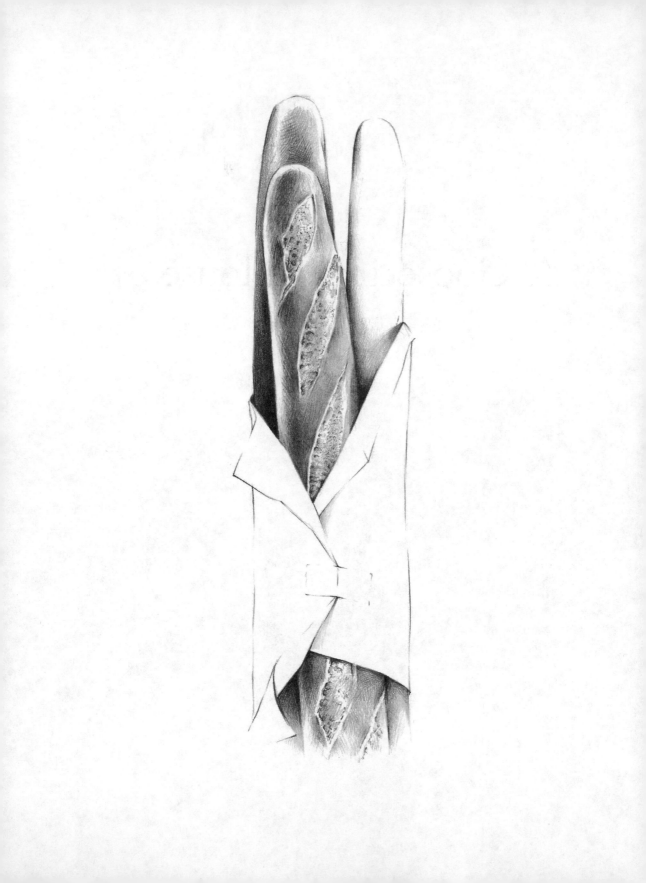

———⟨⟨⟩⟩———

ONE

A God in France

"The destiny of nations depends upon how they feed themselves
... The pleasure of the table reigns among other pleasures, and it is
the last to console when others are lost."
— *Anthelme Brillat-Savarin*

"In France, one dines. Everywhere else, one eats."
— *Montesquieu*

ONLY IN FRANCE could a loaf of bread come with a technical support
phone number and an instruction manual thick with philosophy. Lionel
Poilâne, who produces such bread, would be a mere baker in any other
country. To the French, he is a national treasure, an artist whose medium
is a 100-ton oven. In his black velvet string tie and gray workman's smock,
tossing his Prince Valiant hair to punctuate a point, he assures a nation of
a mere 60 million inhabitants that they still hold the lantern for billions
of less enlightened mortals.

"Bread is the soul of civilization," Poilâne remarked one morning in
the seat of his empire, a little redbrick *boulangerie* on the rue du Cherche-
Midi. That is, a people can be defined by their daily bread and the quality
of meals they create around it.

It is hardly news that the words food and French are inseparable. Back when heads were piling up in baskets in a Paris square, and revolution in France shook the world as nothing had before, a pudgy, balding savant reminded citizens to keep their priorities straight. Great human events are fine, Anthelme Brillat-Savarin observed, but let's not forget lunch.

Literature that followed stirred imaginations everywhere, but France's great writers were often happier with a fork than a pen. "The only irritating thing about eating," Alexandre Dumas *père* remarked, "is that when you are done, you are no longer hungry."

French society revolves around greengrocers who know each of their tomatoes personally and cheese sellers who can spend half an hour discussing the pros and cons of a particular slab of brie. On New Year's Eve, whatever the rest of the world does to celebrate, the French sit at large tables and eat themselves senseless. While others wondered where to be on December 31, 1999, Frenchmen were deciding which bottles of wine they would open.

Not long ago, northwestern France flooded, and television cameras found an old man who saw the worst of it. He told of crops under water, drowned animals, buildings swept away. But he kept his priorities straight. A lot of people pitched in to help, he concluded, "and we were seventeen at lunch."

The rise of French grandeur owes more to kings' and emperors' chefs than to their generals. Its decline is measured by lines at Pizza Hut. No economic indicator is more reliable than the aisles at Fauchon, the temple of fine food that stocks more mustards than there are days in a year. An improbably fabulous dessert of *tomate confit farcie aux douze saveurs* at Alain Passard's Arpège is enough to excuse any rudeness from the Paris cabbie who brought you there.

Over centuries, the dinner table has remained an anchor for families and friendships, the heart of what is finest about France. Each course requires separate effort, part of a whole. Children learn their values and their manners at mealtime. Nothing important gets signed, sealed, or delivered without the clinking of glasses and the rattling of cutlery.

And nothing is so sacred as Sunday lunch. In French, you only have to say "*dimanche midi*." The eating part goes without saying.

• • •

GOOD FOOD, with all the *art de vivre* around it, was partly why I moved to Paris in 1977. For my first real taste of France, I rented a fat, fish-faced Citroën with cushy seats, and I headed south. North, east, or west would have been just as good. But I had heard a lot about Raymond Thuilier and his three-star *auberge*, L'Oustau de Baumanière at Les Baux-de-Provence, a medieval village atop starkly beautiful mini-mountains, Les Alpilles. By the fifth course, with desserts, coffee, and *digestif* yet to come, it was clear I would not leave France any time soon. And the food itself was not the half of it.

A friend and I had been shown to a sun-splashed table by the tinkling waters of the pool fountain. The maître d'hôtel, untroubled by layers of grime from our morning of castle-crawling, displayed exquisite courtesy.

We each looked at the menu. I saw duckling with lime and luscious red mullet afloat in basil-laced olive oil. My friend, an artist from Vermont, saw the *chef-propriétaire*'s vivid paintings on the cover and his delicate calligraphy. I eyed the cheeses and pastries on trolleys in the corner. She noticed the spray of flowers on our table, lush purple irises tucked among yellow jonquils, every blossom bursting with life. Had the crisp linen not soon picked up ruby wine spots, we might have gone snow-blind.

It was genuinely, non-metaphorically perfect. Waiters guided patrons toward a symphonic meal with subtle lifts of the eyebrow or flickers at the corner of the mouth. Silver and crystal glinted in the sun. Each sprig of thyme at the edge of a plate had passed someone's rigorous inspection.

So many elements had been put together by the bald, slightly bashful octogenarian at the heart of it all, Raymond Thuilier, that it almost seemed as if he was responsible for the overwhelming pièce de résistance that loomed high above us. And in a way, he was.

Perched on a limestone outcropping, the ruins of Les Baux castle sheltered as many ghosts and myths per square foot as any place in the Old World. This was where troubadours played the big time, and highborn ladies of surpassing beauty decreed in the Courts of Love that marriage should be no obstacle to amorous dalliance.

Medieval barons of Les Baux traced their nobility back to Balthazar, one of the gift-bearing Wise Men, and a Nativity star radiated on their armor to make the point. But a jealous King Louis XIII tore down the walls in 1632, and gave the fiefdom to Monaco. Two centuries later, someone discovered aluminum, giving the world the term *bauxite*, and gouging deep, ugly cuts in the dramatic landscape.

At the turn of the century, an English traveler found the village to be no more than a handful of squalid beggars, with a Hôtel de Monaco that offered no beds and nothing worth eating.

Thuilier, then an insurance salesman and son of a railway engineer, happened by in 1941. He loved to paint, and the light thrilled him. He couldn't sell enough insurance, or paintings, but he had spent a childhood watching his mother cook in the station cafe she ran. Like a lot of Frenchmen, he often fed his friends at home. So at age fifty-one, at the height of war, in the ruins of an olive oil mill, he created one of the finest restaurant-hotels that France, and therefore the world, had ever known.

By the time I got there in the seventies, the path was well-beaten to his door. The Shah of Iran had just flown in a crowd to celebrate the 2,500th anniversary of his empire. Thuilier, however, was unaffected. He showed us around with the humble pride of someone who knew the underlying master plan. Not his, but His.

"God was clever," Thuilier liked to say, tapping himself first on the throat, then the forehead. "He placed the brain so near the gullet."

This was low-tech France, when it was still hard to get a phone line, but Thuilier's kitchen had what mattered. The marble pastry counters were cooled to exact temperatures. A *salamandre* grilled the top of a fish to a tasty crisp. The wine cellar was all musty charm. In the auberge rooms, each furnished with antiques, guest beds were made up in sheets designed by the chef.

The old man rose at dawn to energize the Baumanière and also his other less costly restaurant down the road. Late at night, when the last pots were dry, he slept. Mornings were spent at the Hôtel de Ville, since he was also the mayor of Les Baux. As a ruler in the realm of food, he wore the ancient mantle of a barony he had restored to life.

DURING THE NEXT quarter century in close proximity to the French, I rocketed through the foreigner's usual love-'em, hate-'em stages, but experience confirmed what was obvious from that first taste. Good food, with all that is behind it, is the defining metaphor of France.

France is a feast, all right, but there is nothing movable about it. Its richness is a broad blend of ingredients, artfully put together and laid out with purpose. Taken individually, some aspects are about as pleasant as a mouthful of raw garlic. Together, it all works to exhilarating effect.

It is simply a matter of point of view. Even before the new American virility drug was approved in France, a chef in the Alps smuggled a supply from Switzerland to make "beef piccata in Viagra sauce with fig vinegar and fine herbs." Pfizer declared, "The objective of a medicine is not to be in a sauce." But the New Jersey drugmakers were wrong. In France, one way or another, everything is a sauce.

I saw that to appreciate the French, a foreigner had to keep in mind the same three cardinal rules for enjoying a fine French meal: Remember that France is essentially *prix fixe* with *service*, such as it is or isn't, *compris*. Take things on the terms offered, without asking too many questions or demanding substitutions. And, always, eat the cheese.

Encroachment by microwaves and McDonald's has not altered the proprietary notions that the French hold over anything edible. This extends from star chefs in Paris to housewives on backstreets in Béziers. Most would rather reveal to foreigners the location of missile sites than the secret of keeping an endive safe from bitterness (don't get it wet).

Something new does not threaten, it is simply digested. Fast-food burgers came to France just before I did, and I stopped with a friend at a local franchise on the Lyon *autoroute*. She was from Idaho, a "catsup" state. That's what she requested.

"*Comment?*" demanded the teenaged girl behind the counter. "*C'est quoi,* catsup?"

"You know, for the fries," my friend said. "*Sauce tomate.*"

"Ah," the girl replied. Correcting my friend's French with a slight condescending sneer, she said, "*Vous voulez dire:* ketchup."

Ketchup soon joined the everyday vernacular along with doughnut and double cheese. When something suddenly flows smoothly after some sort of obstacle, that is *l'effet ketchup*.

When I first got to Paris, the only place to find tacos was in my kitchen. Now they are everywhere, sort of. A French taco, known as *un tacos*, is usually lettuce, some cheese, meaty bolognese sauce, and a sweet tomato salsa piled onto a flat tortilla. How else could you eat it with a fork, as any Frenchman can tell you is the proper way to do it?

The French have plenty that is all their own. Producing superlative edibles for centuries has made up the framework of socioeconomic structures. Roquefort, for instance, is not merely cheese. It is a complex network of shepherds, dairymen, *fromagers*, geologists, hewers and haulers, and business executives. New space-age industries may have nothing to do with food, but, when dinnertime rolls around, watch how the salaries are spent.

Frenchmen also love ideas. A standard encyclopedia of homegrown intellectuals runs to 1,200 pages. And none of them meet to muse without at least a Proustian madeleine.

And politics. France remains a world power. Yet for all the effort François Mitterrand put into defining his place in history, what many Frenchmen remember most is a last supper described in a biography by Georges-Marc Benamou. Nearly gone with prostate cancer, Mitterrand called in close friends for a final forbidden feast.

The president began with oysters, flat *belons*, not too salty, the way he liked them. He had called from a state visit to Egypt to be sure they arrived. Alone in a corner, he ate a dozen, then another, and then, pausing briefly to let pass a spasm of pain, yet another.

More food came before it was time for the *ortolans*, a finch-like bunting from southwest France treasured for tender flesh but a fiercely protected endangered species. His old pal Henri Emmanuelli had brought a dozen, and they were served by a gendarme.

The small band dined as the court did at Versailles, with large napkins masking their faces to hide the grisly gnawing and spitting of tiny bones. Some guests declined diplomatically; diners outnumbered birds. The rest attacked with frenzied relish, each occasionally peeking from behind his cloth to see if anyone got an extra ortolan.

"François Mitterrand emerged first from behind his steaming napkin," Benamou wrote. "Overcome with happiness, his eye sparkling, his glance full of gratitude toward Emmanuelli." One bird remained in the hot oil, and the gendarme-waiter circled the table. When he reached Mitterrand, the bird was still there. The president speared it.

All told, Mitterrand ate thirty oysters, foie gras, a slice of capon, and two ortolans. Not long after, he passed into history.

Brillat-Savarin would have loved that last supper, as much for its meaning as its menu. For him, few pursuits measured up to savoring culinary pleasure. "The invention of a new dish," he wrote in *The Physiology of Taste*, "brings more to the good of mankind than the discovery of a new star."

Roland Barthes noted: "The discourse on food is like a grillwork window frame, in front of which strolls by each of the sciences that we call social or human." And Pierre Gaxette took the idea to its logical extension.

"*La cuisine*," he wrote, "is not a bad observatory for studying *la Grande Histoire*."

But if the rise of French civilization could be measured by the knife and fork, so could its fall. And, as the millennium waned and a new sort of world took shape, warning signs were clear.

I had heard reports of France's culinary demise since first moving to Paris. Increasingly, casual conversations revealed distressing testimony. Monsieur Turpin, my friend the Île Saint-Louis fruit-and-fowl man, retired in disgust. When I last saw him, he was glumly singeing pinfeathers off a pheasant, his walrus moustache bristling with indignation. "*Ces gens-là*," he muttered, jerking an elbow toward a cluster of young French people shambling past, "they are eating while they walk."

During the 1970's, one had to work hard to find a bad meal in France. By the 1990's, it took no trouble at all. Now it seemed that everywhere I looked, someone was fretting over the future. France would dissolve into a mere bouquet of flavors in a stockpot known as the European Union. Worse, the juggernaut of "globalization" would trample historic borders, obliterate ancient customs, dilute a unique society, and leave only ubiquitous golden arches where great restaurants had been.

The glories of France were rooted in the kitchens of Versailles, so prodigious that when Louis XIV died the royal coroner found a stomach twice the size of your average eighteenth-century glutton's. Now vendors sell hot dogs at the gates of Versailles, and French tourists track melted ice-cream goo across its polished courtyard stones.

Was the Sun King's radiance finally in eclipse? Did this, I wondered, mean France was finished?

ROBERT DANTCIKIAN, a butcher with a bedside manner, purveys choice cuts in the Provence city of Draguignan. His small shop jams solid on Saturday mornings when townsfolk and villagers from all over the Haut Var come to market. Handsome and hearty, he always seems amused. For a Parisian lady in gaudy gold, he trusses rich red filet mignons. With equal care and affectionate teasing, he slices veal thinly for an old widow on a pension. However long the line, he asks about sons in Canada, comments on a hairdo, and listens to grumbling about local crises.

Half of Robert's customers ask him what they should have for dinner. Some want advice on cooking. All leave with something they hadn't planned to buy, cheerfully handing over 200-franc notes to Robert's wife, Jackie, who totes up bills with a pencil at computer speed.

He speaks meat. When I first explained to Robert my recipe for chili, he took time to ponder. An hour later, he handed me a kilo of hand-carved strips from just inside the ribs; he had determined that the moisture in that particular cut would best allow the beef to get tender while absorbing spices thoroughly.

By prior demand, he produces brochettes of lamb, soaked for a day in his magic marinade and sprinkled with a private mix of *herbes de Provence*. Otherwise, there is always a surprise. It might be a *daube provençale* he had spent all Sunday cooking. Or a succulent chicken that found its way south from Bresse. Once, after briefing me at length about a garlic-loaded *côte de boeuf*, Robert winked at Jackie and disappeared into the back room. His pal, the president of the Bandol wine cooperative, had just dropped off some remarkable red, and he wanted me to have a bottle to honor the steak. Each December, he keeps a chunk of *foie gras frais* for me, just in case I show up in time for a Christmas dinner.

But on that chilling morning, the surprise was an empty shop, and for once Robert was not smiling. "Business," he allowed, "is *moyen*." That translates to "average," but it means "awful." This was no surprise. French unemployment approached thirteen percent. Politicians talked darkly of cutting away at the social safety net. Across the country, Frenchmen nibbled at their small reserves and worried about what might happen next. Those with jobs or businesses worked harder and longer for less result.

"People are eating less, and they are eating cheaper," Robert said. One by one, his customers sneaked away to buy chicken legs in cellophane and Styrofoam at the Continent *hypermarché* for half the price. His butcher friends, faced with the same problem, laid off helpers. It is a simple enough calculation. If people figure they can't sit down to enjoy a meal as they know they should, why spend the extra money for the best ingredients? For a man like Robert, this is not an economic crisis. It is the end of life as he knows it.

Back in Paris, however, I went to see the artist of bread, Lionel Poilâne. His brother, Max, is also a baker, whose bread many prefer. But more than a baker, Lionel is an acknowledged curator of old French artisanry, a modern keeper of the ancient faith. He had a different viewpoint.

When I laid out the various grim scenarios I had heard for an altered state of France, he replied with a single unspellable word, something on the order of, "*Pfaff!*" A theatrical grimace filled in any doubts about its meaning.

Poilâne sells plenty of his pricey bread, which strengthens his point. He believes that respect for the old order of things, good food included, is indelibly imprinted in the collective French psyche. When I asked if he did not see an identity crisis in France—a dynamic tension between wanting to be like everyone else but different—he tossed his hair impatiently.

"That is a stupid way to put the question," he said, with a kindly smile at the fool who posed it. "I don't identify with anyone." It was understood that "I" was synonymous with France. "If I remain myself alone, then nothing can change me. I am only who I am."

This might have suggested arrogance. Yet Poilâne, the emblematic Frenchman, is humble in his way, a generous spirit, and a true believer in his art. He is merely an emblematic Frenchman.

France is under pressure, he acknowledged, but it is also at work perfecting a simple means of salvation. He calls it retro-innovation. When adopting what is new, Frenchmen must remember the value of what is old. Poilâne, son of a neighborhood baker, has gone global. Order forms in English and Japanese invite visitors to receive a round sourdough *miche* each week, or each month, at their home address. The leaflet adds, "Want to butter up a bread lover?" Only a faxed American Express number is necessary. Or, there is also an e-bread link on the Internet.

Yet with all the machinery for mass-production bread, for instance, Poilâne's dough rises in traditional straw baskets. He requires his bakers to touch every loaf.

"You must use your hands," he says, fluttering his own delicate fingers to make the point. "The hand is a marvelous thing. With it, you can spank a baby, make a sculpture, create a symphony. In the end, that is why we are different. We are a culture of hands. We use time differently than Anglo-Saxons. The Americans live to work, and the French work to live."

So there I was, with conflicting views from the butcher and the baker. (The only Frenchman I knew who made candlesticks had sold his shop to a tourist art gallery.) The question pressed: Was France as we knew it doomed to melt away, a casualty of a figurative form of global warming? Victor Hugo had once mused, "France, France, without you the world would be alone." Were we finally on our own?

True enough, France is locked in a struggle between what it wants to be and what it does not want to stop being. Frenchmen try hard to be like everyone else in a turbocharged omnicultural world of byte-sized syllables. Yet different. This would be a tricky balance for any society. For the French, it can border on a national psychosis.

Philippe Labro, a novelist who loves irony, explained it like this: "We French are incapable of making the changes in our lives that the reality of the new global economy demands. So instead we now change governments every two years and pretend we are changing our lives."

Globalization has a distinct American accent, but to the French, the U.S. model is no answer. They are troubled by America's income disparities and lack of a social safety net. They worry when French kids kill people, or themselves, in the name of imported American cults. *Le drive-by*, for a gang shooting, is not only a new French word but also an occasional reality. French society works. City streets are safe at night. Villagers take pride in their old stones and fresh flowers, preserving traditions for themselves rather than the tourist trade.

It is not for nothing, Frenchmen of a certain age assure themselves, that an old German metaphor denoting profound well-being manages to remain fresh: "Happy as a god in France."

Along with food, Frenchmen love the idea of free rein on the open road. All but the most deprived of modern adults share a childhood memory: piling into the family's Citroën, the kind with sofa seats and freight-elevator suspension, for Sunday lunch at a country auberge lost among flowering trees. In Germany, cars are built for speed and serious purpose, with firm seats to which starch-fed burghers are expected to bring their own padding. The French bourgeois equivalent wants comfort after a large lunch. Who else could have produced the Michelin red guide, with which families can plot a trip according to tables at the end of the trail?

All in all, it comes down to a simple Cartesian concept: "I eat, therefore I'm French."

MY FIRST EVENING ever in Paris equipped me well for observing France *à table*. I had come for a brief visit in 1967 on what happened to be the night they closed down Les Halles.

Sense had finally worn down sentimentality at the venerable central market, in the same spot for nearly nine centuries. Trucks that brought fruits and vegetables before dawn to the heart of Paris from a dozen directions snarled traffic hopelessly on their way home. Rat gangs swaggered through sewers and streets, forcing the heartiest alley cats to seek cover. Still, abrupt surgical removal of what Victor Hugo had called "the belly of Paris" could hardly fail to stagger the body politic.

Forever, every caricature of storybook Frenchmen gathered before sun-up at the vast marketplace near Saint-Eustache church. Grimy bérets made their last stand at Les Halles before grimy tweed caps muscled them aside. Each generation added dimensions, as ox-drawn carts evolved into huge refrigerated rigs.

Harsh bursts in incomprehensible dialects punctuated the steady drone of haggling in standard farmer French. Grocers, chefs, and housewives padded a regular beat under elaborate wrought-iron *pavillons Baltard* to select produce still wet with the dew of its own *terroir*. Workers in sturdy French blue coveralls gathered at all-night cafés for a restorative *coup de rouge* or a *petit marc* under the bluish haze of pungent black tobacco smoke. A row of restaurants served steaming earthenware bowls of crusted onion soup, that enduring monument to the French gift for turning leftovers like stale bread and hard cheese into something to kill for.

Just as the last truckers slammed doors and headed back to the provinces, clusters of men in suits and silk ties took their parking spots, hurrying to the ornate Commodities Exchange hard by the edge of the market, just in front of Le Chien Qui Fume café and Le Pied de Cochon restaurant. It was a traffic cop's nightmare and a throbbing headache to public health officials. But it stayed so long where it was for a simple reason. Les Halles was the holy temple of food, hallowed ground for anyone who worshipped the dinner plate. And in the 1960's, that took in just about every resident of Paris.

Les Halles did not die easily. When the last of the petitions was pushed aside, and the demolition order was signed, a giant party roiled through its condemned alleyways. I happened onto this while on the honeymoon of a marriage that had ended by the time the last remnant of the old market was finally hauled away.

Like everyone else, we started the party with dinner. Le Pied de Cochon was jammed, but the maître d' liked the honeymoon part. He produced a battered table from somewhere and threw a cloth over it. Waiters soon brought a succession of oysters, onion soup, a *sole meunière*, and chocolate mousse, the kind of simple tourist fare that makes you want to take a nine-year lease on the apartment next door.

At midnight, the wake for Les Halles was in full swing. People snake-danced and sang through the narrow streets. Students with brass instruments climbed atop the statuary in a huge fountain. Their tubas and French horns blasted "Those Were the Days." At each pause, someone tossed a bottle of wine to the musicians, often missing by several yards. Soon the old cobblestones were redder than they had been since 1789.

By the time we wandered off, the sky was beginning to lighten. We walked down to the Pont Marie, heading toward the Île Saint-Louis, and watched the dawn paint tinges of pink and orange on the Seine. Parisians slept peacefully behind their shutters. The upheaval of 1968 was a year away. McDonald was just another Scottish surname. France was France. Those were the days, all right.

FOR A THOROUGH LOOK at French tastes, going back a century, I had Michelin. A whole series of green Michelin guides, everyone knows, is immensely useful for learning about how Louis the Flatulent outflanked Richard the Wheezer somewhere up the Somme. The Bible, however, is red.

The first Michelin Guide was published in 1900, a slim volume that was free, *"offert gracieusement aux chauffeurs."* It already had those familiar symbols for restaurants and hotels, along with others to help motorists locate a telephone or a rare garage. A twenty-one page section examined the mysteries of inner tubes and how to repair them. The guide began, "This work appeared with the century, and it will last it out." It has kept that promise.

Now the red guide runs to 1,700 pages. These days, it costs twenty-five dollars and still loses money. Only its small staff of anonymous experts is trusted for evaluation, and they never reveal who they are. Demotion from three stars to two drove one chef to suicide, and others to despair. Bestowing a first lone star to a remote eatery seldom fails to change radically the life of its restaurateur, for better or worse. Even more, a second and a third.

I looked through the faded first edition and the gleaming crimson tome stamped 1998, side by side, looking for a place to start. I wanted a three-star chef whom the French hold in godlike reverence, in a historic site of gastronomic glory. It took only a moment to settle on Saulieu, an old coach stop on the road from southern France to Paris.

The first Michelin had a single listing, the Hôtel de la Poste. A star next to it meant only that meals cost between seven and ten francs, wine included. Several decades of guides later, Michelin would add the Hôtel de la Côte d'Or, where Alexandre Dumaine earned the first real stars and held them throughout the 1950's and 1960's. The Hôtel de la Poste, next door, had won its own stars. Saulieu was a holy site for French food pilgrims.

During the 1970's, Saulieu's galaxy dimmed. The Hôtel de la Poste slipped to merely very good, a death blow by standards of the time. The Côte d'Or sank so low that its chef opened cans to make lobster bisque. In those dark days, a new owner, Bernard Loiseau, vowed to cook his way to lasting glory.

Writers like to call Loiseau "Bernard the Bird." If you inject an apostrophe after the "L," that is what the name means. He does tend to flap his arms when swooping down on a hapless *sous-chef* a shade below perfection. But the image conjures up a Little Sparrow, a mere tragic slip of a cabaret singer who pecks at her food. Physically, Loiseau is closer to Big Bird, a jovial and solidly built presence with an endearing goofy smile. Unless, of course, when angry. Then he is an Andean condor on final approach.

Loiseau is a textbook French culinary success story. He started, as most chefs do, as a galley slave to a famed master. In his case, it was Pierre Troisgros of Roanne, who, as a departing reference, muttered, "If this kid ever becomes a chef, I'll be an archbishop." Loiseau scraped together enough money to buy what was left of the Côte d'Or. Meal by meal, he set about putting the place back on the map.

The first star came relatively fast, followed in time by the second. But the third took twelve years. At first Loiseau lived monklike in a room above the kitchen, sallying forth at dawn to shop and staying up well past midnight to fret about his bills. By the time Michelin bestowed the treasured final star, and the old stage stop reverberated with popping corks, his name was made. He borrowed eight million dollars and put it to good use.

These days, the simple Auberge du Relais across the street offers a perfectly good dinner for twenty-five dollars, and it is usually empty. At La Côte d'Or, where the bill can easily surpass two hundred dollars a person, tables book solid weeks, if not months, in advance.

"No, good French cooking is not in peril," Loiseau pronounced. Circumstances were changing, but not the bedrock. "Okay, so often people are in a hurry and only have time to wolf down a sandwich, even a Big Mac," he said. "But the idea of dressing up, going out, celebrating a birthday or a marriage, that is sacred."

The European Union does not scare Loiseau. "I am all for enlarging Europe, but does that mean I'll be speaking German?" he declaimed, flapping his arms for emphasis. "Never. We are French, attached to our roots, and that will not change."

And the subject of omnicultural cooking, known in France as *le World Cuisine*, brought a furious beating of the air. "Let people eat what they want, but they should also have what they know and love. Can you imagine a Thai restaurant in Saulieu? Hah! In fact, all of these outside influences have made us cling more tightly to our basic resources. My goal is to capture that wonderful sense of our grandmothers' cooking and refine it. To know the present, you must know the past."

Loiseau's grandmother might not have recognized the four-hour lunch that followed, but she would have loved it. The pièce de résistance was something on the lines of boiled chicken, what *grand-mère* knew as *poule au pot*. But not exactly.

Poularde Alexandre Dumaine is Loiseau's tribute to his predecessor. It requires a tender Bresse chicken. Farmers from Bresse, near Lyon, produce what Brillat-Savarin called, "the queen of fowl, the poultry of kings." He was not exaggerating. Henri IV conquered Bresse in 1601 and raved about the chickens. The bird is stuffed with carrots, leeks, and its own liver. Black truffle slices are slipped under its skin. Then it is steamed at length over a blended stock of chicken and beef and vegetables, flavored with port and brandy.

Two waiters brought the clay pot to the serving table, with towels wrapped tightly around the lid to keep steam from escaping. One whipped off the top, infusing the large dining room with its aroma. The entire room froze—forks in midair, glasses touching lips, sentences left half spoken—and every set of eyes was fixed on Bernard Loiseau's version of poule au pot.

I would be back for more questions. And more chicken.

———

ALONG WITH *le world* cuisine, of course, there is *le world* everything else. "Frenchmen" is no longer much use as a collective noun. For one thing, there is the language. Molière's proud tongue, which took such pleasure in probing intimate places of the mouth to make sounds only the chosen few could get right, is now dangerously diluted. Not long ago, most Frenchmen would not speak English to foreigners even if they could. Now, many insist on speaking English even if they can't.

Americanisms are everywhere. One night, I watched *NYPD Blue* in English on a French channel called Jimmy and noticed the subtitles. "Let's play it by ear," an amorous cop told his love interest. That was translated, *"On va au feeling."* A television game show is named *Le Bigdil.* "The Big Deal." One popular phrase, pronounced *"ze apifiou,"* refers to a privileged minority. That is, "the happy few." Menus are often multilingual, even if approximate. One in Aix-en-Provence described a salad: "lettuce, tomato, egg, lawyer." *Avocat,* the French word for avocado, also means attorney.

Studies show any number of shifts. A decade ago, the average Frenchman spent ninety minutes at the lunch table. Now the figure is closer to half an hour. Wine consumption is dropping. Children show a surprising slide toward obesity. Older people travel more, and farther. Young people are less reluctant to settle abroad to find work.

France is even changing color. Though obvious enough in daily life, this hit home when France hosted the 1998 World Cup soccer tournament and, to everyone's shock, beat Brazil to win it. Within minutes of the final whistle, the Champs-Élysées was blocked solid with a million hugging, yelling, leaping bodies. As World Cup victors do, they chanted, "We are the champions!" But they also roared a cheer with the cadence of a train engine: *"Tous ensemble, tous ensemble."* All of us together.

The French team was called *Les Bleus,* The Blues, but its colors ranged from gleaming ebony to Saint-Tropez suntan to a light shade of pale. A France that had gone into the tournament deeply divided over race and immigration policy was suddenly color-blind. Only blue, white, and red registered on the scale.

The hero playmaker who scored two goals was Zinedine Zidane, born and raised in a nasty Marseille suburb, the son of an Algerian night watchman. No anti-immigrant bonehead wanted to send him back to North Africa, at least not before the 2002 games. Lilian Thuram, from the French Caribbean island of Guadeloupe, scored twice in the semifinal against Croatia. And even diehard white supremacists of the National Front chanted, "Thuram Pré-si-dent."

Commentators drew the obvious conclusions. Max Gallo, an author and thinker whose favorite theme is unifying the French against all odds, wrote: "We all shivered, amazed, because these voices weren't of violence, revenge, aggression, xenophobia, but of enthusiasm, of joy, of pride. And of youth. . . . This France that exulted was not embittered, aging, hateful, racist, consumed by its fears, closed, suspicious, but welcoming, open, and patriotic."

But euphoria subsided. And in France, there is always the other extreme. Within weeks of the World Cup parties, the editor of the *National Hebdo*, a weekly close to National Front leader Jean-Marie Le Pen, prescribed "police raids and concentration camps" to solve the problem of illegal immigration. Hitler, he observed, was merely pushed to such means by an inferior race who gave him no choice.

One lunch hour in Paris soon after the World Cup, I watched a small but noisy demonstration of Asians demanding papers to stay in France. I mentioned this to the butcher-caterer who often fed me at midday, a salt-of-the-earth Frenchman with easy humor but firm opinions. This, he replied, was significant.

"They always used to shut up, peaceful, and not make trouble," he said, referring to Vietnamese and Cambodians whose nations once belonged to France. "Like the Portuguese used to be. Never heard a peep out of them. Docile."

"What does that mean?" I asked, surprised at his vehement reaction.

"It means they're eating too well. We're giving them too much. They got nothing else to do, this new generation, so they open their big mouths. We ought to kill them all, and we'll have a little peace."

He was not joking. Evidently, he saw the twitch in my unsuccessful poker face.

"That's not pretty," he said, his face harder than I'd ever seen it, "but that's how it is."

My now-former butcher was certainly not part of any majority. But neither was he alone.

In the end, I realized, "Frenchmen" for the outsider's purposes still means what it always has, an undefinable bouquet of national characteristics, each reinforced or cancelled out depending upon whom one comes across and under what circumstances.

Edith Wharton took a stab at describing this in an essay from France in 1919. She recalled this passage from an old guidebook depicting the people of remote Mediterranean islands she had approached years earlier:

"The inhabitants are brave, hospitable, and generous, but fierce, treacherous, vindictive, and given to acts of piracy, robbery, and wreckage."

That, Wharton said, caught the contradictory French spirit exactly. And she concluded: "No civilized race has gone as unerringly as the French toward the natural sources of enjoyment; none has been so unashamed of instinct. Yet none has been more enslaved by social conventions, small complicated observances based on long-past conditions of life. No race has shown more collective magnanimity on great occasions, more pettiness and hardness in small dealings between individuals.... No people are more capable of improvising greatness, yet more afraid of the least initiative in ordinary matters. No people are more skeptical and more religious, more irritable and nervous, yet more capable of a long patience and a dauntless calm."

IF PARIS WAS particularly long on the irritable and nervous, I found balancing patience and dauntless calm in the back pocket of Provence where I retreat regularly to tend olive trees. My mountainside neighbors grow food on rocky ground, raise food in hutches or flocks, pick food off trees, hunt food in dense forests, dig up food under old oaks, or collect food where it crawls at a snail's pace. And all of them eat food with consuming passion.

Down the hill in Draguignan, small-city dwellers shop for food at the Saturday market exactly as their forebears did for more generations than anyone's memory can span. The Saturday market is a microcosm of a bigger France beyond. "Le Breton" sells fresh fish from a converted van that looks as if it just happened to stop while passing through. He has been there twenty-five years and still stays up to date on news of the fleet off the faraway Brittany coast. Bernard André, the Savoyard cheese man, each week comes up with something new to try. "Ah, a tasty cheese, a fine wine," he declaims with a silly grin, "what more could the people want?"

Just as it always has, the Saturday market brings old friends together to catch up on the gossip. Françoise Romana, well into her eighties, seldom fails to come down with her son, Jeannot, and a load of homegrown potatoes, chick peas, leeks, melons, and eggs. Next to her stand, Yves Van Weddingen, a young Belgian who left his suit and tie in Brussels, sells his goat cheese.

From sunup to noon, the marketplace is packed, throbbing with its vital purpose: to provide families from miles around with the ingredients for Sunday lunch.

My little farm, Wild Olives, is situated well for a look at non-Paris, France. And there is another advantage: It attracts friends and curious visitors whose own expertise offers illumination for my half-seen insights. Ari Weinzweig, for instance.

Ari runs Zingerman's Delicatessen in Ann Arbor, which applies funky science to everything from pastrami to truffle oil. He is particularly up on cheese. Before dawn one morning, we rocketed down the A8 autoroute toward Nice Airport discussing the Teutonic tendency to ban raw milk cheese, at least within the European Union. This, of course, is generally a needless precaution and a potential death blow to France's best cheeses. It was early, and we were late. Cheese laws could wait.

I dropped Ari at the airport and took the long way home. It was barely 6:00 A.M. on Sunday, and on a tape, the Eagles were singing "Tequila Sunrise." Soon I saw a Pastis Sunrise over the Mediterranean. It was magnificent. As the dark blue-gray dawn turned to day, through a range of pinks and oranges, the Côte d'Azur slowly woke up.

In Antibes and St.-Juan-les-Pins, only the bakeries were open. I could smell each before I saw it. A few trucks delivered fresh fish; others carried the day's newspapers to wrap them in. The air was fresh and clear, warm for early April, and there was not a jogger in sight. The odd hound was being walked, and some families made their way toward church.

Just before seven o'clock, I was on the narrow coastal road to Cannes. I'd had a *pain au chocolat,* still warm from the oven, and a shot of jet-black coffee. Morning light revealed wisteria in deep purple, and irises in the same hues. White yachts bobbed in port, and the sea sparkled beyond.

Up ahead, a battered little Peugeot wagon poked along in the single westbound lane. My own Peugeot was straining at the harness. This is a noble old mount, a 504 convertible that I've had since it came off the line in 1979. It is metallic brown and named, for reasons I've forgotten, Jaws.

Ol' Jaws had already done 125,000 kilometers of autoroutes and backroads, but that morning he was clearly eager for more. Each time the station wagon ahead of me slowed to take a gentle curve, Jaws's motor growled with impatience. I prevailed, however, and kept him cool. When we eventually passed the wagon, I was happy to have given the driver a break.

At the wheel was a gray-haired man in a pressed shirt, the sort of old duffer the French call *pépère*. Whatever he was thinking about, it wasn't speed. The backseat was piled high with bags. My bet was they were full of food, and he was headed to his granddaughter's for Sunday lunch. He was looking at the flowers, the water, and life in general, happy as a god in France.

TWO

Feeding Time at Froggy's

"WATCH WHAT YOU SAY to this dope," Jean-Pierre Delay yelled across to his neighbors when I dropped by his stone house in Saint-Restitut, in the lush Rhône country near Grignan and Nyons. "He's a damned American, here to write about French cooking. Trying to steal our secrets, suck away our spirit, bring us those disgusting hamburgers—"

"Welcome!" a friendly looking middle-aged man hollered back, rolling his eyes at the tirade.

Delay nearly exemplifies why the French came up with the word *rouspéter*. Harrap's dictionary offers "to resist, grumble, gripe, grouse, bellyache, protest; to show fight," and none of those definitions does remote justice to a first-rate French rouspéteur. But Delay does not quite pull it off. He is too nice a guy. Even in his finest hour, a veiled self-mocking grin lurks where a poker face should be. As he did this time, he usually breaks into a throaty laugh before the rouspéteur's requisite coup de grâce insult.

Delay does far better in his role as *père de famille*, and that is why I am there. Fatherhood in France means only peripherally having one's own children. Mainly, it defines the man at the head of the table who carves the goose finely enough to serve however many relatives and friends show up for dinner.

In his sixties, Delay is the patriarch of a family that spans France and also, at any given moment, everywhere from the Khyber Pass to the Mosquito Coast. As luck would have it, he is the father of Jérôme Delay—Froggy to his friends—the admirable photographer with whom I cover distant mayhem for the Associated Press. Over time, I oozed into honorary membership in the clan. This is a particular treat at feeding time. Even more, I realized, this family tie brought into focus my two decades of French-watching.

France is made up of separate regions, from vast former duchies like Normandy, Burgundy, or Provence to tiny old fiefdoms with sharply defined boundaries invisible to the outsider's naked eye. But subtle subcultures and societal dysfunctions make generality based on regions a risky business. Static geography is all wrapped up with daily life, a long-simmered stock of traditions, tastes, alliances, and enmities.

Therefore, you can't handily divide France up into large sectors such as the Northeast, the Midwest, and the South. Instead, think in terms of breakfast, lunch, and dinner. And these are best appreciated from within the circle of a family that is all over the map.

Jean-Pierre was born near Valence, in the bosom of Rhône wine country. His father worked for the railway, but Jean-Pierre decided to teach. At school in the Ardèche, he met Annie Blondelet, from deepest Burgundy, whose father was a hero of the French Resistance. They married and found jobs in Cosne, a few miles from Sancerre on the Loire. That is where Jérôme was born.

All of this family lore came out slowly, over time, almost invariably in the presence of good food.

I first met Annie's mother, Paule Blondelet, over a satellite phone from Sarajevo under siege. I had just flown in to join Froggy, hauling a duffel bag of essentials in short supply: *saucisson d'Auvergne, pâté de campagne,* foie gras, fresh coriander and basil, a tolerably soft Camembert. Before preparing dinner for our colleagues, we called Paule at her home near Saulieu for her crêpe recipe.

Months later, we stopped by her assisted-living apartment in Saulieu, a little studio in a complex of older people with time on their hands. Warned she would have company, Paule was perfectly powdered and rouged, hair tidily set and curled. We talked about politics and a France gone by. Mostly, we reviewed her diet and the beloved dishes she was forbidden to enjoy. When I asked what she would have if allowed anything, her face settled into a beatific smile.

"A huge platter of *fruits de mer*," she said. For a moment, conversation stopped as her fantasy tract played on a crushed-ice mound spilling over with belon and *fine de claire* oysters, mussels, large clams and smaller *praires*, sea urchins, saltwater crayfish, and those tiny, tasty shrimp known as *crevettes grises*.

I met Christian, Jean-Pierre's brother, in a patch of France he created in Venice, California. He and his American wife, Joanna, ran the French Market Cafe, which served meals and packaged delicacies no Frenchman abroad can survive without. Christian was a perfect deadpan Delay. His glasses suggested a serious demeanor, and his face reflected subtle twitches of ironic humor.

"Would you like to order something, or shall I just feed you?" he asked. Silly question. A fabulous foie gras with a sweet Sauternes was followed by *confit de canard* in garlic-laced sauteed potatoes. Fresh salad leaves were dressed exquisitely in an olive-oil vinaigrette. The Côte du Rhône red had just enough snap for a lazy afternoon. At nearby tables, young Frenchmen in fashionably ample trousers smoked smelly black tobacco and read *Paris Match* borrowed from a wooden rack of nearly current Paris papers.

Christian beamed. *"C'est l'Ardèche,"* he said, and it very nearly was. Soon afterward, he sold the cafe and came home to the Rhône to think about what to do next. At last check, he was still thinking, on a beach in Mexico.

Mostly, I met the family at Jean-Pierre's retirement *quartier-général*, a medieval village house in Saint-Restitut, just off the Rhône River where the Drôme gives way to Provence. It is near the rich little town of Saint-Paul-Les-Trois-Châteaux, where his aunt, Tante Puce, has dispensed unforgettable meals for more than half a century from the same rambling farmhouse kitchen surrounded by old fruit trees.

Cooking had come to Jean-Pierre by French osmosis. On the spur of the moment one night, he threw together a meal to remember. A decent dinner is hardly surprising from a chef who spends half his life studying his craft and, with a bank loan, builds an elaborate kitchen and hires skilled hands to help. More impressive is when some poor guy's son asks him at the last minute to feed a dozen friends, and all he has is a stone sink, a crate of tomatoes, and a village grocery shop that is closed for the day.

Jean-Pierre's pièce de résistance was *tomates farcies*, served with a perfectly dressed salad and followed by cheese.

"I suppose you're going to make me look like an idiot by giving recipes that everyone knows," he said when I asked how he prepared the meal. "All you do is go to the charcuterie to buy your *farce* (stuffing) and then you cook it in a tomato. Big deal." That, of course, did not stop him from expounding in detail, a maestro perfectly aware of what musicians of differing skills might make of the same score.

To start with, good cooks who take the logical shortcut of buying farce have got to know where to get it. Except in the remote reaches where choices are few, this is a lifelong challenge. Suitable butchers are found only by trial and error, on the strength of recommendations by trusted friends. When one is located, he must be watched for variations in humor which may affect his work. If he is thoughtless enough to retire or die, his successor must be scrutinized.

Jean-Pierre is happy with his source. The farce is a blend of ground lean pork meat, white and fresh, spiced with herbs. To this, he adds egg, garlic, and parsley.

"You have to work it with your hands," he explained, flexing his fingers as Poilâne did when figuratively kneading his dough. "Put in the whole egg and squeeze it into the mix, over and over. It feels wonderful to the touch."

With the filling set aside to rest, Jean-Pierre attacks his tomatoes. The tops are sliced off carefully and saved. Insides are emptied. Camargue sea salt is sprinkled thickly into the hollowed-out tomatoes and left for twenty minutes to absorb excess moisture. A little butter is spread into the shells.

"By now your fingers are good and greasy," Jean-Pierre said, loving it. "You place the tomatoes in a greased round pan, maybe eight or ten of them, and shape your farce into each one. Among the empty spaces, you put potatoes, peeled and cut into squares. Fit them in tight so the tomatoes can't move. Bake the pan for half an hour at 220 degrees (centigrade), then put the tomatoes' tops back on. Add a little olive oil—that's obligatory in our part of France—and cook another fifteen or twenty minutes."

As he said, big deal. No one gives stars for workaday stuffed tomatoes.

But they were a smash hit. The potatoes baked to a crisp brown exterior. They drew off just enough moisture to infuse themselves with taste and allow the tomatoes to remain firm.

The salad dressing was simpler still: vinegar, salt, garlic, mustard, oil. It's all in how you do it.

That same afternoon, Jean-Pierre and I rocketed down a country road on a wine run. We headed toward Suze-la-Rousse, yet another ancient stone town with an imposing castle perched on a steep hill above it. The restored fortress was now a wine university, famous in France for its fine tuning of advanced oenophiles. We, however, went to the wine filling station.

The large open-fronted store offered a row of six huge barrels, each with the hose and pistol grip of a gasoline pump. Customers brought their own containers, from plastic jugs to giant jerry cans. Labels announced various types of reds and rosés, with prices marked in large letters. Except for the *appellation d'origine contrôlée* Côtes du Rhône, which rang up at eight dollars a gallon, the bulk wines each cost less than five dollars a gallon, cheaper than gas.

"We're not buying that stuff," Jean-Pierre snorted from among the racks of pricier bottled Côtes du Rhône, curiously sensitive when I teased him about the gas station pumps. A sense of humor is fine, but some things are sacred.

Jean-Pierre maneuvered along the twisting two-lane blacktop, skirting tiny villages with their requisite church spire and mossy stone walls. He frowned as we passed large tracts of ancient forest cut to make room for more vines. Then he looked up and, happy again, gestured grandly toward Mount Ventoux, which rose grandly above Provence in the middle distance.

"That's my mountain," he announced with enough pride to suggest he had piled up its tree-fringed rocks all by himself. "I love this part of the country." Wherever else Jean-Pierre had roots or permanent visiting rights, this was home. He liked it all: the hard life that somehow seemed easygoing, the rich, lovely land with history predating Gauls and Romans.

Soon, with no prompting from me, the subject shifted back to food.

"Eating well is important," Jean-Pierre explained, in a rare serious mood. Since Annie commutes to a job in Paris during the week, he is often alone at mealtimes. "I try to duplicate the old flavors I remember from my mother, my aunt. The idea is simple, good family food. It's not that easy. They were wonderful cooks who spent a lot of time at it. Still, I suppose I do all right."

He had just made himself a two-pound *épaule d'agneau*, a lamb shoulder with potatoes steeped in laurel and bacon. By reducing laurel leaves with water, the potatoes cook into a *bombine*, a rich flavorful gravy.

"If friends drop in, I'm ready," Jean-Pierre said. "Then it just depends on the weather. If it's a little cool, I can heat the lamb and top it with bombine. If it's warm, I'll serve it cold, with mayonnaise or aioli. Either way, it's wonderful the next day."

Jean-Pierre's real speciality, he added, was fish.

"I do incredible fish on a bed of leeks," he said, concluding the conversation with a dismissive wave. "Maybe I'll tell you about that some other time. First I need to know what's in this for me."

SAINT-RESTITUT, by its nature, seems to demand good cooking around a family table as a requirement to residence. France is full of such heartland places, which are collectively known as *la France profonde*.

As legend has it, the village was founded about the time B.C. changed to A.D. Restitut was the blind man in the gospel whose eyes Jesus Christ healed with his own saliva. He took the Latin name Restored, to honor his new sight. Then he set off westward in a boat with neither oars nor a sail to wash up in the Camargue, a popular landing site of the day for holy pilgrims.

Restitut made his way to Saint-Paul-Les-Trois Châteaux, not far from the Roman stronghold at Vaison. He then moved on to build a fortified chapel at Saint-Restitut, near Stone Age ruins, from where he dispensed spiritual guidance to the region around.

A new church was built eleven centuries later, and it remains in fine condition. Its Provençal-Romanesque walls are thick and sturdy, decorated at the top by stone friezes. A tower over the crypt rises above the red tile roof. Sculpted capitals top columns flanking the elaborately arched doorway. The tiny structure, somehow squat from the outside, is in perfect proportion within. Jean-Pierre fell in love with the village for the local bistro, Annie says, but she followed him there for that thirteenth-century church.

"The French love their old stones," Annie told me. Her job is helping to preserve national patrimony for the Ministry of Culture. "As a rule, they take good care of their of old heritage."

Saint-Restitut is a jewel, with each facet lovingly looked after by someone with a stake in the place. Narrow cobbled streets wind up a hill and around the church. Occasionally some Parisian tourist scrapes paint off his BMW before he learns that old Restitut planned the village for donkeys.

The few businesses in town thrive with local customers: a newly restored hotel, a hairdresser, a restaurant, an odds-and-ends shop. The young baker is there only because the village council gives him a financial break to survive.

Every square inch of dirt is planted in something lovely. Hollyhocks soar from the tiny patches between paving stones. Geraniums burst from narrow planters, leggy and tall and ablaze in reds. Roses climb up the roofbeams, and flowering vines drop from second-floor terraces.

But most remarkable are the aromas, always changing with the season, that waft from kitchen windows.

"You won't see that eighty-year-old woman next door, because she's a witch and is always extremely busy," Jean-Pierre remarked one night. I tried to picture a MacBethian cauldron that could smell so good. In fact, I eventually figured out, he had not said *sorcière*, but rather *saucière*. Instead of boiling newts' tongues, she spent long days simmering sauces.

"Places like this show the old French cooking we know is not in danger," Annie said. "We have so many regions, and in each one the dishes and recipes and traditions are different. People are attached to what they grew up with, and also develop tastes from regions they get to know. We can absorb new dishes, new ways of preparing meals, without losing what we have always had."

French children are raised to think about food, she said. "For Sundays and holidays, we always knew what we would eat. The staple was roast beef. For Easter, it was lamb or pigeon." The first meal that Jérôme's American wife, Suzette, ate with her new family happened to be the ritual August 15 feast. "We had fourteen dishes," Annie remembered. The meal lasted from midday to nearly nine P.M. "God knows what she thought."

Suzette was not scared off. Her own young daughters, Pauline and Juliette, each eat like well-raised French kids. It just happens that one of their home regions is Tennessee, and they also love barbecue.

In the Delays' part of the Rhône Valley, regions come together in a mouth-watering fashion. Nearby Nyons is olive country, with its spicy but mellow oil. But the butter line starts at Valence, just to the north. The cream of Lyon is not far beyond.

The Delays' food orbit—I define this as the farthest distances one can drive to lunch and return for predinner apéritifs—is a Frenchman's dream. It stretches between two wonderful under-discovered chefs, Régis Macon at Saint-Bonnet-le-Froid in the Auvergne mountains and Reine Zamut at Lourmarin by the Durance. For fun, there is the Café des Fédérations, and its fabled animal innards, in Lyon. For fancy, there is Le Petit Nice on the water in Marseille.

But why leave home? Everything grows nearby, from succulent melons to herbs that thrive on drought. Richerenches, close by, is the truffle capital of France. Farther south in Provence, hardly anyone keeps cows. Rhône beef is tender and full of flavor, as is the lamb. The pork is as good as the fowl, and wild game is still abundant in neighboring forests.

Côtes du Rhône wines, powerful and velvety, come from grapes like the Syrah, which the Romans domesticated. Vineyards climb up steep rock terraces built by Caesar's legions, who had to be kept busy.

Aromas of meals past scent the history. Madame de Sévigné wrote her mouthwatering reflections on food at the eleventh-century château of Grig-nan, while visiting her nobly wedded daughter there. When Madame de Sévigné dropped in during the seventeenth century, it took months to make the rough and risky trip from Versailles. Now, Paris is three hours by train.

One afternoon Annie took me on a tour of Romanesque villages, with their restored churchs and ancient squares. Each offered at least one in-viting new *bistrot* run by a young couple who had sunk all their savings and spare time into feeding people who jammed every table for lunch and dinner. In the hilltop village of La Garde Adhemar, a vast muncipal herb garden descends below the church. People visit simply to sniff, or to pinch off dinner ingredients.

Annie's big finale was a bit of living patrimony, the ramshackle farm of a woman everyone knew only as Grand-mère.

No one would think of stopping at Grand-mère's sign by the road, a fading and peeling shingle with the center punched out. Just barely, you can make out the message: Goat cheese for sale. This is just as well because Grand-mère does not sell to importuning passersby. When we found her,

Annie identified herself as the niece-in-law of Marie-Rose Salard, Tante Puce. This brought a warm smile.

"Come in," the old lady said, splurging to switch on a feeble lightbulb hanging from the kitchen ceiling. We settled in for a half-hour disquisition of the tribulations of modern life. Grand-mère's son was the only help she had, and he was busy making ends meet. The chickens alone were a handful, let alone the twenty goats and everything else.

Nosy inspectors from Brussels seemed to be snooping around the neighborhood. If she could not scare them off, she was doomed. As it was, this would likely be her last year. Too much work.

"I still go to the weekly market at Saint-Paul, but I stay in the car because I have no permit to sell," Grand-mère said. "It just gets harder and harder."

Eventually we went outside for cheese. A half dozen white pellets remained in her showcase, a rectangle of mismatched bits of raw, battered wood to which pieces of window screen were loosely nailed. Hygiene patrols be damned, the cheese was wonderful.

At the risk of a Jean-Pierre tirade—"What, you think I'm not capable of shopping for my own kitchen?"—I could not pass up the juicy red tomatoes at a few pennies a pound. Then I selected some melons that exuded sensual perfume from their rough skins.

"I'll take them back to Paris with me," I remarked.

At that, Grand-mère cackled with pleasure.

"You're taking my produce all the way to Paris?" she said, shaking her head slowly to take in the concept. "Imagine that." She grinned through flawed dental work and raised the price a few francs.

ON A COLD BLUE DECEMBER, I came back to Saint-Restitut for Sunday lunch. Though convened at the last minute, it was prepared with all the care Napoléon took to take Austerlitz. Michèle did the cooking, with help from her sister, Françoise, and her mother, Tante Puce. It was served around Jean-Pierre's oval table, seven feet across. The rest of us contributed by making appreciative sounds and trying, unsuccessfully, to persuade Jean-Pierre to let us help wash the dishes.

Jérôme, Suzette, and the girls were not expected before eleven P.M. on the night before the lunch, but I pitched up about seven o'clock. Annie, just in by train from Paris, was finishing a light supper.

"What, you never heard of phones?" Jean-Pierre said, by way of greeting. I sat down.

"Well, I happen to have a little bombine here," he went on, lifting a heavy lid to display something wildly appetizing beneath. "Maybe you can have a small sample of gravy, but surely you understand I can't give you what a father has made for his famished son."

As he said this, he forked a thick slice of roast pork onto a plate and made it disappear under a mound of tender potatoes and onion-rich gravy. I had to stop him by brute force from adding more. With my portion gone, Jérôme would not have starved had he shown up with a hitchhiking rugby team.

I had just missed the star attraction of the next day's lunch. Michèle had prevailed upon her butcher to find a lamb from the flock at Clansayes, just to the west, where one family still raised the makings of *gigot d'agneau* the old way. Sheep graze on tender meadow grasses in the open air. The butcher personally carved off a haunch and delivered it.

Jean-Pierre inserted garlic cloves under the skin, salted and peppered the lamb, and then took it to the baker next door. He had the only oven in Saint-Restitut big enough for the job.

I could already smell our first course. That would be truffle omelet. Michèle had visited her secret connection. He agreed to part with an aromatic handful of his finest fungus, selected from what he would take the next morning to the Richerenches market. These were put together in a container with eggs straight from a farmer's hen, porous and fresh enough to absorb the earthy scent.

The next morning, Jean-Pierre led me to Michèle's lost-in-the-woods house.

"You know what that is?" he asked, pointing to half a dozen pots of bright green cat grass on the kitchen counter next to a box of cat food.

"Cat grass," I said.

"Nope," he said.

It was wheat. Early each December, traditional Provençal families buy a sachet of wheat seeds from farmers who use the money to feed poor kids. The seeds are planted on moist cotton in small beakers.

"If you have *une main heureuse* (that means a green thumb but also 'a happy hand') and the shoots grow tall and green, that means you'll always have money in your pocket during the next year," Michèle explained. From the evidence, she would be loaded. "We put the wheat on the Christmas table as decoration. Who knows how far back that tradition goes, but I like it. These things are important."

Michèle Ramin is the Cartier version of an earth mother, a good-hearted country woman with fashionably coiffed blonde hair and invisible makeup. She wears sensible shoes and a tailored jacket. Judging from Tante Puce, her beauty is the unfading type.

She was waiting for Sophie, her twenty-five-year-old daughter, to come home so they could make the crèche. For that, they would gather forest moss, branches, and ferns as backdrop for heirloom *santons*, carved Nativity figures. The thatch-roofed manger would be erected, but the baby Jesus appeared only after Midnight Mass.

Sophie had a taste for hot Mexican food, Michèle said, but she loved the old recipes passed on from her grandmother. And she was a terrific cook.

The Ramins' house was built a few decades ago, but Michèle oversaw each detail. The carved-stone hearth came from a small castle. It glows in coals or blazes fire from fall to spring. Heavy beams add warmth and strength. The kitchen exudes a sheer joy of cooking. Pots and implements hang every which way. Spices and flasks fill the shelves. Only cookbooks are missing.

"Try some of this," Michèle said, offering a luscious quince paste that was the basis of a Christmas dessert, one of thirteen that tradition demands each year. She picked up a fat, ripe yellow quince and held it to my nose. "It's a holiday smell. As a kid, I remember how much I loved it. We'd make bread and put a ripe quince inside while it was still hot. Then the bread would give off this wonderful smell."

A quince? I had no idea quinces could smell so good. But then Michèle started on squash.

"We have one we call a *gégérine*, a sort of big, round, flat squash," she said. "You cut it and scrape the insides very carefully to avoid getting the skin. Cooked with sugar, it makes a wonderful jam."

Michèle wore a homespun apron decorated with a cheery pumpkin she had embroidered herself. She collected kitchen linen from a time when dish towels were meant to last. Wooden armoires were stuffed with nineteenth-century fabrics, coarse but elegant, that she had found at antiques fairs.

Our lunchtime lamb would be accompanied by potatoes, but in a respectable French kitchen, there is no such thing as just potatoes. By far the most popular vegetable in France, the potato comes in dozens of varieties. The Auvergne's speciality is a small tender tuber known as the *truffole*. But Michèle had selected a pile of substantial brown jobs, like russets, for her fabled *gratin dauphinois*.

By the time I volunteered to help peel the potatoes, she had a dozen of them stripped down and floating in water. She used a wood-handled peasant's knife, whacking away sizeable chunks rather than mincing around with a potato peeler. She set them on the counter next to a deep oval earthenware dish.

Michèle crisscrossed the bottom of the dish with olive oil. She sliced potatoes thinly and made a bottom layer. Next she shook out a layer of grated Swiss cheeses, a blend of Emmental, Gruyère, and Appenzeller. Michèle liberally studded the first layer with chunks of garlic, diced with the green vein removed. She added three dollops of *crème fraiche*, her favorite salt, and then repeated the process for a second tier.

"I always use *fleur de sel* from Guérande," she said. "It has a softer, distinctive flavor." The French have nearly as many types of salt as potatoes. The best is skimmed from evaporated seawater on islands off the coast of Brittany or in the Camargue.

After more cheese and cream, Michèle made a top row of potato slices. But just before, she laid two fat pats of butter in the dish. That took a separate blade. "The knife that cuts garlic shouldn't cut butter," she said, almost to herself. With a final flourish, she poured in almost a quart and a half of fresh milk. And the dish went into the oven for an hour and a half at 180 degrees (centigrade).

"I don't really have a recipe," she said, "I just do it the way I feel like doing at the time, depending upon what I have. Sometimes, there is no garlic. The amounts, that's all pretty much by sense. And everyone does it differently. In Lyon, they boil the potatoes first in milk to make them softer."

That, of course, was basic family food. Michèle got fancy when her husband, Pierre, came back from hunting or fishing. Game birds, venison, and wild boar are each prepared according to old French recipes that take hours, if not days. Fish can be simply grilled, but that is only one of countless variations.

"I like to roast *sanglier* with a *poivrade*," Michèle said, telling me how she made her rich red wine-based sauce that was enlivened by black pepper and given texture by cooked-down liver and fatty pork cubes. "Or in a *daube* or *civet*." Daube, a stew of meat, hearty wine, and vegetables, takes a mere day to cook. A civet takes that long just to describe.

Had it not been the dead of winter, we would have gone in search of greens. I could just imagine what Michèle might do with a simple ripe tomato.

Jérôme had brought a magnum of 1990 Saint-Émilion. I hijacked Michèle's son, Bruno, an expert in local wines, who picked out an armload of Côtes du Rhônes. The *chèvre* and Roquefort had been set out to take on room temperature. Tante Puce had sneaked in a mystery dessert to go with the chestnut-cream log Michèle had baked. We were ready for Sunday lunch.

FOR A FRENCHWOMAN who has cooked for most of her eighty-something years, making an omelet is as easy as breaking eggs. Tante Puce amassed a dozen bright orange yolks and whites in a glass bowl. With quick flicks of a sharp knife, she sliced in truffle wafers until the eggs were nearly black. Then, with a pinch of good salt, she beat the mix and put it aside.

Ideally, when your grandnephew is not racing off to the ski slopes at three P.M., the eggs and truffles should sit two hours. Otherwise, whenever. The only trick is that the omelet must be lightly cooked so the truffles stay moist and tender. There can be no better cure for a dislike of runny eggs than infusing them with truffles.

Whatever the baker did to Michèle's magic lamb, it was exquisite: crispy outside, pink and juicy within. Jean-Pierre had sent it off expertly seasoned. Natural gravy, trapped in the pan, kept it moist.

The gratin dauphinois, to no one's surprise, had come out perfectly. A crunchy top layer locked in all of the flavor beneath. "I don't know what you did to try to impress this guy," Jean-Pierre said to Michèle, "but these are the best you've ever done." He had probably eaten variations of that particular dish a thousand times, but he wolfed down a second helping as if he had just discovered a new taste sensation.

We were twelve at the table. Michèle's husband was off hunting, but Bruno was there, along with Françoise and her husband, Michel. Jérôme's daughter, Juliette, snuffled with a cold but bravely occupied her place. Pauline, too, politely suffered the table talk.

France was in an uproar at the time. President Jacques Chirac's Gaullist party was falling apart. A woman he opposed had been elected chairperson, and a former sidekick had started a splinter party. A newly decreed thirty-five-hour workweek had not beaten high unemployment. Scandals plagued the government. Crime was high. Frenchmen had second thoughts about the European Union and a common currency.

None of this came up even once, of course. We talked about food. Françoise and Michèle engaged in a heated discussion with their mother about edible thistles: how to cook them, when to pick them, what gloves to use. I mentioned to Michel, a meat merchant, that the lamb was from Clansayes. He gave me an all-knowing look of doubt. "We will see," he replied. When it arrived, he agreed that it was sufficiently white, but saved face by explaining how it might have been better cooked.

At my prompting, Françoise told me her favorite tales of the kitchen. No earth mother, Françoise is a fast-talking, wisecracking, type A with a different sort of elegance. She is spokesperson at the nuclear power plant nearby, a source of Saint-Paul's wealth and occasional center of controversy. Career aside, however, she also loves to cook.

Françoise's speciality, in bird season, is thrush *á la broche*. She skewers a row of thrush and roasts them over coals, with bread arranged underneath them to catch the drippings. When they are done, she takes one from the spit, debones it and liquifies it in a food processor with mustard and vinegar to make a sauce for the fire-toasted bread.

Annie recalled meals past, which rattled long forgotten ghosts. Jérôme, who always looks as if he is about to burst into laughter, raked Michel over fire for having—perhaps inadvertently—trod on his favorite Dinky Toys. It was a trauma then, but, with the value of mint-condition Dinky Toys having since skyrocketed to dizzying heights, it was a fresh tragedy. "I can forgive," Jérôme intoned, "but I can never forget."

The inevitable cheese platter offered *picodon*, the Drôme chèvre speciality. And when dessert followed, Juliette and Pauline had their reward.

Tante Puce had made *oeufs à la neige*, the classic country favorite that can turn out from merely good to good beyond belief. Hers was in its own class. Peaked mountains of beaten egg whites, delicately carameled, floated on a golden sugary base.

And then we had the coffee.

This was nothing more than dimanche midi. Christmas dinner would be something special, with the three separate tablecloths, the endless courses, and all the rest that tradition demanded. Stripped to its basics, our meal had been no more than a bunch of relatives sitting down to scrambled eggs, meat, and potatoes. That, of course, is like saying France is just a country. I left the table a very happy man, with a great deal more to see.

—◁≪≫▷—

THREE

Roquefort on the Run

FINDING THE VILLAGE of Rieisse is easy enough. Just drive south from Paris about four hours, turn left at Millau, climb the harrowing switchbacks up the south bank of the Gorges du Tarn, and, once up on the craggy limestone high plateau, head straight until your car tumbles two centuries back in time.

At Rieisse, any resident you happen to see will be a Libourel or an Arnal. Earlier this century, as many as twenty-nine families raised sheep in this hardscrabble stone settlement in the heart of the Causses, the dramatic moonscape west of the Cévennes. Now there are two: seven Libourels and three Arnals. Each clan has a nonagenarian patriarch, and one is a near carbon copy of the other. Both old men are hoe-handle straight and burnt red, with sharp noses, clear eyes set in a nest of leathery wrinkles, and tight mouths that seem amused at some private thought. Their flat grimy motoring caps, blue jackets, and green gum boots could be a local uniform. It is best, though, not to confuse the two. Neither family has exchanged a civil word with the other for three generations.

Rieisse is as close as I could get to the roots of France. True enough, the first Frenchmen were redoubtable homegrown Gauls, joined later by marauding Franks from Germany, who commingled with the descendants of Phoenicians, Greeks, Celts, Romans, Vikings, and other early tourists who never went home. Over centuries, French kings shaped a nation that reveres the idea of civilization. Yet the grand historian Fernand Braudel, along with every barstool savant, asserts that France began as a nation of farmers, and its soul remains in the soil.

The Revolution was fed strength by serfs who wanted more than to slave on someone else's land and survive on black bread and wild greens. One's terroir, home ground, has ever since been a treasured part of a Frenchman's identity.

Today, "farm-fresh" is no falsehood on a menu but rather a distinction that justifies a handsome premium. For most of the year, urban shoppers who can afford it merely pay more at the checkout counter. When they can, families pile into the car and look for roadside stands or, better still, rural *bourgs* where farmers shuffle out of their barns to sell fruits and vegetables, eggs and cheese, or cured meats and sausages.

There is nothing to buy at Rieisse, although if Lucienne Libourel takes a liking to you, she might offer a squash the size of a bowling pin. Lucienne's daughter, Agnès, closed her snack bar rather than convert it to new European Union regulations. A few customers a day in summer, if that, seemed not to justify a stainless-steel kitchen, a morgue-sized freezer, a knee-operated sink for an employees' rest room, and separate doors for food coming out of the kitchen and dirty dishes going in.

Odile Arnal used to sell eggs, but she decided not to invest in the date-stamping machine required by the standard-setters in Brussels. All that is left is the family's habitual lifeline, the little truck that comes by regularly to collect sheep milk for Roquefort Société. But even that is now in doubt.

Odile and her brother, Roger, both unmarried and nearing sixty, are the last of the Arnal line. They might decide to refurbish their milking operation to satisfy France's new European partners. They might even laugh off the plan from Paris that limits the French workweek to thirty-five hours. Like the Libourels, who sell meat, not milk, their working week is closer to 135 hours.

Both families are on the job by 6:00 A.M. Except for a sacred midday meal, they stay at it until maybe 10:00 P.M. The animals' routines vary little. With grain to coax out of poor dirt, nature determines priorities. Emergencies add a little spice. Hauling, chopping, repairing, canning, and all the rest must be fit in when possible. On holidays, they take out their separate cars and drive half an hour to Mass. They come home for a slightly more elaborate meal, each at their own table. Then, only after counting sheep, they climb into bed and close their eyes.

Excitement is confined to midweek. On Tuesday, the baker drives up and honks his horn. A few minutes later, he is off to the next bourg. On Wednesday, the fruit man appears and vanishes. And on Thursday, three horns are honked: the fishmonger's, the butcher's and, yet again, the baker's.

At least, I remarked to Roger Arnal, it was a good, healthy life. He was content, right?

"Oh, *alors*, content?" he mused in reply. "I was born to be doing this. I'll die doing this." Those were more words than Roger had spoken in a month to anyone but his sister, his father, or his 250 sheep.

RIEISSE IS A STILL-LIFE illustration of what the French call "rural desertification." In Africa, that means too many people on fragile land result in a widening desert. In France, it means the opposite. Vast fields grow nothing more than wildflowers and weeds. A generation ago, an amusing ditty went, "How're you gonna keep 'em down on the farm, after they've seen Paree?" Now that is a national crisis.

France is Europe's largest country in area, and it is the least densely populated. Fifteen percent of its sixty million inhabitants cluster around metropolitan Paris, and half the nation lives in forty urban areas with populations higher than 150,000. Many of the rest are in towns of the 20,000-inhabitant range.

The countryside still attracts. Just about every Parisian family that can swing it spends a month each year, and long weekends, at their *maisons secondaires*. These range from inherited feudal estates to crumbling stone cabins lost on forgotten hillsides. Small fortunes are spent on *maisons phénix*, ugly new constructions in the countryside where city folk can pass a few healing hours scratching in the dirt.

But the real farming infrastructure is dissolving. Until the 1960's, most rural dwellers were still in tiny settlements like Rieisse or larger villages nearby. Now changing times are spinning them off, as if by centrifugal force, to growing small towns dotted across provincial France. A third of Frenchmen were classed as *paysans* just after World War II. Now the figure is nearer seven percent. And only one person in ten still living in rural areas actually works the land.

In the thirty years from 1967 to 1997, at least 50,000 rural businesses shut down, victims of agricultural consolidation. Back then, France had three million working farms. As the millennium ended, the total was near half a million. Perhaps 1,200 towns and 15,000 villages were slipping toward ghost-hood.

Strictly speaking, a hamlet needs a church to be considered a village. In practice, the determining factor is a bakery; as Lionel Poilâne had said in Paris, bread is the soul of a village. But that requires a customer base. Few young Frenchmen embrace the idea of waking at 2:00 A.M. to labor alone by a hot oven for income that might not match the national minimum wage. As a result, more and more villages drop down to a category known as "SB." *Sans boulanger.*

All of this is worrisome enough for a nation that treasures its rural roots. The implications are more dramatic still for the old arts of producing the specialty foods and quality ingredients that underpin French cuisine. With each disappearing farm, wherever it happens to be, a priceless piece of culture and tradition vanishes forever.

Rieisse, for instance, is in the Lozère, the least populated of France's ninety-eight states, or *départements*. It lies atop the Causses, wide open plateaus and deep gorges of eerie rock formations that span the Lozère and parts of the neighboring Aveyron. The name comes from a local word for *chaux,* meaning lime. Geologists marvel at the deep caverns and crevices gouged out over time by wind and water. Gourmets, however, are more interested in the singular blue sheep's milk cheese that these caves produce.

Driving through the Causses, the casual tourist sees flocks of sheep loping across rocky pastures, making sharp ewe-turns and then gamboling back again. The consummate Frenchman, however, sees Roquefort on the run.

These shepherds, their flocks, the Renault trucks to carry raw milk, the alchemy of *Pencillium roqueforti,* and months of patience in the caves are all that stand between him and a life of Velveeta cheese.

Some villages and small towns band together to pool their resources. Neighbors help one another to repair ancient slate, red tile, or thatch roofs. The luckier ones persuade the government to keep the school open and the baker to stay put. Those with nearby tourist attractions can organize fêtes to bring in extra money and amuse their kids.

But there are also plenty of the unneighborly kind.

Driving through the Lozère, I turned down a dirt road near Cassagnas at a sign that proclaimed, "Espace Stevenson." Late last century, Robert Louis Stevenson had tramped across wild country, among wilder peasants, to write his amusing little book *Travels With a Donkey Through the Cévennes*. A streamside hamlet off Route 106 alleged itself to be one of his stopping points.

I found no remaining spoor of the Scottish author, but Evelyne Dumas was happy to tell me what little she knew. She was a retired nurse from Marseille who spent as much time as she could at her mother's old place, still marked in fading paint, Hôtel-Restaurant de la Gare. Once a narrow gauge train brought fresh travelers each night to the valley. Now the tracks are gone, and so are the travelers, and so are most of the villagers with whom they came to do business.

"Oh, everyone claims young Stevenson passed right past their door, even though the poor man would have had to make twenty trips to cover all that ground," Dumas said. "It gives someone a commercial advantage over others, see?" Literary pilgrims from Britain, who rent donkeys and buy picnic supplies, are one of the area's main summer resources.

Dumas had caught me by surprise. I first spotted her as I drove past, a grim, broad face with a hard mouth and unhappy eyes peering over her low terrace wall. Hers was the sort of hostile mien that suggested to foreigners that French people hated them on principle. Risking nothing but a brief Arctic blast, I turned back and approached her. She could not have been nicer. That look was merely her at-rest neutrality toward a world she examined on merit. I seemed friendly enough and interested in her neighborhood. She was happy to answer all questions at length.

No, she said, families were not eating the way they used to. "The products aren't the same anymore," Dumas said, citing the usual suspects: chemicals, mass production, time pressures, the economy, poor upbringing. "But a lot of people are trying to fix this, with a sort of return to terroir, learning from their grandmother's recipes." These were almost the same words Bernard Loiseau had used in his temple-kitchen at Saulieu.

"My cousin up there in Cassagnas is doing just that in her restaurant, and it is a great success," she added. "People care."

I brought up Marseille, and Dumas answered as I suspected she might. "Black and white now," she proclaimed. "The Arabs on one side, the Europeans on the other." It was a trifle more complex, I knew, and I'd go back to Marseille. But I pressed her a bit. She replied with a litany of crimes she had heard about—muggings, burglaries, and such—leaving me to assume the ethnicity of the perpetrators and victims.

"You understand, I have nothing against immigrants," she said, "but the Arabs just don't adapt. They speak their own language, cook their own food, have their own religion."

This was a line I'd heard before. Often. And that feeling seemed to deepen the farther one got into the depths of France, what people call *la France profonde*. It wasn't so much a visceral reaction to skin tones or facial features as good old-fashioned racism was in America. It was a fear of change brought on by alien elements, a threat to the very soul of Frenchness. National Front orators struck a chord each time they raised the spector: Do you want a muezzin in a minaret drowning out the bells in your church tower?

And then Dumas changed the subject with a question of her own: "Do they cast spells where you come from?"

Before I could answer, she was launched.

"Around here, they do. A lot. People believe in secret spirits, supernatural healing, and curses of all sorts." Even in Marseille, she said, people talked often of the *scomoun*, a vague evil spirit that can throw off your *boules* game or muck up your digestion. Deep in the countryside, such beliefs were stronger.

She pointed vaguely westward, where a narrow road dissolved into a mountainside of trees. "In that village up there," she said, "someone had a fat, beautiful cow, and the neighbor was jealous. His own cow was puny and gave hardly any milk. So he had a spell cast on the neighbor's cow, and it wasted away to skin and bones."

I asked a dumb question: "Why didn't he have a spell cast on his own cow so she would fatten up and give more milk?" Dumas shook her head gravely from side to side. French peasants did not do it that way.

"You know, there's nothing else to do in the country, so you have to amuse yourself by telling stories about your neighbors," she explained. "You gossip, exaggerate a little, and after a while, it can fester into a real war. Then in time, people forget the original cause. It just goes on. So many of these little places are seething with that sort of thing."

That cursed cow business sounded more like something her mother had told her back during the heyday of the Hôtel-Restaurant de la Gare, while simmering stock by the iron stove. But it could have happened the week before. If Madame Dumas liked Cassagnas, I thought, she would love Rieisse.

NO ONE TODAY has a clue what started the feud between the Arnals and Libourels. Talking to each family, in fact, I got the impression that neither one acknowledged to themselves that blood ran particularly bad in Rieisse. Hate thy neighbor has simply gotten to be the normal state of affairs. But the atmosphere is pretty hard for outsiders to miss.

During the mid-1980's, there were subtle signs of a thaw, a nonspecific global warming. France was not doing badly. French families could load up their cheese platters with fine Roquefort cheese and spend a little extra for a farm-raised gigot of lamb. The weather did nothing extreme. Claude Libourel and Roger Arnal, non-friends but contemporaries since their infancy, seemed to be making smaller circles around each other.

Then one morning, Claude's sheep barn caught fire. His wife, sister, and aged father helped him haul buckets of water toward the blazing old wooden building. But, according to Libourel memory, Roger stayed back and watched it burn.

Relations got so bad that when the families decided to separate their fields with a costly electric fence, they each bought their own and set up parallel barriers rather than share a single one.

Sometimes the feud is merely amusing. Once, when a storm knocked out the phones, workmen who reconnected them accidentally switched the lines. Two weeks passed before the families realized what had happened. They get few calls, anyway. And neither spoke to the other to mention any anomaly.

Sometimes it is pathetic. Early in the 1990's, old Marcel Libourel dozed off at the wheel of his Citroën 2CV, and he smacked into a plane tree along Highway D16 from Florac. His wife, in the passenger seat, died in the crash. The Arnals all appeared at the funeral, but no one spoke.

And then there was Le Millionaire. This is one of those popular lottery games. You buy a card at the tobacco shop and scratch off foil to reveal symbols underneath. If several match, you win. If they all match, you win big. A television program whisks you to Paris to compete for serious prizes.

A Swiss tourist happened to pass by one day and gushed to a Libourel about the villagers' good luck. He had just seen someone from Rieisse win 300,000 francs, about $50,000. No, he assured, he was not on drugs. Rieisse.

When confronted, Roger Arnal replied, "Yes, that was me. I am hiding nothing." He was miffed that anyone might think he was holding back. His good fortune was a mere detail that would surely have come out in conversation, had the villagers indulged in conversation across family lines. The program had aired at 6:00 A.M. when the entire population was occupied with sheep. It is not clear whether Roger's sister, Odile, even saw him.

Details were quickly hunted down. Roger had driven from Rieisse to Montpellier, his first foray beyond neighboring towns since his army days. From there, he was flown to Paris and taken to a fancy hotel in a Citroën XM with black leather seats. All the while, according to village sources, he luxuriated in the splendor as though he was born to it. Then he quietly wheeled his little Citroën Visa back into Rieisse and returned to his sheep.

"His total expenditure was thirty-three francs, and that was a mistake," reported one Libourel, who had taken pains to glean facts. "He didn't realize they were picking him up, so he bought a shuttle ticket from the airport. He did not even buy a little Eiffel Tower souvenir or perfume for the woman who sold him the ticket." There is no Arnal version on record.

And so it goes. One day while I was there, Roger beat frantically on the side of a barn, clearly trying to sort out some difficulty with his flock. Claude cast an eye in the general direction and then shrugged. "Must have some problem," he observed, making no effort to learn what it was and even less to help resolve it.

That was just one more missed opportunity. Claude needed Roger badly and, most likely, vice versa. Claude wanted to retire before working himself to death, but the meager pension allotted to farmers would not support his family. Roger and Odile, he reckoned, might be interested in the same thing. The Libourels owned expensive machinery for planting the grain both families needed to feed their flocks. The Arnals had a costly automatic milking system. Cheese brought in more money than meat. So Claude had what he thought was the perfect plan.

If he leased land from Roger, a local bank would front five years of rent money at low interest. This was because rural bankers knew how French farmers thought; no one trusts anyone. Thus combined, the two could split the labor and the profits, coming out far ahead financially with some time to get a life.

Only one thing stymied this perfect plan. Claude and Roger were not talking to each other.

THE IRONY IS that if the Libourels and Arnals got past the feud, they would probably like each other. Individually, they can be a charming lot.

Lucienne, Claude's wife, married into Rieusse, but she comes from just across the plateau, on the barren section known as the Naked Causses. Lucienne and Claude had two daughters who married two brothers named Machin from yet a third Causses village. Chantal moved away with her husband, but Agnès and Alain settled into a house they built. In 1991, their son Gaël was born. David followed four years later. Alain, unlike the others, has a job.

"I'm lucky, because this is the only way I could stay in this place," he told me one morning. "I'm no farmer, and I have no interest in becoming one." Instead, he is a water engineer, employed by a string of villages across the Causses to find underground sources, keep them flowing, and maintain an elaborate distribution system.

Like most of rural southern France, water supply is straight out of Marcel Pagnol's *Jean de Florette*. Subsurface veins are located, often with the help of a water witch and a forked stick, and boreholes are sunk. If rains are steady, levels remain constant. But it is always guesswork and the grace of God.

"Our problem is that in summer when the levels are lowest, the demand is the highest," Alain explained. "The old-timers never had a problem because they didn't use that much, and they knew how to make it last. I don't know if the Arnals even have a shower, and I'm sure they don't have an indoor toilet. But summer visitors are used to their luxuries, like flushing and taking baths. That is a terrible problem."

In the best of times, piped water is used only for vegetable gardens and flowers. Fields of wheat and barley for the sheep depend on regular rainfall, just as in the African Sahel. When rains fail, scant working capital is spent on commercial feed.

Alain is also a handyman, one of those people who can do anything. His two-story house is topped with a perfectly laid slate roof, in the old way. The cinderblock walls clash with the ancient, irregular stone that built the original homes, but Alain still managed to capture the old lines and styles.

The front part, originally meant to be a snack bar–café, is now rented by the week or the night to tourists, hikers, and the occasional pilgrim who needs a break on the road to Conques.

"We love this life," Alain said, to the enthusiastic nodding of Agnès. "Take me to Paris, and I've got to leave immediately." They wake with the roosters, pack their boys off to school a half hour down the road. He goes to work, and she starts a full day of chores. After lunch, Alain gets out his tools and attacks yet another project. "At night, we watch TV and go to bed. We hardly ever go out to dinner. Once in a while, we'll go to town for a movie and anything we need. That's enough."

Town is Millau, a bustling little city from the Middle Ages, an hour away down sharp hairpin turns and along a gorge of breath-catching beauty. It's not Paris, and most people there don't want it to be. You can get your hair styled, your car overhauled, and, in a pinch, your heart transplanted.

To approach the touchy subject of neighborhood relations, I told Alain about Madame Dumas' stories of casting spells. He chuckled. So did Agnès.

"Well, that happens," he said. "Of course, here we get along pretty well, but in some places, you can really get a feud going. Local jealousies, small slights, that sort of thing." He fell silent after that, and I moved on.

Like everyone else, Alain worried about the rural exodus and what it might portend for the future. In the villages he knew, at least a third of the inhabitants were over sixty. At the same time, he expressed some optimism. More and more people came from the city to set up secondary homes. They put money into old ruins, restoring them. This, at least, breathed in some new life.

Just down the edge of the gorge, a carpenter from Millau had acquired the ruins of what had been a beautiful, sprawling farm. He was putting up the old walls, room by room. A young nurse from Paris, whose job with an aid agency took her to distant disasters, bought a piece of it to restore as her home base.

"Something better be done to reverse this process of desertification," Alain concluded. "Otherwise, the city will take over completely, and we'll be left with nothing but an aseptic, mass-produced life with no flavor or reality to it."

He told me about a friend who visited often. "The guy's son was in class in Paris, and the teacher asked everyone to draw a chicken. He was the only one to put in two feet, tail feathers, and a beak. The other kids' chickens were trussed up, wrapped for the supermarket shelf, ready to be cooked."

Alain stressed the point that the danger was more than old ways sliding into folklore. "This is primordial, preserving this type of life," he said. "Once you lose the rhythm of the animals, of man, of nature, then all is lost."

As we talked, Gaël and David frolicked in the garden. As things stood, the pair of them constituted the entire future of the centuries-old community of Rieisse. They seemed happy enough among the rock terraces, rusting tractors, and cheery flowers around old ruins. I made a note to check back with them in twenty years.

Before going, I tried another stab at the forbidden subject. Had any Libourel or Arnal ever invited the other home for a meal? Alain did not understand my question. It was obvious enough that the Libourels and Arnals would each gather regularly around their own tables. And it did not occur to him that I might think there had been a social mingling of families.

When I made the question clearer, he and his wife consulted for a moment. No, they decided—at least not in the lifetime of any of the four generations still alive in Rieisse.

Later, Lucienne and Claude simply rolled their eyes when I broached the subject. Lucienne, the good-humored outsider, seemed amused. Claude, the dour son of local soil, snorted in ill-masked disdain. Instead, we talked about mutton.

The Libourels own about 1,500 acres of Causses scrubland, a blend of wild grass and piney woods shrouded in lichen. Succulent mushrooms grow among the limestone rocks, but the open spaces are hell to plow. When everything was done by hand, Claude worked like a donkey. Now he just works very, very hard.

Each reasonably warm day, he herds his 210 sheep out for breakfast. At night, safe in their tin-sided barn, the flock munches away at raw grains.

Claude, like his son-in-law, worried about the future.

"Big farms can't produce quality the way you can when you know every animal and care about every detail," he said. "Most people these days have no idea what lamb really tastes like. When you automate and raise herds that are too large, you depend on chemicals, awful stuff to make meat grow faster and last longer."

So far, he said, he was holding the line. But small producers were dropping out at an increasing clip, and one day he would have to follow. Economies of scale are tough to beat.

"Every year, there are 30,000 fewer farmers in France," Claude said. "That doesn't sound like much, but if you figure it out over ten years . . ."

For a moment, as he thought about that, Claude's weathered eyes wandered off to the middle distance. "You know," he said, smiling happily at a picture he'd formed in his mind, "every year we keep a few lambs for our friends and ourselves. They eat nothing but wild flowers and their mother's milk. That is what lamb ought to taste like."

"I HATE MUTTON, never touch the stuff," grumbled Ferdinard Arnal, late the next afternoon. "Give me beef, pork, chicken, anything. But lamb? Paf!" He did, however, love his cheese.

From all the stories and a few distant glimpses, I had expected entirely another character. Arnal was a friendly old guy, with wry humor playing across an amused mouth that suggested the French comedian Bourvil. If he was normally *fermé*—closed up—and suspicious of strangers, as I had been warned, he was definitely having a good day.

We talked for an hour, standing in the sun on the little patch of common ground by the long-unused stone bread oven and the equally disaffected schoolhouse. With very little prompting, and aided by a cane, Arnal reenacted Rieisse history.

"Back then, the snow was like this," he said, marking off a good fifteen inches on his cane. "Now, hardly anything, and when it comes, it goes away overnight. Same with the rain." (Official records bear out that patterns are changing, but they differ from his details. For French farmers, notoriously, it is always too hot, too cold, too wet, or too dry, even when it's perfect.)

Crops used to be better. "That soil just clings to the top of limestone rock, only about this deep," Arnal explained, showing a mere ten inches of the end of his cane. The women grow potatoes, green beans, onions, squash, lettuce, and, weather willing, tomatoes. Men raise grain for the animals. "In the days before tractors, that was work," he said, his cane imitating a plow.

Arnal pointed to the abandoned bread oven, the symbolic remains of the village's lost soul.

"You won't believe this, but we used to go get wood for that thing and bring back oxcarts full," he said. The cane was a swinging axe. "It took a few hours to heat up, and we had fresh bread for everyone. Don't think we've used that thing much since the war," he said, referring, I think, to World War II.

I asked what the family did with their sheep's wool.

"Not much, anymore," Arnal said. "You know, it takes a damned lot of work to shear, and card, and spin. People can buy factory yarn much cheaper. We just buy a sweater when we need one. But it sure used to be different. All day, we'd make yarn." Tucking the cane under his arm, he spun an imaginary wheel, accompanied by a whirring sound from deep in his throat that was likely faithful to the real thing.

I noticed his old green gum boots and asked if he knew about how many pair he had worn through in his life. He replied that he used to wear wooden sandals. When I asked about vipers, his cane flashed to life again, and he showed how he handles importune snakes. "I must have killed forty a year," he said. "Now, they're pretty much gone," he added, as if he regretted it deeply.

Then we talked about the European Union. He spat first before offering an opinion. "Pretty soon you won't be able to cut down a tree around here without their permission," Arnal said, spitting again. "What do they know about us, our conditions, what we do? Who are they to run our lives?" He meant Brussels, but also Paris. And, for that matter, the nearest city, Millau.

I did not bother to ask Arnal about the euro, a new common currency that was replacing the French franc. Even the young people in Rieisse, and much of rural France, still calculated in terms of old francs, which had two extra zeros. Ten thousand "new francs," for example, comes out as *"un million."* The price of an egg is usually "one hundred francs." New francs came out in 1960.

Arnal remembered when the school was full of laughing kids and a whole range of vehicles stopped at that little clearing with things to sell. It seemed like the right moment to pop the question. Again, I brought up Madame Dumas and the cursed cow.

The old man grinned. "She told you the truth, that woman," he said. Then he smiled to himself and stopped talking.

I tried another approach: "If one family here produces meat and the other milk," I observed, all innocence, "it seems like you could make more money by joining up as a cooperative."

Arnal's grin widened. He flung his cane back over his shoulder and said something like, "Poh, poh, poh." That is one of those peculiarly French sounds that translates, very roughly, to, "Are you out of your flipping mind?"

With no further preamble, Arnal began to reminisce toward a purpose. "In the old days, you know, we had a pretty nice little village here. At night, we'd all play *belote* [a sort of pinochle], talk after work, drink wine. Now, it's everyone for himself. Each one goes home to his own affairs."

But why? I asked.

"You know," he said. "People. Jealousies. One gets a fifty-horsepower tractor, and the other thinks, 'I can do better than him,' and he gets a sixty-horsepower tractor. Each one wants to be a little richer than the other. And it goes on."

As he spoke, Arnal looked around at the old schoolhouse and beehive oven. He took in the newer additions. Against a tree, there was the back-seat from the 2CV in which Madame Libourel died, on which old man Libourel sits in the sun and muses, just as his adversary of nearly ninety years was now doing. With his cane, Arnal slowly scratched parallel lines in the gravel.

"I guess," he said, before ambling away, "it is just the patterns of life."

THAT NIGHT, Odile Arnal invited me in to watch the milking. Roger, bashful, eyed me cautiously and then accepted my presence. The two dozen sheep whose turn it was to dine and give milk could hardly have cared less.

Sister and brother looked remarkably similar in their matching green coveralls and large-lensed spectacles. Both, like Claude Libourel, had the snaggletooth look of a childhood short on dentists. Roger spoke softly and hesitantly. Odile's deep voice boomed. They were hard at work but gracious, nonetheless.

The Arnals' vast sheep barn was a complex affair. The milking apparatus amounted to twenty-four sets of clear plastic suction cups and pumps in a center pit, like the lubrication bay at a gas station. Two ranks of twelve stalls, similar to the starting gates at a race course, faced the pit from either side.

When one lot was through, Odile herded the twenty-four ewes through one door, and Roger let twenty-four in through another. The fresh arrivals jostled for a spot, as in musical chairs, but with enough places for everyone. After the last ewe rammed her muzzle into the grain trough in her stall, blocks closed to lock the sheep in place. Both sets of gates rolled backward until hind legs were near the pit. Odile and Roger swiftly affixed cups to udders.

After a few minutes of low rumbling from the pump, milk stopped flowing through clear tubes into the stainless steel tank in the next room. Then it was time for the next batch.

The whole process takes an hour and a quarter, more or less, morning and night. It goes on from February, lambing season, until the end of summer. A healthy Lacaune ewe might give three liters of milk a day, about nine dollars' worth at average rates. It is not a bad business if you don't mind no days off, middle-of-the-night emergencies, and a never-changing messy routine.

"This is not for everyone," Odile allowed, with a tight smile. Soon, she added, it might not be for her, either. It was the European Union. Unlike dairy farmers, they did not have to sterilize each udder and use plastic sleeves when milking. But the new regulations called for expensive changes. For one, the Arnals were supposed to cover the clean concrete floor of the milking shed with ceramic tiles.

"You think these sheep give a damn what they stand on?" Odile fumed. "It makes no sense. The milk won't be any cleaner. All that will happen is that the smooth surface will freeze in winter, and we'll slip and break our necks. This is progress?"

Another concern, too fearsome to mention, lurked in the background. What if the European Union relented to pressure from some quarters and banned all cheese made from raw milk? Already, a special permit was required, with rigorous codes to follow. Some of France's cheese might survive that, but certainly not Roquefort or the unctuous *bleu de Causses*.

Not long earlier, a cheese monger friend handed me a sliver of Europeanized tomme from the Vendée. It was creamy and yellow, but my grimace told him he had made his point. Pasteurized milk, from a cow, a goat, or a ewe, had its limits.

As Odile and Roger worked, a thought crossed my mind that I decided not to express. If they gave up their flock, what would they do? Move? To where? With unemployment near twelve percent in France, and legions of fresh university graduates still pounding the pavement, what were the chances of two retirement-age sheep farmers who could not survive on an agricultural pension?

We talked around the edge of politics. They did not like parties that promised too much change. Though hardly endangered by immigrants, they liked the conservative tone of the housebroken elements of the far right. France is France. Keep it that way.

For good measure, I also talked to the Fruit Man, the Butcher, the Fish Lady, and the Bakery Guy. Each had a name, but none was anxious for me to learn what it was after I began asking specific questions about their business. I might have been a tax spy. Trimming the edge off taxes is a national sport in French cities and a requisite to survival in the countryside.

"Families out here still eat well, like they used to," the Fruit Man assured me. "The women cook proper dishes, and they all gather together at fixed mealtimes to appreciate them. That is what this rural life is all about. They grow a lot of their own stuff, but not everything. I sell twenty-two tons of stringed garlic in the season."

He hits a few dozen isolated villages a week, starting with his first spring fruit. In August, he has peaches, nectarines, melons, and tomatoes. He ends his route after apple season in early fall. "Between those times, they're on their own," the Fruit Man said. That means driving to Millau every three weeks or so and putting a dent in the shopping mall supermarket.

"It may not be long before they have to do that all the time," he added. He could also market his fruits and vegetables through some conglomerate, saving himself predawn mornings, a lot of gas, and extra labor for prime quality. "I've been at this seventeen years, and I'll eventually have to stop. I don't know how many *courageux* are out there to take over." The word means "courageous" only peripherally. Zealous is more like it. Or, as the Fruit Man would admit with a laugh, nuts.

The Butcher merely confirmed what was obvious. His regulars were dropping like flies. Young people moved away if they could find something elsewhere to do, or even if they couldn't. Old people moved in with urban relatives or to retirement homes. Also, he confirmed, in the heart of sheep country, he did not sell a whole hell of a lot of mutton.

The Fish Lady, jolly and eight months pregnant, was running behind schedule and could not linger to chat. But a glance at her wares told me what I wanted to know. A morning's drive from the sea, lost in the back pockets of rural France, she had it all: mussels and oysters, shrimps and fish soup with *rouille*, succulent sea snails, a huge tuna, stream trout, and at least a dozen sorts of salt-water fish with clear eyes and a fresh feel. With all the *rouget, limande, loup, daurade,* and the rest, her open-sided Renault van might have been the Saint-Tropez Saturday market.

The Bakery Guy had more time. He was actually a photographer from Paris who made the rounds because he loved the countryside and the people he met along the way. Like me, he had a thing for moribund old stone villages.

"Look, it's simple to understand," he offered. "The bases of bourgeois life are getting vastly more complex, so things have to change, and the countryside is changing along with it. Some people can cling to their old ways, and some can't. Outsiders are moving in. It's amazing when you try to find an old place to buy. Everything is being snapped up. City dwellers go rural to get back to their roots. Others just want a vacation home. But life is changing."

There were other reasons. The tiniest towns each have their monuments to those fallen in World War I. Nearby Saint-Chely-du-Tarn lists forty names, nearly half as many as its year-round population. And the school system helped draw away the best and the brightest. I stayed with a friend whose grandfather was born in Rieisse. When he was young, his teacher proclaimed him gifted, so he was sent to Millau and then on to study engineering. He kept the family house but moved on.

The Bakery Guy's route took him past some hideous new homes, built with garish new materials, or garishly phony replicas of old materials. At the same time, some lines were holding fast.

"It's the peasant mentality," he said. "They resist change by nature. Their way worked for their grandfather, and it works for them, so why change it? Some people might think that's backwards, but it is what holds traditions together. Look, these rural people are exactly like islanders. They live by themselves, surrounded by empty space. They don't go out to the world. The world comes to them. It's the same. So instead of boats, it's cars. What's the difference?"

THE LIMESTONE CAVES at Roquefort, where the Arnals' milk turns to cheese, are open for visits. In fact, the 1,700,000 cheeses that pass through Société's eleven-story vaulted Cave de la Rue outnumber tourists by a mere ten to one. In France, food draws, and this is the Lourdes of cheese. Maurice Astruc, the *maître affineur* whose bushy mustache crawls from the middle of one cheek to the other, delivers his patter as if auditioning for a satire on Ye Olde France. All the place lacks is someone in a sheep suit with a painted-on goofy grin to hug the children.

That aside, however, a certain hallowed air stirs within those ancient cliffs of the Combalou Plateau towering above the narrow Soulzon River, a short ride south of Millau. Roquefort cheese has been ripened in those caves for at least 500 years, if not a great deal longer. The interplay of specially cultivated mold with the natural flora of raw ewe's milk and the cold, humid currents from clefts in the underground chambers is precisely the sort of high technology that the French revere.

According to the Institut International du Fromage in Paris, ancient Gaul was divided into three cheeses: Roquefort, Comté, Cantal. Brie de Meaux joined the list in the eighth century, among a lot of others.

When Charles de Gaulle once cracked that it was impossible to govern a nation with 246 cheeses, he was a bit off the mark. Counting carefully, you can find more than 300. Of those, thirty-three are protected by a set of strict guidelines, with an appellation d'origine contrôlée. Roquefort alone accounts for a tenth of the 175,000 tons of French cheese made each year.

In 1666, the Parliament of Toulouse, with royal authority, prohibited anyone but inhabitants of Roquefort from selling cheese under that name. Between 1845 and 1900, production increased by six times, and 300 producers made Roquefort. Gradual takeovers have reduced that number to eight.

Roquefort Société grew from a local producers' cooperative started in 1842. Now it is big business, owned partly by Perrier, with advertisements featuring Maurice's mustache on bus benches all over Paris. Along with French feta cheese and a range of other products, Société turns out seventy percent of all Roquefort. It is not, of course, necessarily the best. Many cheese lovers find more flavor and moisture from the handful of independents, such as Papillon, who produce the remaining thirty percent.

All Roquefort producers make their cheeses using variations on the same ancient theme. Rennet is stirred into the sheep's milk along with starter bacteria, which makes essential acids and also carbon dioxide gas to carve crags where blue mold can grow. Curds are separated from whey and packed loosely into steel forms. Powdered blue spores of *Penicillium roqueforti* are sprinkled onto the forms, which are then put together to make a three-kilo cheese.

Over the next days, the cheeses are dried, turned, and salted. At about eight days, they go into the caves. Each is pierced with stainless-steel needles so the blue mold penetrates evenly. Under the 1979 rules of its appellation d'origine contrôlée, each Roquefort is supposed to spend at least three months maturing in the limestone caverns. Few actually do.

The secret, cheese makers say, is in the mold. Most comes from specially made rye bread gone green. Until about twenty-five years ago, Société affineurs left their loaves exposed in the caves to pick up wild penicillia in the air. For more consistency they began baking bread in glass bottles and then injecting pure strains of mold. Others have their own techniques.

"Americans are developing a real taste for Roquefort," Patrick Striano, Société's enthusiastic director of marketing, told me. "It is the only raw milk cheese allowed into the United States because we convinced the FDA that the penicillin mold kills anything that might be harmful." With hand gestures, he described the mounds of studies compiled over years to accomplish that.

That raw milk business was a bit more complicated. Raw-milk cheeses aged more than sixty days can be imported into the United States, but some authorities are gunning for even that exception. In Michigan, for instance, there is a movement toward a total ban. Both the European Union and a United Nations agency are also pushing for restrictions. French cheese makers cringe at the thought.

Striano was right about changing American tastes. Still, if Roquefort is marbling its way into the United States, the way those blue pockets spread in wheels of cheese, there is still some way to go. Americans import 300 tons a year. France, with a fifth of the population, consumes 14,000 tons.

AT THE EDGE of Millau, a sprawling shopping center features a hypermarché, discount emporia, and a late-night bowling alley. That is where the golden youth of places like Rieisse sneak away for an occasional big time. But the heart, soul, and belly of Millau remain where they always have, under the wrought-iron scrollwork of the covered market, *les halles*, hard by the tenth-century watchtower, in the medieval center of town.

One August 15 morning, only a few merchants rattled around in the vast halles. Josette Chaniez, third-generation butcher, had plenty of time to talk. With tidily permed black hair, two-tone plastic framed glasses, nice teeth, and a neat blue cardigan, she looked like a pleasant schoolmarm. She was thrilled to learn where I came from. For reasons she was eager to explain, she loved Americans and despised the English with equal passion.

While the English are inelegant and aggressive, she said, Americans are rich and enterprising, if not without faults. "Whenever a French person goes to the United States and then comes back home, he has the impression that everything is so small," Chaniez said. "The scale is so different. There are so many opportunities. It is a terrible problem for us, because so many of our young brains are moving there to make a living."

Nonetheless, she said, Americans could be pretty silly. They made up lies about a good president. Well, she added, thinking about that, in any case, a president's private life is no one else's business. And besides, she concluded, the French still knew how to live better.

"It's true that the French are not eating as well today, but it's a question of means, not changing tastes," Chaniez said. "You've got to pay for good merchandise, and many families can't do that now. They go to the supermarket for meat. But they'll be back. As soon as things get better for customers I lose, I start to see them again."

While commercial butcheries were making inroads, she said, farm beef was actually getting better. "In the old days, cattle had to work for their living," she explained. "A cow pulled a plow or a cart, and then when it was too old, it was slaughtered. Now beef is grown only for meat, and it is fed and butchered for just the right tenderness."

It costs more, and good beef does not keep long. But, Chaniez said, there is still a market for it. "Peasant farmers are starting to realize they can earn more and work less if they concentrate on quality rather than volume," she said. "People I know who tried selling to big companies gave it up."

Cash flow aside, she said, producing good meat was much more satisfying. "You can see the difference," she explained. "Real beef is a bright, live red . . ." She stopped a second and then pointed to a gorgeous beef fillet of shimmering crimson, neatly trussed like a package from Cartier. "Like that."

When good beef is aged to purple, it gets even better, but I did not raise the question. Josette Chaniez had more to say. Mainly, she wanted me to know that Americans were wonderful even if they did not understand food, or seem to care. "Everything is so sterile and regulated," she said. "It is awful for French people who go there."

One of her displaced customers, for instance, played saucisson roulette with U.S. Customs. Friends regularly sent him her specialty pork sausage through the mails, hidden among a load of books. "Sometimes it gets through, and sometimes it doesn't," she said. "For him, it's worth the risk."

A few aisles away, Catherine Got did not think the French were still eating well. Over the seventeen years she had sold cheese, she had noticed a steady decline. People were losing their long-acquired tastes. A postprandial cheese platter was still the style, but its absence no longer was tantamount to social suicide.

Got felt that bigness had affected the quality of some cheeses. She much preferred Papillon and other small producers over Société. By and large, though, the problem was simply a change in preferences.

"These days, people eat *produits frais*, yogurt and processed creamy things they buy at the supermarket and eat quickly," she said. "I would say that compared to when I first started, my average customer buys one-quarter as much cheese." With a fleeting look of pain, she added, "Even Roquefort."

FOUR

⸺◁◇◇◇▷⸺

Another Roadside Attraction

WHEN I MAPPED OUT that first trip to Roquefort country, my eye fell on the name Conques-en-Rouergue. Years earlier, my sister Jane had come back stricken with concern after church-hopping in the Aveyron. She had come upon a gem, a hallowed waystation for pilgrims headed toward Santiago de Compostela, and its roof was falling in. Poor Conques, she lamented. Someone has to help save that church.

A fabled tympanum above the great western doors of the abbey church featured 124 polychromatic figures, carved in stone by medieval monks with passion and humor, depicting the Last Judgment. Priceless stained glass colored the light that fell on treasures within.

From its lonely spot in a patch of wooded hills on the small-scale Michelin map, Conques looked as if hardly anyone had been there since Jane's visit. If that precarious Romanesque roof had lasted since the 1200's, chances were it had not yet collapsed in a pile of slate. I'd sound the alarm. This was the stuff of Mother Teresa.

For good measure, I took along Jeannette Hermann, my stalwart companion, who organizes tours to little-known places. Surely, she could help this French backwater find a suitable following.

The first obstacle to our mercy mission, as it happened, was finding somewhere to park. A young woman in a Conques Tourist Board T-shirt and frayed change apron sent me to the annex lot because a great sea of cars, minivans, and tour buses had choked all available spaces at the entrance to town.

Winding around to the back way in, I found an empty spot. A kid hurried up to tell me that since no white lines were painted around the perfectly good space where I had parked, I would have to go another quarter-mile farther. But first I had to fork over the equivalent of four bucks for a parking sticker.

God, I knew, works in mysterious ways. This might be a test, and I was not daunted. In any case, I was in an unflaggable mood. It was time for lunch. No serious crusade in France begins on an empty stomach.

Jeannette and I approached the highly recommended Hôtel Sainte-Foy, and we located a vacant table on a lovely terrace overlooking the church. It was shaded with wisteria, and planters were ablaze in scarlet geraniums. Succulent aromas wafted from the other tables, which buzzed with happy mealtime chatter.

A waiter approached, pleasant but firm, and informed us that it was seven minutes after two. The kitchen had closed only moments earlier. I explained the parking delay. I pleaded and added the hint of bribery. He consulted the chef. Sorry.

We scurried to the smaller Hostellerie de l'Abbaye across the plaza, much less attractive but with an encouraging clatter of plates echoing from the dining room. I asked the young man at the desk about lunch.

"Are you crazy?" he wanted to know. "It's nearly two-thirty." In fact, it was 2:16.

"Yes, but . . ."

"It's the law in France," the young man said, puffing up as much importance as his scrawny frame allowed. "Restaurants close at two o'clock. Lunch is from twelve to two. Soon it will be less."

"Since when?"

"Since the Socialists," he said, not specifying whether he meant the Socialist president with the conservative prime minister or the subsequent conservative president with the Socialist prime minister. In either case, it was crap.

Jeannette, meanwhile, was desperate for a ladies' room. She asked the bartender, who pointed amiably toward a door across the room. As she headed for it, a stocky woman who looked as if she had just dismounted from a broom ran out and barred her way.

"Where do you believe yourself to be going, madame," she demanded. This was not a question.

"To the bathroom," Jeannette said pleasantly. She has the angelic face of a harmless innocent, which melts most such barriers, and the tidy, be-jeweled look of a traveler with real luggage. But she might as well have been Dorothy facing the Wicked Witch of the West.

"The bathrooms are for customers," the woman shrieked. "This is a hotel."

The whole scene was so preposterous—the young prig followed by the old harridan—that Jeannette and I just looked at each other and laughed. We walked out, but I was overcome with curiosity. I went back in and asked the clerk for the name of the proprietor.

"Why?" he demanded.

"Because I'm—"

"Do you have a salesman's license? You have no business asking questions."

When he saw me write the hotel telephone number on a pad, he leaped forward, halfway over the counter, and yelled, "What are you noting down there?"

Just then the old woman approached, shrieking louder still and waving her arms.

"Call the gendarmes," she ordered.

"Exactly," the clerk said. He reached for the telephone and dialed the equivalent of 911.

This was a dilemma. I was dying of curiosity to know what the cops would do, in fact, faced with a foreign perpetrator, who had politely asked for lunch in a restaurant and an accomplice who wanted to use a hotel bathroom. I even had a French press card, which formalized the right to ask questions.

But in a small town in the rural back hills, who knew whose brother-in-law held local authority? And, more important than that, we were hungry. I left, laughing harder, and we found a friendly refuge on a terrace just across the street.

"Ah, yes, them," the waiter said with a little chuckle when I told him what had just happened. Apparently we were not the first to have found an unusual reception. This, in contrast, was a friendly bistro with more relaxed hours. But it was after 2:30, and the kindly waiter, who doubled as assistant cook, said he could only serve us a Roquefort salad.

"Not even an omelet?" I asked.

He shook his head. The stove was just inside the door. Surely, there were eggs in the refrigerator. But I'd had enough fights for the day.

Later, at my request, the owner came over to chat. I complimented him on the sparse, cold salad.

"Paf," he said, making a face. "That's no meal."

It was not actually what we had in mind, either, I told him, but he did not offer to do any better. Instead, we talked about the state of food in France.

"All this fast food, Coca-Cola, it makes me sad as a Frenchman," he said. "It offends my pride. Before, in the cities, everyone left the office at midday and had a proper lunch. And now"—he paused to purse his lips as if to expel the next word quickly and completely—"sandwiches."

The nearby city of Rodez was once thick with fine tables, he said. One could still find a decent meal, but the future trend was unsettling.

"Do you realize there are two McDonald's in Rodez?" he asked, with a snort and a thump on the table. "Two! And that's the only place kids want their parents to go. My own kids! For me, that's a real sign of the times. Two of them. It is *dégueulasse*."

"Disgusting," I agreed. "Where are they, exactly?"

And there you have it. Nature is not known for its tolerance of vacuums, and the monster international chain learned that lesson early on. For me, it was a simple calculation.

Dinner was impossible until, say, eight P.M. If I worked quickly, I could save the ancient Conques church in an hour or two, and get back on the road toward Draguignan. One choice was to stop at a café for a frozen industrial pizza slice or a baguette, stale by late afternoon, with sliced ham of dubious quality. Another was to shop around for the fixings of something tasty, which could be amusing. But that would take time and might expose me to a lurking big sister of the hotel hag across the street.

Or I could roll up to a McDrive window, say a few words into a speaker, hand over not many francs, and wheel away with an acceptable warm sandwich that, at the worst of it, would probably not give me ptomaine.

It is easy enough to see why an American traveler on budgeted time would want to take every opportunity to find good French food. But the long-termers? M. F. K. Fisher once wrote of being stopped by a young American in Marseille who was in acute culture shock. A luncheon club network had selected him as outstanding student and sent him to France for a grand tour. In city after city, local nobles fed him their specialties. After three weeks, he was ready to kill for a hamburger. Fisher and her daughters sent him after a sort-of hot dog by the Gare Saint-Charles. That was early in the 1960's. Now, he would hardly be beyond sniffing distance of a Big Mac anywhere in greater Marseille.

By the end of 1999, nearly eight hundred McDonald's restaurants were scattered across France, from the Champs Élysées to remote crossroads deep in the countryside. That is not counting the Belgian version, Quick, or all the rest.

McCustomers, in fact, are only marginally American. The French have taken in the place as their own, shortening the name in popular slang to two syllables pronounced "Mahc-Doe." Kids in their late teens love to hang out in the immediate vicinity and do wheelies on their Hondas. A certain sort of young professional stops in for a quick lunch or post-film bite. But just as the Conques restaurateur explained it, the real devotees are very young French people with their parents in tow.

If Americans are used to a certain level of permissiveness, French kids suffer through a restaurant meal. They're supposed to sit in quiet dignity while their elders prattle on about boring stuff. McDonald's, therefore, is kiddie heaven. A *blanquette de veau* might be tasty to a preschooler, but its heavy cream is not secret sauce you can let drip down your cheeks. *Pommes rissolées* have their place, but as ketchup-bearing missiles to launch against a younger sister, nothing beats *les frites McDo*.

Then there are all those toys, gifts, rides, games, clowns, exotic American names for things. The kid tug factor is massive. And when busy parents calculate the bill and the time spent, compared to real food in a proper place, it is often an easy sell.

Up to now, there has been plenty of resistance among parents. An occasional *attaque de Mac* might be harmless enough, but what about the family table, tradition, a svelte figure, and decent nourishment? The big question, of course, is what next? What happens when all these McDo Generation kids grow up and have their own kids? If the push is equaled by a pull, God help us all.

BUT MY MISSION in Conques was to save a church roof, and I hurried across the old village square to assess the damage.

I found no damage. Actually, some other writer saved the place, beginning in 1837. Prosper Merimée, who was also the first Historical Monuments Inspector in France, found the whole structure in grave danger of collapsing. With all the urgency of the times, a vast restoration program began in 1873, which has been going on ever since. When my sister Jane visited, the roof needed attention. But that seemed to have been fixed, and no one remembered the details.

If some French and European Union funds had repaired the church, a torrent of money went into a European Center for Art and Medieval Civilization. The multistory building, starkly modern among the ancient slate roofs and gray stones, amounted to 2,600 square yards of floor space, not counting a garage for eighty cars.

Looking around, I noticed the church and the old town around it seemed to be doing quite well on their own. The price, however, seemed to have been some sort of Faustian pact with the tourism devil. Nearly half a million people a year stop in Conques. The parking lot receipts alone could probably rebuild Notre Dame. Eighty thousand annual visitors pay five dollars to see the old treasure. And the little book and souvenir shop is busy enough to be dealing on the Internet.

"Oh, Sainte-Foy is in good hands," assured Father Jean-Régis, as he rang up yet more postcards. Jean-Régis, a jolly if underfed Frenchman with idiomatic English that sometimes fails him, is abbot in charge of the church. He also lends a hand when gift shop customers besiege the small staff. With thinning hair, owlish glasses, and a beatific smile, he is hand-crafted for the part. "We are Norbertine fathers here," Jean-Régis explained. "Our order is very big in the States. Near Philly."

Sainte-Foy began as a Benedictine abbey, built from the ninth century on the campsite of a godly hermit named Dadon. Charlemagne poured in wealth, but the abbey badly needed holy relics. In 866, monks from Conques solved that problem. They visited a church at Agen which sheltered the remains of Foy, a twelve-year-old girl put to death by Romans for rejecting pagan gods. And they made what history calls a "furtive transfer." That is, ignoring a pesky commandment, they stole Foy's bones. Conques rocketed in stature.

At its peak, Sainte-Foy ranked among the most beautiful structures in southern France. By the time Merimée showed up to save it, it was in ruins. Half of its old stones had gone into local houses. These days, Conques is again an important stop on the annual westward pilgrimage to Spain.

Perhaps 1,200 real pilgrims walk through each year, Jean-Régis said, some having been on the road for two months. In the old days, they slept in the church. Now pilgrims blend into the roiling multilingual crowds that fill the square for much of the year.

Jean-Régis was philosophical about the state of faith in France. Three-quarters of all Frenchmen call themselves Roman Catholic, but fewer than four percent attend mass except on rare occasions. People over the age of sixty-five go to church three times more often than those under eighteen. The total of priests has dropped by half since 1970. Muslims in France number about five million, far more than Protestants.

"No, I don't think that the church is losing its place in society, as a comfort and a guiding light to people," he said. "But, yes, particularly among young people, there are changes. We will see."

It was a hot July day. Inside the cramped shop, voluble Italians were grappling over a guidebook. Outside, by the tympanum, a tour director explained in Japanese what I assume her colleague nearby was talking about in German. Conques had its charming aspects—all those overlapping gray slate roofs and walls and lovely old woodwork—but I had had my fill of Medieval-land.

Father Jean-Régis was also fading. He had eaten lunch, and a siesta was in order. "*Miam-miam, dodo,*" he said, in mock kids' French. Then, for his new American friend, he added an accented English version: "Time to heat the sack."

Actually, we heat the road. After a brief McDo stop in Rodez, we drove on home. For the hell of it, I turned on my computer to see what I might learn. One hit offered a virtual visit of the medieval town. The first two search engines I tried came up with 2,803 related websites in a dozen languages. Whatever else Conques might need, it wasn't a savior sounding an alarm.

THE ROAD HOME from Conques, which took me back again through Millau, produced a surprise. I had just covered the soccer World Cup all around France. Millau was host to what it proclaimed as the World Cup of Pétanque.

Boules, as pétanque is more often called, is sort of a cross between aerobics and a nap. Moments of strenuous body English to put backspin on the heavy steel ball are interspersed with desultory shuffling around to smooth imaginary lumps of dirt in the line of fire. The organs most exercised are the larynxes of sideline kibitzers. Betting is intense. Routinely, one hears of some unfortunate who lost his restaurant by backing the wrong team.

Forsaking the doubles, triples, women's, or mixed play, with 1,500 players in all, I focused on the tête-à-tête championships. This was the real thing. In each match, two guys face each other in a showdown to the end. Although a handful of Japanese and assorted others signed up, a *boules mondial* in France is about as international as the World Series.

Players start by tossing a tiny wooden ball into the dirt ahead. Each has three balls, and the idea is to end up closest to the marker. If one player's ball is near the marker, the other tries to blast it away. The first one to reach thirteen points wins.

In the semifinals, I liked a tough-looking, unshaven bruiser named Éric Bartoli. He was a Corsican from Marseille, born to boules. Just as I expected, he wiped out his opponent in nothing flat.

In the finals, Bartoli's opponent, Christian Fazzino, wore a T-shirt with baggy blue nylon pants and heavy Hush Puppies in the hot sun. He was short, sunken-chested, and slightly hunched, with a mousy black mustache, an overbite, and an almost apologetic scuttling walk. Zelig plays boules. No match, I thought, as Bartoli bowled away the guy's best placement and took a 5–3 lead. Fazzino threw the next ball wild, and my attention wandered.

A square-jawed old man next to me was discussing with a friend what they'd had for lunch (a tasty stewed chicken with green beans served in a gigantic tent that filled to overflowing as soon as morning play halted) and was musing about dinner. The people behind me were grumbling that they needed a *pastis*.

I glanced back to see Fazzino's second ball drop squarely on Bartoli's, bombing it halfway to the Spanish border, and stop dead exactly in the vacated spot. His third ball rolled up to within inches of the marker. Fazzino pulled ahead and never looked back. My man was skunked.

Fazzino, an electrician from Montluçon, turned out to be a three-time champion of France and had anchored winning French teams in a handful of international playoffs. He held the record for competition bombing: 992 hits in 1,000 throws. Now in his forties, he had been playing since the age of six. As any Frenchman could have told me, you can't judge a pétanque player until you see him toss.

Unlike the soccer Mondial, this one was free. People just showed up and squeezed into the stands. Fans watched with varying interest, ignoring loud-speaker commentary. Only once did ears perk up and strain to catch the details: The announcer read out that evening's dinner menu.

Because the tournament took place over an August 15 weekend, traffic into Millau on Highway 109 was jammed solid for twenty miles. On that particular national holiday, as on the June 21 Fête de la Musique and on Bastille Day, France holds a giant block party. Every village, town, and city dances in the streets.

Millau was having an African weekend. Women from the Ivory Coast served steaming pots of chicken in peanut sauce, its normal lash of hot peppers dampened for local tastes. Volunteers sold tickets and served in a downtown square. The dinner, advertised from 8:00 P.M. to 9:30 P.M. sharp, began long past nine o'clock and petered out at midnight. Even at a block party, the French sit down to be served, course by course. Before dessert, the square throbbed with an exotic beat.

I watched a reggae rocker in dark glasses, long tangled dreadlocks, a broad hat, and bright African robe. He twirled a laughing white-bread Millau blonde to the amusement of people who happened to look up from their food. By then, the last boules tournament stragglers had shown up, and dancing room was scarce on the town plaza.

In neighboring restaurants and on the terraces of private homes, other dinners were in happy progress. Someone had roasted a spitted North African *mechoui* of tender Aveyron lamb. Huge bowls spilled over with *aligot*, a local delicacy based on mashed potatoes and old cheese. There was much clinking and murmuring, with an occasional burst of raucous guffaws.

All together, the scene was encouraging for anyone who fretted over the future of France. On the margins, aged ladies in baggy stockings sat chatting on benches, just as old women like them had done for six centuries. Little kids listened with respectful attention when their elders spoke.

The aromas were mostly familiar and all were delicious. Strange new spices intrigued many and seemed not to bother anyone.

It was a lovely Saturday night in the heart of France. And I was looking forward to Sunday lunch.

PLACES LIKE THE Aveyron backcountry inspire deep reverence for the crimson Bible. The Michelin Guide, in fact, is not easy to love as an institution. It can be arbitrary and pigheaded, ignoring some excellent tables for unexplained reasons while touting others best left undiscovered. It is kept purposely opaque by a diffident director who stays in the shadows. Ratings are based on limited visits by anonymous inquisitors; a chance dribble of sauce gone astray on an otherwise blameless plate can be deadly for a chef in hock to his shoelaces. It all counts: decor, ambiance, attitude. That these things are subjective, vulnerable to the odd human slipup, is beside the point. Three-star chefs must be infallibly consistent and routinely perfect.

The laudable purpose is to aid consumers who pay dearly for a culinary experience. In human terms, however, the pressure can push a chef's fragile psyche into the red zone. A sudden star can wreck a wonderful out-of-the-way place as easily as it can improve its fortunes. New customers appear, one-time passersby with guide in hand, bringing high expectations. Regulars drift away, discouraged at too many full houses and put off by rising prices. What was homey tends to get snooty, as ambitious chef-propriétaires dream of that second star.

But what would France be without the Michelin Guide? One shudders to think.

That Saturday afternoon, I had found a single star at a place called Sauveterre-en-Rouergue. Le Sénéchal's specialities were listed as *foie gras chaud* and roasted figs in dark sugar and almond cream. It was a mere hour and a half from Millau, and, yes, they had a table free.

Why Michel Truchon had only a single star is one of those Michelin mysteries. By the guide's rating system, that means "A very good table in its category." The top rating—defined as "worth a trip," although Michelin does not specify from where—implies one of the best tables in France, and that is saying a lot. But two stars denotes "An excellent table, worth a detour." I'd make that detour any time.

Whatever pressure it might put on the owner's cash flow, a one-going-

on-two-star status at a relatively large place is usually terrific for the customer. All that fanatic extra care in the kitchen and attention to detail in
the *salle* comes at bargain prices.

For about eighty dollars, I could have tried Truchon's personal "back-
from-the-market" menu. Nothing was specified; it all depended upon the
chef's mood and what he had found to be in particularly good form that
morning. Instead, I looked at a few simple stalwarts.

Brittany lobster with fresh coconut and pork crackling seemed intrigu-
ing. So did pigeon stewed in a game ragoût, truffles, and Marcillac wine.
There was a promising piece of Aubrac beef—just the heart of the fillet—
done *au jus* in wild mushrooms. And a saddle of rabbit stuffed with fresh
herbs.

I settled for poached foie gras in a truffle-laced vegetable bouillon followed by large crayfish tails roasted in Ligurian oil so rich and sweet that
I could picture an old lady near San Remo hauling her taggiasca olives to
the village press. Jeannette had her foie gras wrapped in a fresh, wilted
cabbage leaf in a nest of (real) bacon bits and (really from the) garden
vegetable julienne. Then she had an amazing salmon in hazelnut oil,
cooked just until it flaked away in moist chunks, with young spinach in
beurre cru and *fleur de sel*.

The first course, in fact, was an abstract painting on a plate, an *amuse-
bouche* of avocado mousse, tomato, and a bit of chèvre set in an artfully
shaped dribble of Balsamic vinaigrette.

Service on the terrace was, as the French love to say, impeccable.
Centerpiece flowers beaded with fresh moisture despite muggy August
heat. Wines were well-chosen and accessible without a second mortgage. The waiter, probably a nephew of the chef who grew up forking
hay, wore a tux that fit with a snowy white shirt collar. Stone planters
spilled over with deep purple petunias and lush geraniums in a rich
dark red.

The sommelier swirled and sniffed my thirty-five dollar local red as if
it were a 1945 Mouton-Rothschild, and he pulled it off without a hint of
pretense. It was August, and I asked the waiter if the truffles had been
frozen. He recoiled in such horror that I did not pursue the question.
Somewhere, obviously, Michel Truchon knew where to score good summer truffles.

All in all, it was the ideal anti-McDo meal, down to the rich coffee
and chocolate-glazed petit fours. With a sated post–Sunday lunch smile, I

flopped on a chair in the lounge for a coffee, cognac, and a cigar. The lone-star chef, his white tunic slightly spattered with evidence of hands-on attention, sat down with us.

"A certain category of Frenchmen will always appreciate a good meal," Truchon said. "As a culture, we realize that eating well is one of the great sensations in life. It is extremely important, to eat well. Not much, but well."

As a result, he added, a careful chef can find quality if he looks hard for it. "In France, still, there are always people with the passion to do well, who are willing to put in the hours of labor and personal attention to produce the best. You must cultivate your suppliers. I buy my fish from small-time fishermen. I know the woman who raises my rabbits and eggs. She just brought some in fresh this morning. I take the trouble to pick out vegetables and fruit in the market."

Truchon was not boasting. Hardly any propriétaire actually does his own marketing any more, but he probably did. At forty-eight, he looked straight from Central Casting: the square-jawed French chef with black curly hair, crinkles around the eyes. But he also had the slightly haggard air of a driven perfectionist who got up at 4:00 A.M. to go prod lamb shanks and then change into a tie for a tough session with the bank.

He had neither explanations nor complaints about his single star. But, he admitted, a second one would make it easier to cover expenses in the lovely but remote village of Sauveterre, which in itself was worth a detour if not a journey.

Kitchen aside, Truchon and his wife, Chantal, run an eleven-room auberge tucked elegantly into a medieval mansion. The Sénéchal's dining-room annex is in modernistic glass and steel that somehow manages to fit in smoothly with weathered carved stone and gray slate roof tiles. It is all in the proportions, the gardens, and the exterior detail, in the old French fashion.

The village beyond has preserved itself with remarkable skill. Shops on the main square, for all of the modems and halogen lighting inside, look hardly changed over the centuries. Houses and cobblestone streets are lovingly restored. The impetus, it is immediately clear, was not some local code with loopholes but rather the residents' collective will.

Truchon offered a comfortable shrug when I asked if he was ever tempted to try his hand in a big city. "I grew up here," he said, "and I like it here."

SOMETIME AFTER my travels in the Aveyron, I chanced upon a scrap of newspaper that I had long ago clipped and forgotten. It was by Barry James of the *International Herald Tribune,* who, I knew, harbors Quixote tendencies similar to mine. He went to save the church in November 1991.

"To many who know it, medieval Conques is the most beautiful village in the world," he started out. "Or, as some would now add, was." The European Center for Art and Medieval Civilization, it turns out, was built on the town's dirt pétanque pitch, a sacred site in any southern French settlement. Tons of concrete covered up original walls from the Middle Ages. Its futuristic profile wrecked the view and the mood.

Just about everyone in town was against it, James reported, except the mayor, Pierre Riom, who lived elsewhere. A string of witnesses wondered why anyone would choose to study a period of surpassing art and architecture by building atop its few remaining traces.

Conques' charm was "secret, mysterious, and spiritual," one resident noted, and the new monstrosity was not only a desecration, but would also drive off the very people needed to preserve its singular character.

Mayor Riom had also acquired an ancient pilgrims' hospice that he wanted to turn into a luxurious retirement home. That fell through, as did a proposal to sell the structure to a local hotel. When James asked Riom why the empty hospice could not be made into a cultural center, the mayor replied, "It is four hundred years old and conceived in such a way that you can only make little rooms." That is, you would have to be satisfied with adapting to the style of the period you intended to study.

Even lukewarm opponents grew hot when their pure, fresh tap water turned foul and muddy, apparently from the construction. Water began to ooze mysteriously from behind the church.

Back then, it seemed clear, the cultural center was only the focal point of a fight over selling the soul of Conques. James' article noted a large illuminated sign had appeared at the edge of town, urging visitors to try a new "gourmet sensation" called *les Conquises de Conques.* These were chocolates made near Paris, with no roots at all in the region. Riom explained the idea was to pump up publicity and provide a souvenir that tourists could take home.

One paragraph jumped out at me. Father Michel, then abbot at the monastery, said the cultural center was "entirely the will of one man," the mayor, who sold the grandiose project in Paris and Brussels. If governments wanted to lavish money on Conques, he fumed, it would be better spent patching holes in the church roof.

That roof again! I grabbed the phone and called Conques. There had, in fact, been leaks over the choir. French Ministry of Culture money was rounded up, however, and repairs were completed early in 1999. As far as anyone knew, the old church was in reasonable condition and not endangered by water seepage, top or bottom.

The European center, nearly a decade on, was thriving. Its brochures described a rich program of seminars, expositions and guided tours. But what had yet to be explained was why anyone would destroy the real thing in order to create a place for guessing what things must have been like.

The town's plan to sell itself to mass tourism was also a commercial success. Some lovely remnants of old Conques remained, and I was tempted to return in the chilly off-season when I could walk an unbroken line on the stone streets and perhaps get a real meal. Frankly, I did not want to risk it.

Growing up in Tucson, Arizona, I had watched a blend of greed and stupidity destroy the closest thing the United States had to Old World antiquity, the heart of a Mexican colonial settlement with its original plaza, thick adobe buildings, and a fortified mud wall.

Somehow, I had expected better in the remote reaches of rural France, where people have a clearer sense of what is important in life. But this had to do with human nature, not any particular society; power trips and poor taste are universal.

The lesson in Conques, in the end, is the delicateness of the balance. A single man in a small place, elected by a handful of voters to a six-year term, can put an indelible blemish on 600-year-old splendor. The mayor explained at the time that his plans were in strict accordance with the Ministry of Culture guidelines. And they probably were. Who can dictate good sense?

Annie Delay, as it happened, was an expert on Conques. She studied the dossier as part of her job in the Ministry of Culture. Such things happen easily, she explained, because so much money is available from the European Union and elsewhere. Mayors have unimagined power in their fief-doms, and national authorities generally rubber-stamp such projects without comment.

"That is how it works in France," Annie said, with a rueful laugh. "Mayors are usually retired doctors, farmers, teachers. The doctors have the best taste. Farmers mostly want to know how much something will cost. The teachers, they're the ones to worry about."

Back in 1991, the headline on Barry James' piece read: "Does a Me-dieval Town Need the Twentieth Century?" As the twenty-first century approached, it seemed a pertinent question that might be applied to a great deal of France and things French.

BY THE END of 1999, Millau and McDonald's were all over the front pages. The French refused to buy hormone-laced American beef. Wash-ington retaliated, inexplicably, with 100 percent tariffs on foie gras and Roquefort. A sheep farmer named José Bové decided to take action. He led irate farmers to the nearly completed construction site of what was about to be Millau's first McDo. In front of whirring cameras, they dis-mantled part of it and then carried doors and panels on a victory parade.

Bové's group did limited damage, and the place opened on time. But the idea caught on. McDos elsewhere burst into flames. Near Nîmes, a dejected Ronald McDonald was photographed lying nose down in a pile of French apples.

"The Americans took our cheese as hostage, so we hit them where it hurts," Bové explained later in Paris over a breakfast of croissants and French preserves. "McDonald's wanted to compromise by putting Roquefort on cheeseburgers. We told them that was like selling holy water in a sex shop."

By then, the McDo Martyr had spent three weeks in jail for vandal-ism—he refused bail—and was off to protest the World Trade Organization summit in Seattle. He was a hero across France. For those who like sym-bolism, it was all but perfect. In the last days of a millennium, 2,000 years after Astérix le Gaulois resisted Roman globalization, a similarly musta-chioed French peasant was at it again.

Bové the peasant, however, was an ex-Parisian who learned English as a kid when his parents studied biochemistry at Berkeley. He chooses to frame world economics in the simple, earthy terms that crowds love, but away from the cameras he backs up his arguments with thinkers from Thoreau to Thurow.

In fact, as Bové acknowledges, McDonald's is hardly only American. It is listed on the New York Stock Exchange, like France Telecom and Alcatel, but stockholders are spread across the world. In France, ninety percent of its raw materials are local, including the 450,000 French cows and potatoes by the ton it consumes each year.

But it is convenient shorthand for "*malbouffe*," or lousy food, a freshly minted term for any industrial, hormone-laced, genetically altered, or just basically cruddy nourishment.

Bové did not enthrall everyone. "Only in France can one get to be a hero by burning buildings," a senior Ministry of Agriculture official grumbled to me. But he got attention. Prime Minister Lionel Jospin took him to lunch. Mike Moore, the New Zealander in charge of the World Trade Organization, met with him for spirited debate.

The wily intellectual-peasant had put himself squarely at the convergence of interlocking issues. The fundamental problem was linked, in fact, to what bothers so many visitors to Conques. France seems to be deeply troubled by inevitable waves of something new: big versus little, too new versus comfortably old, phony versus real.

The dispute with the United States came as French farmers faced withering profits. Competing supermarket chains, ever larger, forced down prices. And now the Americans were insisting that France buy their artificially stimulated, possibly dangerous, beef.

"Our beef can't be sold at all in Europe," David L. Aaron, the American undersecretary of commerce for international trade, argued. "Even though there are (U.S.) tariffs on European products, they can and will be sold in the United States." He dismissed French concerns as "public anxiety" not based on science.

This was a legitimate issue. Under the Bush Administration, the Food and Drug Administration ruled that genetically modified or hormone-treated agricultural products need not be labeled as such; they were technically no different from natural versions. The French insisted that too many questions remained about biotechnology. They had their own scientists, with some expertise in the field. Besides, they wanted to know exactly what they were eating.

Beyond the issues, there was the principle of the thing. American methods dominated world trade and were altering the way French corporations did business. And now Americans were telling the French what to eat?

Bové made it simple. Astérix, embattled again, faced a whole new sort of Roman.

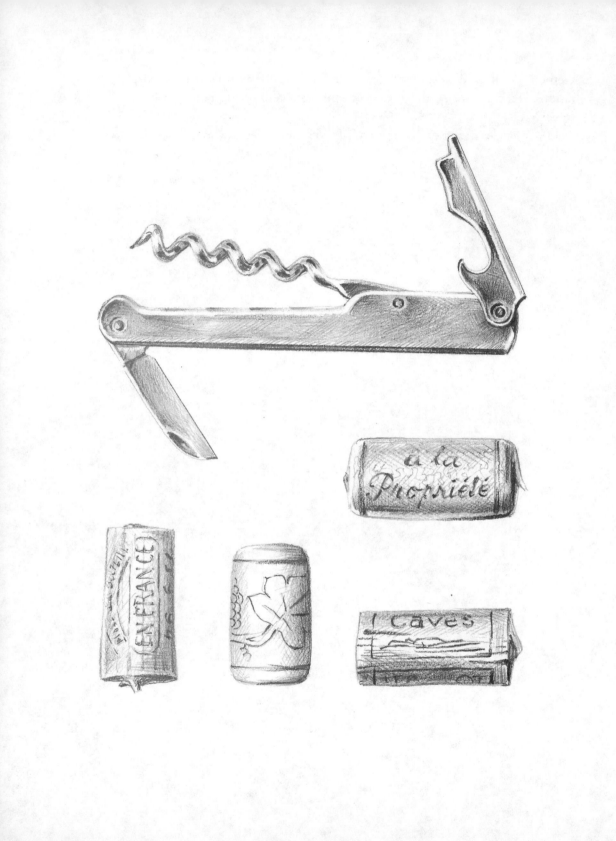

———◄≪◊◊≫►———

Battle of Bordeaux

No sign points to Château d'Yquem near the village of Sauternes. Only discreet weathered Latin letters chiseled into stone, centuries ago, mark the main gate. When your wine runs to the thousands of dollars a bottle, you're not eager for casual schleppers to drop in for a free tasting. Besides, the same family has been making unctuous pale-gold nectar in the same spot since 1593. The 1855 classification of great Bordeaux wines put Château d'Yquem into a category of its own, *premier grand cru*. Anyone who can't find the place by now does not belong there.

In the early 1990's, a French mogul named Bernard Arnault found Château d'Yquem, and the winery director, Count Alexandre de Lur Saluces, decided he did not belong. Arnault wanted to buy the place, along with its old noble name. He had already bought Moët et Chandon, with its signature champagne, Dom Perignon, as well as Hennessey cognac. Both were folded into his Louis Vuitton Moët Hennessey empire, which included the fashion houses of Dior and Givenchy, and was steadily devouring luxury brands across Europe.

Arnault, a short, silver-haired man of fifty for whom the word dapper seems to have been invented, came with a reputation. He rose rapidly in the industrial north, expanding a family fortune made by rebuilding France after World War II. After leaving the elite École Polytechnique, he learned American-style business, managing the Arnaults' Florida real estate. He bought more than he sold. Back in Paris, he took over the bankrupt Marcel Boussac textile holdings, which included Bon Marché Department Store and Dior.

After fourteen years of aggressive deal-making at the heart of *luxe,* he was anointed "the pope of fashion" by *Women's Wear Daily.* The *International Herald Tribune* summed him up differently in a brief caption under the portrait of a determined-looking man with an aquiline nose and ears just short of Ross Perot proportions: "Mr. Arnault has a history of buying firms despite the owners' objections."

A *Wall Street Journal* profile was more specific: "He displays a steely ruthlessness in his business dealings that would make the Borgias look like shrinking violets."

And Arnault's sense of acquisition made Louis XIV look like a monk sworn to poverty. Most wealthy magnates satisfy themselves with a few fancy Swiss watches. He bought Tag Heuer.

In normal circumstances, Monsieur Arnault would have been politely escorted to the gate by a beefy groundskeeper. His timing, however, was fortuitous. The Lur Saluces family was in disarray. Not all were happy with Count Alexandre's firm hand and staunch attachment to tradition. And some were persuaded that multiple millions of francs on the barrelhead were preferable to waiting on nature to produce wealth a little at a time in musty old cellars.

Thus began the Battle of Bordeaux, a punch-throwing conflict hostile enough in its own right but also a revealing symbol of the greater such wars engulfing modern France.

BATTLEFIELDS DO NOT COME any more beautiful. The tidy stone turrets and parapets of the fourteenth-century castle stand on a low hill above vines stretching down to the Garonne River. Château d'Yquem Semillon and Sauvignon grapes grow on 250 acres, and all five premier cru Sauternes châteaux are all within a one-mile radius, watered by streams surrounded by lush growth amid handsome old hardwoods.

Here the term terroir takes on its most complex meanings. The word translates to soil, but that does not begin to cover the nuances. For French vintners and farmers, every piece of land has its own soul. Besides the crucial geology, terroir subsumes culture, history, and bloodlines. And in Sauternes, where a tiny patch might have half a dozen soil types from chalky clay to sand, the significant element is moisture.

All together, a coincidence of nature performs an annual miracle, all within sight of the turrets of Château d'Yquem.

The microclimate of this small section averages ninety-two mornings of fog per year, compared with sixty-five for the rest of Bordeaux. Mists rise off the much chillier waters of the Ciron, a lazy Garonne tributary. The dense Landes forest blocks winds from the Atlantic. With the proper dose of afternoon sun, the grape skins produce *Botrytis cinerea,* or noble rot.

To favor this microscopic fungus and build the fruit's sugar content, severe pruning limits each vine to six bunches. By the time grapes are ripe in the fall, most have lost half their water. Skins have grown a distinctly unappetizing beard of botrytis. Skilled workers harvest grape by grape, returning to each vine up to six times over a month to pick at the perfect level of rot. Elsewhere in Bordeaux, one vine produces an average of two bottles of wine. At Château d'Yquem, one vine produces a single glass.

Once pressed, the must is stored in new oak barrels to ferment. Every three months, each barrel of the strengthening wine is pumped to a freshly washed and sulphur-smoked empty one. This not only separates out sediment but also controls fermentation. After three and a half years in casks and another year and a half in bottles, the wine is ready to leave the château.

But only 100,000 bottles are sold each year, no matter how many are produced. This keeps a stock on hand to fill in during the years when the delicate balance misses a step. If the mists are too thin, botrytis is scarce. If it rains in the fall, grapes split.

In 1985, pickers made eleven passes through the vineyards, waiting for the capricious fungus. They finished in mid-December, in a tight race with the first freeze. In 1992, the whole crop was lost. About once a decade, the wine is not good enough for a Château d'Yquem label, and it is sold instead in bulk as a standard Sauternes. Ah, but those other years.

"Try this," said David Mark, the assistant cellar master, offering me a glass of what amounted to Château d'Yquem nouveau, in a cool stone vault just beyond the treasure trove of stacked barrels. It was a 1994, sweet but fresh with a velvet texture and a lovely long finish. "Normal Sauternes are usually drunk with foie gras, but not this," he said, with a little shudder at the thought. "I love it with a strong cheese, perhaps a good Roquefort."

New Château d'Yquem sells for less than $200 a bottle. But the great years are beyond price. Under the heavy oak tasting table, I noticed a display of the best years, each secured firmly with iron pins. The first had a simple hand-scrolled label: "Château d'Yquem, 1893." Later vintages also bore the name Lur Saluces: 1921, 1929, 1937, 1945, 1967, 1982, 1989.

I could only guess about the earlier vintages, but that last one, I knew, had taxed even the prodigious descriptive powers of American taster Robert Parker: "It [the 1989] is a large-scaled, massively rich, unctuously textured wine that should evolve effortlessly for a half century or more. It does not reveal the compelling finesse and complexity of the 1988 or 1986, but it is a far heavier, richer wine than either of those vintages . . . extremely alcoholic and rich, with a huge nose of smoky, honey-covered coconuts and overripe pineapples and apricots."

Mark, young and friendly, had drawn visitor duty that day. We were a small group: two Japanese women who listened intently to murmured simultaneous translation; a French know-it-all tourist with an overdressed wife; a second French couple who observed in reverent silence; and me.

Visits, arranged by mail and strictly limited in number, start in a grand anteroom displaying mementos going back to the early Renaissance. Mark liked to talk about the noble old wine and its traditions, but he made it plain the domain was hardly frozen in place or time. "Actually, I'm from Burgundy," he said. "They're not racist around here. We're a good team."

It was at least a skilled, hardworking team. We had just emerged, coughing and gasping, from an underground chamber where a crew spent all afternoon burning sulphur bouquets in oak barrels. Outside, others sprayed vines with copper to prevent ignoble rot. No weedkillers are used. Only cow manure is added to the soil every third year. After thirty years, vines are torn out, and new ones are planted. At the same time, centuries-old clay pipes that drain moisture from the vineyards are exhumed and replaced with polyvinyl chloride tubing. And then someone trims the explosion of roses in the central courtyard.

When I asked Mark how the Battle of Bordeaux might affect the team and its way of doing things, he shook his head. "They tell us nothing will change," he said. "I suppose, we'll see." He attempted an uneasy laugh, but this was no laughing matter.

・ ・ ・

THE FIGHT IS ROOTED in a will drawn up in 1925 by Bertrand de Lur Saluces, the unmarried marquis who, at that time, headed the family. He left his entire forty-seven percent stake in Yquem to his nephew Eugène, then three years old. Other smaller holdings had been divided up among numerous family members.

Before Bertrand de Lur Saluces died of heart failure in 1968, he had promised to leave his inheritance to his youngest nephew, Alexandre, who had helped him run the château. Although he mentioned this in at least one letter, lawyers found only the original will, written before Alexandre was born.

Nine days after de Lur Saluces' death, two of his nephews, brothers, agreed secretly to set up a company that would give each of them half control of their uncle's properties, including his share of Château d'Yquem. The company was never established, but the agreement is at the heart of the issue.

While Eugène has hardly set foot on the property, preferring to devote his life to charitable work, Alexandre has run the château with firm attachment to its old roots. Its prestige has been maintained, if not enhanced, over the past thirty years.

On November 28, 1997, Bernard Arnault announced that he was the new owner of Château d'Yquem. His company, LVMH, had bought a fifty-five percent stake for about $100 million. Alexandre de Lur Saluces was caught off guard. He was in Singapore, expecting to meet Arnault in Tokyo to discuss his intentions. Arnault, meantime, had acquired not only Eugène de Lur Saluces' shares, but also those of more than forty other family members, including shares of two of Alexandre's three children.

Uproar followed. Alexandre argued that Eugène's deciding stake could not be legally sold. Family meetings degenerated into shouted insults and swinging fists. A dozen lawsuits in French courts froze the sale. In one, Alexandre alleged that his adversaries manipulated the serious mental "weakness" of his seventy-five-year-old brother, Eugène.

"Earthquake in the wine world!" declared the Paris daily, *Le Monde,* describing an unprecedented sale of the "most prestigious wine estate in the world." Unlike what outside buyers might expect from Médoc, Graves, or Saint-Émilion, it noted, Arnault could not expect large earnings from Sauternes. "I fervently hope that with Yquem, LVMH will twist free of its principles of profit," remarked Bruno Prats, president of the Syndicat des Crus Classés, the leading Bordeaux winemakers' association.

Alexandre's nephew, Bernard Hainguerlot, a financier in Paris, told the *New York Times* that the count had "made life hell for all shareholders [and] that is why we finally decided to sell to LVMH." In *Le Monde*, he denounced references to Eugène's mental health as "monstrous manuevers," which he would refute.

But the count replied, "Mr. Arnault is financing the Hainguerlots to get rid of me. If he gets hold of the château, he will install his fashion models here and start producing a perfume called Yquem!"

If Arnault meant to buy prestige, de Lur Saluces took pains to point out that a good name was no saleable commodity. He traces the château's lineage back to December 8, 1593, when the French crown ceded the land to Jacques de Sauvage, counselor of the king. On June 6, 1785, Françoise Joséphine de Sauvage, dame d'Yquem and sole heiress, married Louis Amedée de Lur Saluces, a colonel in the Penthièvre Dragoons.

"Everything you see here is the fruit of an obstinate pursuit of perfection by my family," he told the *New York Times* in 1997, as the court battles raged. "I feel deeply worried, agitated, and disappointed when I think that the continuity that has created this very fragile environment is now threatened by a corporate shark."

About that time, the respected Bordeaux publisher Mollat produced an elegiac private edition in French and English entitled *Pour Yquem*. Letters from writers, restaurateurs, wine merchants, and journalists evoked past and present glories of the embattled symbol of French grandeur. Arnault, stung by how some portrayed him, added yet more lawsuits to the battle.

Among the essays in *Pour Yquem* was a brief study by a Bordeaux writer named Hervé Lorin, who, according to Yquem insiders not related to the family, came close to capturing the undercurrent of secret dealing.

Lorin is not exactly objective. "Yquem sold!" he began. "The idea seems unthinkable, inconceivable . . . Here is a small study at the bosom of a family deeply divided between the lure of immediate profit on one side and, on the other, the elaboration of an oeuvre d'art and the safeguarding of a patrimony. More than a simple affair of big money, it is also a matter of power (this cancer of the heart) and the eternal problem of artistic creation within a company dedicated only to profit."

A following section entitled "*Le requin et les raisins*" (The Shark and the Grapes), Lorin notes: "Little by little, and not only in the vineyards, the most beautiful blooms of our artistic and cultural patrimony are hijacked at the hands of men to be sacrificed on the altar of the god of profit. This becomes a sad habit. But, after all, Yquem!"

Beyond his Bordeaux-hued prose, however, Lorin lays out some facts and background. This is his version:

At the October 1991 annual board meeting, closed to outsiders, a minority group challenged Alexandre de Lur Saluces' leadership as "too prudent, archaic, and totalitarian," which deprived shareholders of profit. Bernard Hainguerlot, a leader of the attack, accused the count of stockpiling too many bottles and of declaring too much of the recent crop as not worthy of the Yquem name.

In fact, Lorin writes, the Hainguerlot branch seemed to have more than simple management differences in mind. When Bertrand de Lur Saluces fell ill, he also considered his nephew Louis Hainguerlot as successor. When the dying count chose Alexandre, Louis went off to another branch of the industry: as director of Moët et Chandon, which LVMH later purchased.

"Thus the sale of Yquem might well have been no more than the consequence of cold revenge, taken over by a matter of big money. Who, the head of a large holding company or a bitter descendant, led the manipulation?"

That is one version, and the other parties have their own. The realities are complex.

Yquem, in fact, was controlled by two separate structures. One partnership encompassed the physical property of the domain. The other, a limited stock company, made and sold wine. This second enterprise was what interested LVMH.

On September 4, 1998, the Bordeaux Tribunal de Commerce ordered Alexandre de Lur Saluces to execute a sentence pronounced in January and upheld by the Paris appellate court. LVMH was to be registered as owner of the 37.48 percent of shares bought from about forty family members. Delay would carry a 10,000 franc per day fine. Meanwhile, a separate action still had to determine whether Eugène de Lur Saluces could sell his seventeen percent, giving Arnault a fifty-five percent majority.

The recalcitrant count complied, but he also fired off a press release. He would appeal again, he said. Until then, he trusted that LVMH would act as a responsible minority stockholder. He was in charge.

For a while, the Battle of Bordeaux seemed to be sputtering away to a standoff. Arnault was preoccupied with other raids. Mainly, there was the war over Gucci.

A man whose name—François Pinault—might have been concocted by a French playwright for its consonance with Bernard Arnault had sneaked up on his archrival. Worse, it was on the eve of what was to be Arnault's triumphant company rally at Disneyland-Paris.

Pinault, despite his steely blue reptilian eyes that perfectly matched Arnault's, was a different sort of billionaire raider. The self-made son of a Brittany peasant, he made his first money logging on borrowed money. His empire was founded on department stores and large-distribution down-market retail outlets. His fortune was estimated at about five billion dollars compared to maybe four billion for Arnault.

In March 1999, Pinault paid three billion dollars for forty percent of Gucci stock, overnight cutting Arnault's share from 34.4 percent to twenty percent. At the same time, he spent another billion to make a debut in the luxury industry. He bought into Sanofi, which means Yves Saint Laurent, Van Cleef & Arpels, Oscar de la Renta, and more.

Arnault fought back, of course, and that began another lingering conflict likely to last for both rivals' lifetimes.

With all of that, however, Arnault did not forget Bordeaux. At the end of 1998, he teamed up with Belgian financier Albert Frère to buy Château Cheval Blanc in Saint-Émilion, among the world's most prestigious vineyards. When the prized old château came on the market, the billionaire buddies discussed it at lunch in Saint-Tropez and decided to wolf it down before the coffee came.

And then on April 20, Alexandre de Lur Saluces issued yet another communique. The two men had reached an agreement, finally ending the dispute.

The sixth count of Lur Saluces remained at the head of Château d'Yquem, chairman of a restructured joint stock company to make wine. He continued as manager of the partnership controlling other holdings. And he retained the right to pursue his claim against his brother over their uncle's estate. But he approved the sale of Eugène's stock in the winery, and he sold his own. LVMH thus acquired sixty-four percent of Château d'Yquem.

Both men promised to uphold the prestige of their unique wine. Arnault praised his adversary as "completely open . . . dedicated and elegant."

De Lur Saluces cited guarantees "that the values I hold dear are to be upheld." But he also added a final shot:

"Certain members of my family decided to sell their shares in the family estate at Château d'Yquem, in spite of the outstanding financial results obtained over the past few years, thus cutting themselves off from the roots of our shared inheritance. I take note of the fact that four hundred years of family ownership has thus been brought to an end."

DE LUR SALUCES WAS away the two times I visited Yquem, as the battle raged on, and I planned to go back to see him once it was all over. But then he sent me a little book, *La Morale d'Yquem*, which said it all. Journalist Jean-Paul Kauffman spent the first part of 1999 interviewing the count. The book was a transcript.

Early on, a single question dealt with Arnault.

"I directed Yquem for more than thirty years to the profit of a group of family shareholders who should have never complained about its evolution," de Lur Saluces said. "They ceded, in fact, just at the moment when they should have held on to their shares. Because they would not understand and saw no further family solution possible, I thought it more satisfactory to take support from a shareholder who was more solid and, above all, was extremely motivated by the aura of Yquem, by its prestige. I have found a serenity that I have lacked for years."

Mostly, the book was a paean to the count's favorite bunch of grapes. "Some people have gone so far as to ask that their ashes be scattered over Yquem vineyards when they die," he said. "This admiration, this enthusiasm, creates a responsibility in return."

Occasionally, he reflects on jealousies, even hatreds, that divided his family. The picture is not pretty.

At the end, he is blunt. "We had a moral obligation: to do all possible to pass on Yquem within our family," de Lur Saluces said. This was a challenge in France, he added, because of high taxes and strict inheritance laws. When his uncle died, it took him years to find a way to avoid selling part of Château d'Yquem and still satisfy the state.

"With each new investment, I had the sense of working against the eventual transmission of ownership to heirs," he said. "In France, the more one improves a property, the more one makes it impossible to bequeath.

A friend once remarked that we were, in fact, no more than sharecroppers to a state that ransomed owners whose holdings could not escape official surveillance. The passing on of Yquem became more and more problematic. But I did it once, so I had hopes."

De Lur Saluces tempered his earlier judgments of Arnault and appeared to make the best of it. It was a defeat, he said, but a family defeat and not a personal one. Château d'Yquem had belonged to France, as well as the Lur Saluces family. A new partner is welcome if he proves himself worthy.

"Yquem might offer a lesson," he concluded. "We harvest grapes that would be considered lost anywhere else. We give back life to what appears like death."

For all of that, those close to Yquem affirm, Count Alexandre de Lur Saluces is an extremely disappointed man.

In the grand global scheme, this was a small-bore deal for chump change. Arnault tried to spend $8.7 billion for a bigger chunk of Gucci. He lost out, so he bought Pucci. American-style takeovers these days run deep into the billions, with lawyers and investment bankers whose collective fees dwarf the few hundred million dollars Arnault eventually paid for Château d'Yquem. That, for French purists, is simply quibbling about numbers. For them, certain fundamental things of value are beyond price.

Sipping nobly rotten wine at lunchtime on the lawn of the Restaurant Sapien, watching hilltop castles appear and vanish again in the mists across a sea of green vines, I could see the purists had a point. Château d'Yquem had been revered for centuries before there was an "American-style" anything. Among those mementos in the visitors' anteroom is an order from Thomas Jefferson, the United States ambassador, scoring yet another load of George Washington's favorite wine.

What exactly had been sold here? The old domain turned out a definable product, clearly enough, but its value was as much in its timeless traditions and mystique as in its velvety sweet flavor. No faceless legion of shareholders could wrestle such intangible assets onto a balance sheet.

I tried to imagine a fourteenth-century agro-dreamer coming up with something similar in a modern corporate framework: Hey, J. B., I've got a terrific idea for making wine from those disgusting shriveled bunches. It'll take some trial-and-error to get it right, of course. Oh, maybe eighty or ninety quarterly periods of big investment with no return. But, my grandson has a natural nose. He's five. By the time he retires . . .

A young waiter floated up with a bottle cocked and ready. "A drop more, sir?" Instead, I asked him about the battle that just ended across the vineyards.

"It's happening all over around here, the same sort of thing," he said. "Families are splitting up, arguing over inheritances and how things are run. It's easy money to sell and go on to something else. When an old man dies, his land might be divided among his children, and that creates even more tensions. And smaller properties."

As he went further into seamy details about squabbling families who frequented his table, I decided not to ask his name. But I recalled a remark that his boss had made earlier to the *New York Times:* In Sauternes, all the rot was not noble.

Sauternes, in fact, was a perfect crucible for the sort of adjustments France would have to face. Partly, it was the way of the world. The waiter's remarks about dividing up land reminded me of conversations I'd had in Rwanda. With each new generation, more land units that once were substantial, and then merely viable, become too small for their original purpose. But that was only a part of it. Little pieces of France such as Château d'Yquem represented a facet of the world that modern times threatened to wipe clean.

Lamented or not, the feudal era that survived the French Revolution did not quite make it into the third millennium. Large corporate frameworks are now the standard, even for businesses still held by ancient families.

At the heart of it all is Shakespeare's old question: What's in a name? Does a well-loved old label describe a specific piece of reality or something much bigger behind it?

If the product deteriorates, the answer is clear. Pressure for profit could force hired executives faced with quarterly reports to hustle up nature a bit, or relax some old rigid lines.

But what if the purchaser defends the quality, adding new resources to enhance its prestige? Alexandre de Lur Saluces, though hardly happy at the forced turn of events, reported his hands remained free—at least at the beginning—to run Château d'Yquem as he saw fit. The answer would evolve in the traditional way of Sauternes. With time.

ARNAULT'S ACQUISITION of Cheval Blanc as a first course in Bordeaux must have been particularly tasty. His nemesis, Pinault, had not long before lost his own battle of Bordeaux for Château Ausone, another grand Saint-Émilion vineyard.

Pinault bought Château Latour in 1993, which whet his appetite for more. He liked the perfectly preserved stone town of Saint-Émilion and the gentle rolling vineyards around it. Saint-Émilion's 12,000 acres of grapes, protected by Unesco as a world heritage site, produce fifty-five classified *grands crus*. Pinault especially liked Château Ausone. Not only were its vintages highly prized, but it was also rife with family feud.

In 1953, the château was divided equally between two owners, Alain Vauthier's grandfather and a granduncle named Dubois-Challon. The uncle married a much younger woman, Helyette, in 1958, when Vauthier was five. "We had a fairly detestable family atmosphere," he recalled. When Dubois-Challon died in 1972, Helyette inherited his fifty percent of Château Ausone. She lived in an opposite wing of the old mansion, and for a long time the family communicated by registered letter and legal summons. Their spectacular discord over when to pick the grapes in 1989 made the cover of *Wine Spectator*.

Early in 1997, at the age of seventy-eight, Madame Dubois-Challon sold her half of the seventeen-acre estate for sixty million francs. That worked out to 1.5 million dollars an acre. Under French law, the other owners had a right to match the price. Vauthier, his sister, Catherine, and his mother pooled their resources. An uncle co-signed their note. They made it.

"I have always lived here, and it would have been very hard to leave," Vauthier told me a year after the dust settled. "I don't know what impact Pinault might have had, good or bad. A terroir is stronger than any man. But I am very happy to be here and Ausone remains in the family, where it belongs."

But few Bordeaux lovers breathe easy these days.

North of Bordeaux, on the Médoc wedge between the Gironde River and the Atlantic, Serge Barbarin showed me his cellars. Like the de Lur Saluces, his family married into an established vineyard. But that was only in 1963, and the roots of Château Biston Brillette were a mere two centuries deep. Barbarin's hearty red Moulis was noble enough but hardly the fantasy of any wine snob.

Yet, at the other end of the Bordeaux spectrum, Biston Brillette's fifty acres of vineyards produced 140,000 bottles of good wine a year. And Serge Barbarin, at thirty-seven, was holding his own frontline.

"What went on at Château d'Yquem is going on everywhere, just on a smaller scale," Barbarin said. "Outside investors are coming in, for one reason or another. Big producers buy up smaller ones. It's a clear tendency, and I see it getting stronger."

If big was not necessarily bad, he said, conglomeration carried serious risks in his line of work. Making good wine requires someone's loving hand, up close and personal. Over generations, families get to know their terroirs, their varieties, their techniques. It is a lot of work. Temptation is strong for young vintners, or old ones, to sell out.

I went to see Barbarin because I had stumbled upon the château nearly twenty years earlier, and I loved the wine. At the time, Michel Barbarin was not sure his teenaged son, Serge, would follow him into the cellar. And Serge didn't. He dabbled in the tourism business and began to study architecture. But he realized wine was in his bloodlines, and he came back to Moulis.

Once a vineyard loses its force, Serge said, it is extremely hard to bring it back. And it is harder still for a young vintner to start out from scratch.

"These days, it just doesn't pay, if that's your motive," he explained. "A young guy starting out can put an investment of thirty million francs into a winery or a million francs into a bar and tobacco counter, and the difference in real profit isn't that great."

The Barbarins, like most of their neighbors, resisted a popular new trend to make *cépage* wine from a single type of grape.

"I know the Americans like their varietal wines," Serge said, "but we still believe you get a better result by selecting and mixing. The idea here is not so much to bring the wine to the customer, but rather to bring the customer to the wine."

This might have sounded a trifle arrogant from another source. He was simply saying what he felt. Serge spoke almost reluctantly, sometimes with a self-mocking chuckle. I remembered his father as being eager to promote his product. He seemed more interested in making wine than selling it.

The Barbarin method is classic and time-consuming. Fermented juice is blended and aged in oaken casks. Every three months during the initial stage, wine is pumped from a full barrel to an empty one to separate out what has settled. The work never slows. When the crop is in and pressed, it is already time to worry about the next season. Vines are pruned with countless cuts. Each is sprayed with a copper compound against fungus and watched closely for insects or disease.

And then there is marketing. A class of brokers, *les courtiers*, make a business of finding good wines at reasonable prices for established merchants, *les négociants*. With wine from well-known châteaux, brokers are hardly necessary; their two-percent commission amounts mostly to a tax on tradition. But what small producers can't market through a broker, they have to sell directly or by word of mouth.

As all vintners do, Serge finished his tour at the tasting table. I liked the 1996, with a full, fresh power likely to get better and better. Before coming down, I mentioned, I'd unearthed a bottle of 1981 that I'd bought from his father on my first visit. Serge looked doubtful.

"That's a bit on the limit," he said, trying to be kind. "You better open it fast and hope for the best."

I had opened it, I said, and it was wonderful. That made him happier than if I'd asked to buy half the cases left in his shed.

NEITHER ARNAULT nor Pinault bothers to stop at the simple concrete structure marked "Petrus" on the narrow road out of Pomerol. It is hard enough to persuade Christian Moueix to sell a few bottles of his wine, let alone his château.

If one could reliably determine the "most prestigious" winery in the world, Château Petrus would likely win. Perhaps Château Margaux. Or Mouton-Rothschild, or Lafite-Rothschild. Or Romanée-Conti in Burgundy. But there is something about Petrus.

"Château Petrus, the legendary Merlot wine estate . . . has probably received more 100-point scores from this magazine over the years than any other wine producer in the world—and for good reason," *Wine Spectator* wrote. "The wines of this property show a wildly lush and exotic character that simply cannot be duplicated. The wines of Petrus do not charm you with their finesse; they excite you with their flamboyance and generosity."

Here is my purely subjective measure: When I left my car to go in for a visit, I shed my leather jacket in favor of a cashmere sports coat. And when I stood in a small room with the entire 1998 vintage—only two thousand bottles' worth in oak casks—I felt badly underdressed.

For France, Petrus amounts to a few minutes of history. It was first mentioned in Tastet & Lawton's notebooks in 1837. If its wines came to

Paris for Napoleon III's 1855 World's Fair—the one for which brokers drew up that famous list of Bordeaux growths—no one made a fuss over it. Until the end of World War II, Petrus was owned by a family named Arnaud.

Madame Loubat began buying into the château in 1925. By 1945, when the war ended and Bordeaux had one of its best vintages ever, she was sole owner. Jean-Pierre Moueix, a Bordeaux négociant, acquired exclusive rights to sell Petrus in 1947. After she died in 1961, he bought shares from her nephew. Moueix's son, Christian, has managed Château Petrus since 1970.

The place is tiny. Its thirty-seven acres fan out from a modest nineteenth-century mansion, with its *chais*, the wine-making vaults, attached. A converted stable for the tractors sits just across the road. Fixing a value would be an interesting exercise.

"Cheval Blanc is just over there," observed Frederic Lospied, when I asked about outsiders buying into Bordeaux. Lospied, a gentleman of impeccable manners, works on the négociant side of the business and is detailed as host to a trickle of visitors.

Unlike the Château d'Yquem grapes, the Merlot and Cabernet Franc of Petrus are supposed to ripen perfectly, round and full, for the mid-September harvest. At a mere forty meters above sea level, Petrus is the highest point in Pomerol. Its heavy clay soil, different from the sand and gravel found elsewhere, holds rainwater longer at the surface. Roots expand horizontally.

Vines are ruthlessly pruned in winter to leave only six to eight buds per plant. And in July, grapes are thinned by up to a half to concentrate growth for a final yield of no more than three tons an acre. No fertilizer is added and vines are sprayed as little as possible.

At harvest, a regular crew of about 150 brings in the grapes within twelve hours, over two afternoons. "We get a great number of volunteers," Lospied said, with a small chuckle. "We are flattered but, of course, we don't use them. That would be a little difficult. Our harvesters have been doing this for up to twenty-five years. There is a certain skill."

Pressed juice ferments in concrete tanks, which, since 1990, have been equipped with computer-driven heat exchangers; these are coils that run the depth of each tank. After the blend, typically nine-tenths Merlot and the rest Cabernet Franc, young wine is stored in new French oak barrels. It is aged about twenty months and often takes another decade lying still in a bottle to reach its full maturity.

In an average year, Château Petrus turns out 3,500 cases. During 1998, with erratic rains and long hot summer days, the production amounted to only 2,000 cases of what promised to be among the finest wines of a century.

"Shall we taste some?" Lospied asked, perhaps the least necessary question I had ever heard. He uncorked a half bottle and poured out intense, luminous color. The highly complex nose hinted of fruits and spices. The texture, rich and complex, was supple on the tongue. A blast of lovely ripe tannins shook to the core my lifelong predilection for Burgundy.

Lospied appreciated his mouthfuls and then carefully spit them into the silver lined barrels provided for that purpose. But I'd be damned if I was going to spit out Petrus. We sipped and talked.

No, he said, Bordeaux did not suffer unduly from scandal in the early 1990's, when some producers were caught adding sugar to their wine. But yes, he added, Bordeaux suffered from greed in 1997. After two very good years, producers raised their prices significantly in 1997, confident that another good year would justify. But 1997 was mediocre, and buyers howled.

"You can lose a customer in a matter of minutes, but it can take years to get him back," he said. "I think everyone got the message, however. People are not willing to pay any price, especially when there are excellent wines elsewhere. Bordeaux lost a lot of market share over that."

But Château Petrus is doing fine. One-quarter of the 1998 would go to the United States, more than would stay in France, to be parceled out by Seagram Château & Estate, its principal importer. Over decades, bottles would most likely change hands at prices well into the thousands. The 1961 Petrus that made most experts' wines-of-the-century list runs to more than $2,800, not much less than a 1945 Mouton-Rothschild or even a 1921 Château d'Yquem.

Eventual high prices have no direct impact on the Château Petrus accounts. The wholesale price to Seagram is a secret, but Moueix remarked to the *Wine Spectator* in 1999: "I don't make that much profit on my wines. The highest price I sell wine for is fifty dollars a bottle." But a 1995, say, retails above $500. And Sam Bronfman of Seagram explained: "It's the job of the marketing person to make wine as valuable as possible. Petrus commands a lot of money in the United States because it is great."

But that is part of the new economy, and the society around it. Money is how you keep score. After well-heeled revelers raided their cellars for millennium parties, rare Petrus grew that much rarer.

Whatever the prices, Christian Moueix is happy making Petrus. And, barring the unforeseeable, Lospied added, new wine will be made eventually by his children and their descendants. As the level in our half bottle dropped down, he concluded: "Some things are not for sale, monsieur."

<><><>

SIX

Burgundy at a Snail's Pace

AMONG THE RICH, rolling hills of Burgundy, man and God were in perfect sync for the last season of the millennium. Chardonnay grapes and Charolais cows grew fat, from the first spring rains to the dappled light of Indian summer. Pinot noir and potatoes survived a brief early cold snap. Bumper harvests of plump, juicy fruit warmed the hearts of vintners and farmers from Chablis to the edge of Chalon. In the village of Alligny, deep within the smoky gloom of Paulette's place, someone actually smiled.

As France weathers its way into a different sort of world, Paulette Millot manages to miss out on change. But it is not easy. In her half-empty bistro, and in thousands like it all over the country, the past does daily battle with the future.

"Ah, oui, life as we knew it is ending," Paulette lamented to me on one gray afternoon. Her remark was remarkable mostly for its length. She was not in the habit of wasting so many words on a nonregular.

Paulette once had to serve invading German troops and now business is so slow she is happy to see the odd Teutonic tourist stray off the autoroute. Her grandmother opened the bistro back when Alligny, a languishing village near Saulieu, was a wealthy farming center with shops and a comfortable hotel. In its heyday, it offered three meals a day instead of just drinks.

For three generations, the one-room pub bound together a community where vintners fretted over rain, grandmothers bragged about their boeuf bourguignon, and the priest lingered over cognac.

Now Paulette is eighty, bent and so nearly blind that she sneaks a finger into the glass so she pours the right amount. Regulars sit by the potbellied stove on chairs antiques dealers would kill to own.

"When I go, Alligny is finished," she said, probably not exaggerating. The only shop in town is a bread dispensary, not even a real bakery, with a few shelves of groceries.

On any given evening, men in filthy wool caps grumble that the European Union might ban their raw-milk cheese. Women in muddy boots fear their sons might become hooked on Paris and leave the farm. They still talk in long-gone "old francs," with two extra zeros. They're suspicious of this new European currency called the euro.

Long moments go by as patrons sip in silence. Sudden diatribes excoriate the weather, or Brussels, or a boss, or a hired hand. Meanwhile, Paulette shuffles from table to table on thickening ankles, peering from behind bottle-bottom lenses, with her half smile of doom. As embers die in the potbellied stove, the view offers little cheer.

But, of course, that is one extreme. In France, there is always the other.

Just up the road from Paulette is her life-long acquaintance, Paule. In ordinary circumstances, a retired career civil servant of nearly ninety would be Madame Blondelet. But, as she happens to be Froggy's grandmother, she waves away such formality.

Paule lives alone in an apartment for the elderly, but she often sees family and friends. She gets by comfortably enough on the pension she earned working in the town hall at Château-Chinon. In her day, she dealt often with François Mitterrand, who was mayor then. She loves politics. With no office to go to nor anyone in particular to impress, she still does her hair and dresses like the elegant Frenchwoman she is.

"Our old foundations will remain solid," she told me one afternoon. "We have to change. Everyone does. But that does not mean we have to give up what is good. The more that France modernizes, the more we hold onto our values."

Some things alarm Paule as she keeps watch on a society evolving with time. She handed me the semiannual village newsletter, with an outraged letter from the mayor. Kids had vandalized the communal Salle des Fêtes. They were caught, and the damage repaired, but Alligny was not used to such things.

"These poor morons who wanted to bring to us one of the scourges of today's urban civilization realize nothing of the life we are developing here," he wrote. "They don't see this center belongs to us all because of our common efforts, the very foundations of democracy. We know in our hearts that the rural world protects the values at the base of our society, and we won't be distracted by those who have lost their way, whose only expression is destruction."

When Paule sees fear in France over restive youth and the effect of four million immigrants on the social fabric, she is frightened about where such fears might lead.

A levelheaded liberal, she is hardly one to bear blind grudges against the past. But she watched how it all happened, from Weimar to the Third Reich. Paule was already thirty when Nazis invaded France. She sheltered her children in Alligny and covered for her husband's activities in the Resistance.

Now she sees the National Front, a France-first party that blames society's worst ills on North African immigrants and globalization, as a symptom of some things that are going fundamentally wrong.

But mostly she is optimistic, confident that France will keep a healthy balance. The key, of course, is the old family dining-room table. Froggy and I had just stuffed ourselves with Bernard Loiseau's cooking at the nearby La Côte d'Or, and I mentioned his philosophy of defending traditional recipes and ingredients.

"He's right," Paule said, "and that's what keeps us together. We are going back to our basic resources, to our families and traditions, as a counterweight to all this change."

As evidence, she described in loving detail all of those ritual gatherings, when great-grandchildren hover at her elbow as she roasts a haunch of lamb. We spoke of holidays past, and she reeled off menus with elaborate care. After three-quarters of a century, she remembers each course of the meals that celebrated communions, marriages, and births.

Paule has a lot of time and is happy to discuss these themes at length. But she can sum them up in a single phrase, overworked but nonetheless the crux of what will save France, or won't: family values.

· · ·

AND, OF COURSE, the family car. Two hours before sunrise one morning, heading out of Paris on an icy southbound freeway, I was not particularly surprised to find a traffic jam.

First, there was the Saint Vincent festival at Chablis. On the last weekend in every January, Burgundy towns take turns as host to a Bacchanalia honoring the patron saint of wine. Second, it was the start of the winter school break, when Parisian families direct themselves lemming-like toward the ski slopes. Third, I was in France.

I had gotten up early so I could reach Chablis, about an hour and a half away, before the parade started. Saint Vincent festivals begin with brass bands accompanying nobles of seventy Burgundy wine fraternities, *confrèries*, who march at dawn with their vineyards' standards on their shoulders.

It should have been a quick trip. French drivers routinely cruise the autoroutes at ninety miles an hour, even when still asleep at 5:00 A.M., and the road surface looks like coconut sorbet. But French drivers also tend to crash when the weather is bad. I was stalled miles behind a smash-up, grateful not to be in the ambulances speeding northward, but still a little miffed.

I need not have worried. Organizers had predicted 150,000 people would jam the few medieval streets of downtown Chablis. When I reached the freeway exit, however, the other cars sped on toward Chamonix. No sensible Parisian hurries to stand in freezing wind at dawn just to watch a bunch of red-nosed old duffers in silly tricorns on parade. They would arrive when the wine-tasting caves opened.

Even the locals were late. Gendarmes clustered on street corners had no idea about the parade route. A kid with a trombone trotted along, his band tunic askew, and I asked where the marchers would start. "How the hell should I know?" he replied over his shoulder, without slowing.

But it wasn't hard to find. Trumpet blasts and thumping drums reverberated down the stone lanes and ricocheted into the main square. The band out front carried a banner reading *"Fanfare Les Enfants de Chablis 1862."* Although a few horn players looked as though they might have been in the original troupe, most members were enthusiastic teenagers.

One by one, names to dream by paraded past: Puligny-Montrachet, Pommard, Vosne-Romanée. Some groups numbered in the dozens, chevaliers with solemn faces as they trundled along their emblem, usually a carved, painted saint on a fancy litter. Others were small knots of youthful vineyard workers, waving at friends and laughing. And most had clearly begun sampling each other's products well before breakfast.

Toward the end, a man and a woman loped along the edge of the parade, giggling as their black velvet robes flapped in the wind. They were late and trying to find their assigned position. Between them bounced an elegant gold-painted saint on a pulpit labeled, "Gevrey-Chambertin." The next time a funereal sommelier served me that lovely red as though it was meant to be worshipped in silent awe, I'd remember the parade. Wine, however fancy, is supposed to be fun.

In the gray cold, Chablis was ablaze in bright color. Townspeople had decked the place in crepe-paper flowers. Purple wisteria hung from arches in the streets. Red roses studded little fir trees on every corner. Yellow tulips bloomed from frozen window boxes. Floats and life-sized figures decorated each front yard. In the main square, a gigantic bottle poured (not actually) white wine onto a huge revolving globe. Like Sherwin-Williams paint, it suggested, Chablis covers the world.

This was a street fair as only the French can produce. Fat sausages sizzled over open fires. In the depths of ancient wine caves, short-order cooks served platefuls of snails in garlic and butter. There were no games or cotton-candy stands or flags to wave. Instead, there was wine to taste. Each visitor paid the equivalent of five dollars for a glass that hung around the neck on a ribbon. Thus armed, the crowds converged on forty thousand bottles offered by the town's dozen wineries.

If this was Burgundy, it was also France. Before any serious tasting began, band members gathered around the monument to war dead, a ubiquitous feature of any French town. Nearby stood the twenty members of the Confrèrie des Piliers Chablisiens, in three-pointed hats and cloaks of gold and green. And, under a snapping Tricolor, a crowd of moist-eyed people sang "La Marseillaise" like they meant it in the morning chill.

I didn't stay long. A free-for-all is not the best way to savor wine. And I was not eager to try my luck again with those ambulances when that Chardonnay-besotted mob returned to Paris.

This was, in fact, the second time I'd come across a circus in Chablis. On my earlier trip, there was only one visitor instead of 150,000. But since he was a bushy-bearded Cuban general with a barrel chest and army fatigues, he caused enough stir.

Fidel Castro, on a diplomatic tour of Europe, had stopped in Burgundy to visit a French chicken king who kept his besieged island in poultry. He traipsed dutifully around the fowl-packing plant alongside a host bursting with pride. He brightened visibly when it came time to climb back into his black Renault sedan for a thirty-mile ride through the countryside to J. Moreau & Sons winery in the center of Chablis.

Throughout the trip, Castro was much more friendly than the goons around him. Occasionally, I shouted questions at him, trying my best to use a Cuban accent, which is essentially rapid-fire Spanish spoken as though you're choking on a chicken bone. He answered each time, as guards hustled him along. Fairly confident of the outcome, I waited while he and his hosts finished a four-hour lunch.

When Castro emerged unsteadily, I yelled, "Comandante." He shifted course in my direction and knocked aside Cuban and French guards like so many bowling pins. We chatted amiably, and he punctuated his remarks with a friendly jab of an index finger that all but pierced my sternum.

Finally, I asked about his mission of diplomacy.

"I don't know what my visit to Europe did for Cuba," he said, with a booming laugh, "but it did a lot for me. I love Chablis wine."

MICHEL LAROCHE IS thrilled when anyone loves Chablis wine. After four generations of Laroches struggled to earn enough from their vines to make ends meet, he has built a thriving enterprise. In 1999, when *Wine Spectator* rated his Grand Cru Les Clos 1996 as the white wine of the year, he nearly fainted with pride. And then, his flinty Chardonnay was a hit of the New York Wine Experience.

A quarter century ago, a third of Domaine Laroche wines went to the United States. But the word Chablis has gotten to be attached to such dubious domestic bulk fluids that Americans tend to retch at the sound of it. By 1998, Laroche was selling less than two percent of its production in America. Now that is changing fast.

"We have worked for years to show Americans that Chablis is not something you drink out of a jug," Lorraine Carrigan told me, when I returned yet again for a more leisurely look at the northernmost part of Burgundy. An Englishwoman of uncommon energy, Lorraine is Laroche's official cheerleader but also a committed lover of his product. "I think they are beginning to catch on."

Chablis, like Champagne, is named for the fragment of France from which it comes. It is extremely hard to produce since the fragile buds must survive March and April in a place where nasty late freezes are a matter of course. Vines require a limestone soil called Kimmeridgian, named for a Dorset village, with the crushed fossil oyster shells that give it its rocky, acidic crispness.

During the Sun King's seventeenth century, poets were already writing that Chablis and oysters were worth any man's fortune. Today, vintners have refined old skills to season the wine by aging it in matured oak barrels. It is bad enough that decent California wine calls itself Chablis. When screw-top skid row rotgut goes by that name, feelings run high.

Reasons for this go way beyond snooty. Like all appellations d'origine contrôlées, Chablis defines a microuniverse. It comprises less than ten thousand acres of vineyards on hillsides and valleys laid out according to their exposure to the sun. Its chalky soil is so whimsically distributed that much of that acreage produces only *petit chablis,* with less power and meant to be drunk young. Weather patterns go from very hot to damned cold, with scattered rainfall that must be generous in early summer.

And, like everywhere in France, there is tradition. Monks migrated from Tours in 877, a few steps ahead of the Vikings. Invading Norsemen could get their boats up tributaries of the Seine and the Loire. But Chablis was just enough of a walk from the Yonne to be safe. When the Vikings left, monks found the Yonne was handy for sending wine to Paris.

Early monks brought the relics of Saint Martin, remembered for tearing his cloak in half to warm up a chilled beggar. These remained ensconced in the crypt of their thousand-year-old monastery, l'Obédiencerie, until recently. Now the underground vaults contain oaken casks of Laroche's latest Les Clos. When finished, it will not be available in screw-top.

"Wine making is all in the grapes," Laroche told me, in the old church above the vault. "Vintifying requires skills and flair, but these are things you can master. We can hire real talent. If you don't start with perfect fruit, nothing can save you. And if your winery is to be successful, you need a lot of perfect fruit."

The first Laroche began making Chablis in the 1850's, joining a boom that increased cultivated vineyards to 100,000 acres of both Chablis and red wines. Phylloxera wiped out the vines, followed by World War I and then successive heavy freezes. By the 1950's, Chablis farmers hedged their bets with corn and cows, devoting barely 1,200 acres to wine.

In 1967, at twenty-one, Laroche took charge of new land that his father added to the family's original fifteen acres. Now he owns 326 acres and has expanded into southern France, near Béziers.

"I had to change things dramatically," Laroche said. "Especially from the seventies, people were using huge amounts of chemicals. They sprayed too heavily with pesticides and fungicides and herbicides, on a schedule whether it was needed or not. Too much chemical fertilizer. I looked at this—every year, more and more, with steadily growing resistance—and saw that this had to be wrong. So I went back to the way my grandfather did it. Just a little of what is absolutely essential, and only when it is essential."

Not exactly. The Laroche forebears battled spring frosts with nightly prayer. Michel, more proactive by nature, added smudge pots. When the mercury dropped to zero, he fired up those same oil-burning contraptions that Arizona citrus growers used to love. Greasy, foul-smelling black smoke curtained off excess cold.

Later on, Laroche brought in higher tech. A fine spray of water coats the young buds as temperatures drop. An icy crust locks in just enough warmth in the same way that igloos protect Eskimos.

In 1989, Laroche eliminated chemical fertilizer altogether. Instead, each winter he fortifies his vineyards with manure to restore the natural balance.

Next he refined harvesting techniques. Although Domaine Laroche handpicks on steep slopes, eighty percent of the crop is collected by machine. A padded arm grips the base of each vine and shakes it at rates of up to one thousand vibrations per minute. Grapes drop off the bunch onto a tarp, leaving naked skeletons to be cut away at the next pruning.

Harvested grapes are trucked to a vast hangar outside of Chablis, a stark contrast to the ornate stone offices in town. This end of the operation is all business: four units of gleaming stainless-steel presses, with a laboratory, vats, conduits, gauges, dials, bells, and whistles, all linked by a mainframe computer that could run the French nuclear fleet.

The trick is to handle the grapes as little as possible, conveying them up to presses designed to allow juice to drop by gravity without being stained by the skins.

Jean-Pierre Colas, the cellar master, uses his Boeing cockpit technology to work in the old ways he learned growing up outside Chablis. Certain strict rules govern the process. But the nuances depend on flexibility. Colas' own nose and instinct tell him how much of what to mix with what, and which to keep for how long in what size oaken containers.

And at the end of this carefully thought-out process, digitally controlled at every stage, the same old mystery hangs in the air.

"I was so nervous, I could hardly stand," Laroche said, recalling the *Wine Spectator* New York Wine Experience when he opened his laurel-draped Chablis for expectant connoisseurs. The 1996 Les Clos is meant to be aged another five to ten years. If opened early, it needs to stand for perhaps a full day to breathe. "With these wines, you can never be certain. Can you imagine the embarrassment if something had gone wrong?"

Making trouble, I asked Laroche why it mattered what a bunch of Americans thought. He took me seriously.

"They have quite educated tastes in America," he replied. "It's wrong to think that only the French can judge wine. Almost every Frenchman thinks he knows everything about wine. Most know nothing."

And many, it seems, are paying less attention than they did. I ate lunch at the one-star Hostellerie du Clos, where Michel Vignaud serves succulent Burgundy snails out of their shells, in parsley and garlic confit.

Vignaud, an engagingly humble chef-propriétaire, offered an excellent menu at reasonable rates. Every chair was full. The staff, not numerous, did its job well. Vignaud's wife watched the front, and he seemed happy in the kitchen. I expected a welcome shot of optimism.

"Me, I am pessimistic about the future of French food," he said. "People aren't taking the time to educate their kids about taste, or even demanding quality themselves, for that matter. The economic balance is very delicate for chefs like me. I don't want to be a star. I don't need to be rich. But still, I've got to run my business."

Vignaud explained how Charolais beef farmers were cutting corners to satisfy a need for lower prices. But what really got him going was snails.

"Imagine," he said. "In Burgundy. Ninety-five percent of our snails come from somewhere else."

EVERY EVENING at sundown, it is roundup time at Jean-François Vadot's snail ranch. Vadot puts on rubber boots and enters the stinky, damp gloom of his converted pig shed. His 40,000 head of escargot are penned into sloping metal corrals he designed himself. After laying out fresh food and making a cursory check of his herd, he is finished.

It is a simple process but noble nonetheless. And Vadot, the Burgundy snailpuncher, feels embattled and alone.

"I'm about the only guy doing this, certainly on a big scale, and I don't know how much longer it will be viable," Vadot told me. "Pretty soon, I'm afraid, my customers will start asking me to kill the snails instead of delivering them fresh. It's a question of economics. Even the grand chefs don't want to pay extra for live snails. But if I have to pack the meat here, that will mean freezing . . ."

At the f-word, Vadot paused to shudder. After all the years he struggled to deliver snails on the hoof, it would be an ignominious end.

Once upon a time in Burgundy, *les escargots* were so plentiful that train tracks were diverted to avoid places where steel wheels might crush too many at a time and lose their traction. In the fifties, however, farmers began to discover new ways of living better with chemistry. Those same pesticides and strong fertilizers that horrified Michel Laroche amounted to a holocaust for snails.

To cap it off, railway workers discovered that cutting grass along the rails was too much work with a scythe. Weedkiller did the job much faster.

Now you can spend an afternoon trying to round up enough snails for a simple *douzaine d'escargots de Bourgogne*. Instead, frozen carcasses are flown in from Eastern Europe where snails are plentiful and seldom on anyone's menu. Hungary and Bulgaria, among others, cover nine-tenths of the total market.

"There is simply no comparison between the rubbery, flat taste of a frozen snail and the tenderness of a real one," Vadot explained. He is lanky and balding, a fifty-three-year-old Robert Duvall with that wry deadpan look on his weathered face. You can seldom tell what he is thinking unless the subject happens to be snails. Then passion overcomes all.

"These are endearing little fellows," Vadot said, as one bull snail prodded its slimy horns at his extended forefinger. They are not free range. The snails live hundreds to a small pen, spending most of their time sleeping upside down, stuck to the smooth metal above them. Food is placed on an outside ledge; each snail must muscle aside others and stretch out of his shell to reach it through the bars. This keeps the food off the filthy pen floors. It also means survival of the fittest.

Vadot's snails are *gros gris*, larger than the *petit gris* which run wild, figuratively, in Burgundy. When butchered, their intestinal tract can be lifted out. This eliminates the need for a long cleansing diet before slaughter.

Vadot was born in his village of Blancey, not far from Saulieu, in the faded-grandeur château just out his front door. His father, a dirt-poor farmer from the back end of the Morvan, had come to sharecrop at the château. In time, he earned his own land. Jean-François inherited a struggling little farm and a mountain of debts to go with it.

Neither the pigs nor the cows were enough to live on. An idea to raise ostriches came and went. Likewise, a career in hunting the so-so Burgundy truffle. Then Vadot hit upon snail ranching.

"I invested all my money, and a government agent came out to give me some advice," Vadot says, with bitterness still lingering in his laugh. "Everything he told me to do was exactly the opposite of what I should have been doing. I lost everything. My wife urged me to keep on going. Life is designed so that every individual has a chance to seize the moment. By then I had so much put into this that we figured my moment had to do with snails."

Vadot went to Bernard Loiseau and made a deal. He would deliver fresh escargots. Loiseau would buy them. Both were delighted. As his herd grew, Vadot found other chefs to buy forty percent of production. Now, in spite of a shelf full of do-it-yourself snail raising books, he prefers to pioneer on his own.

Up close, tending snails does not look easy, and it is not.

"Top secret," Vadot replied when I asked what went into the feed. Marine algae is part of it, along with fresh grains and certain sorts of flour. Snails must put on meat, but they cannot be allowed to get too fat for their mobile homes. Shells, though stiff with calcium, need a certain flexibility that comes from diet.

Their sex life is picturesque. Snails are basically male except when two mate, and one of them lays eggs. Reproductive organs are located in the flat part that oozes from the shell under the head. In cages, snails produce eggs every four months.

Snaileries are nothing new. The Romans fattened up snails on bran and wine. Frenchmen developed a marked taste for them after Talleyrand had his noble chef, Marie-Antoine Carême, prepare them for the visiting czar of Russia. No self-respecting kitchen is without its little forks and rounded pincers for gripping shells awash in garlic-parsley butter.

As we left the snail corrals, however, Vadot sounded fresh variations on the grim litany I had heard almost everywhere I went.

"I'm a paysan and happy about it," he said, "but I put in maybe fifteen, sixteen hours a day and don't earn the minimum wage. Now they have a thirty-five-hour week for most people, but who pays for it? Us, of course, with all these special levies and taxes they try to sneak past us. Damn, I can work thirty-five hours in two days. It simply makes no sense."

A quick glance around Blancey supported his point.

"Who do you see here? No one. There's no more school, no more café. You can go a week without seeing anyone else. You have to drive a half hour for bread and all the way to Dijon for a pair of shoes. What kid will stand still for that?"

Vadot's own kids did not seem to mind. But their world seemed to be taking a different shape.

"I can feel it coming," Burgundy's lone snailpoke concluded. "Pretty soon, my customers will want dressed meat. I don't want to kill my snails. I'd do it badly. It takes a long time, and I can't do enough at once. That'd mean spending hours at it and then freezing the meat until the next day. And in the end, if all I produce is frozen snails with that same rubbery taste, what's the point, anyway?"

Vadot walked me back to a car that I felt silly to have locked. He was the only guy around to steal it. He spoke with a final burst of passion, and it wasn't about snails.

"If you're a paysan, and want to do a good job of it, you're dead where you stand," he said. "Aspiring to quality is like going into the priesthood. It's a personal commitment with no balancing reward. That's how it is. You either go along with it or go bust."

As LONG AS I was within sniffing distance of La Côte d'Or, I followed my nose back to Loiseau. If he shared any of Vadot's forebodings, he was not letting on. Since my last visit, Loiseau had launched his little culinary enterprise onto the French equivalent of Nasdaq. He had opened two restaurants in Paris. His picture appeared on a brand of supermarket meals. And he was adding yet more space to his hotel. For him, optimism was a matter of financial survival.

His initial public offering went badly, and the stock was not soaring. His Paris restaurants had gotten mixed reviews. Not everyone was impressed that he endorsed industrial food.

Loiseau, however, is an optimist. *GaultMillau* magazine had just named him among the eight greatest chefs in France, and that buoyed his personal spirits remarkably. On the larger question, he holds that food is the only reliable barometer for gauging the state of Frenchness. And he considers that question an open and shut case.

"People come back to what they love," he said. "It is what anchors them. You can try new things, and you can add nuances here and there. It is a challenge to keep finding the best ingredients you can and use them well."

Loiseau was building to something. Just in case, I edged back beyond his range. Suddenly, his arms flapped open, and he leaned forward.

"But in the end, my cooking does not change," he declaimed. "Anyone can follow their imagination and invent. Hardest of all is to be there, day in and day out, lunch and dinner, making the same thing with the exact same perfection. That is cooking. That is what the French love best."

I nodded encouragement, and he shifted to high drama. "Where does it stop, all of this fanciful innovation?" he asked, expecting no answer. "You try to invent some new dish every night and you end up with, what, sorbet au Chanel No. 5?"

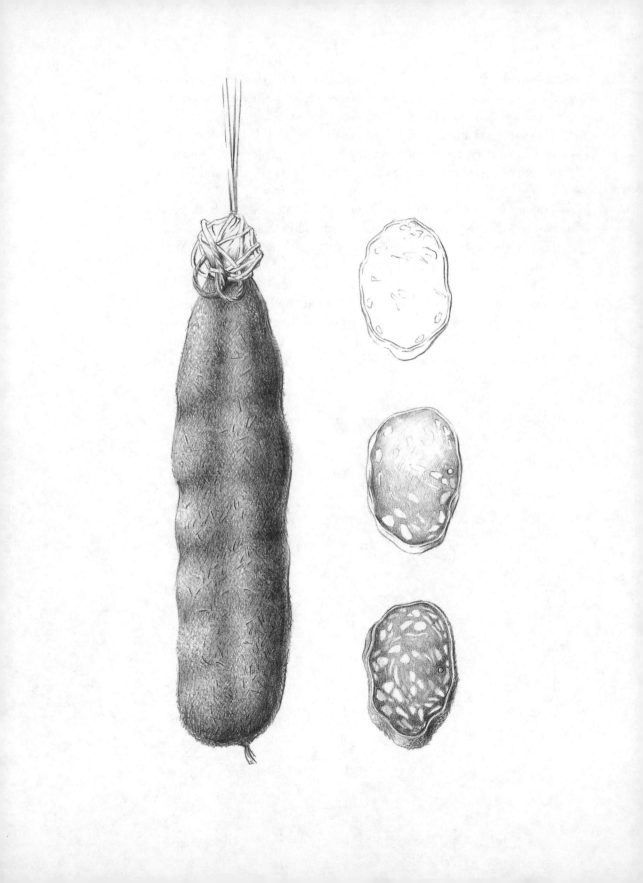

SEVEN

Les Enfants Terribles

OR *SORBET AUX CÈPES*. Right, mushroom sherbet. It is one of many reasons to hurry to—or run screaming from—Marc Veyrat's three-star posh palace of culinary whim on the shores of Lake Annecy.

Veyrat and a small band of high-profile iconoclast friends articulate a different view from traditional chefs like Loiseau. For them, the old school lacks flair and daring. They see no limits, either to ingredients or imagination. As long as you are tossing in South Indian spices or bits of West African cactus, you might as well make ice cream from fungus.

This can go to extremes. Rather than simply adding a few rare wild herbs, Veyrat garnishes one dish with a brick of smoldering pine bark. Who says he can't make pastaless ravioli from underbrush? Enthusiasts call this the wave of the future. Detractors have other descriptions.

The idea is sound enough, and it is rooted deeply in modern French cuisine. Tomatoes and chocolate, for instance, began as exotic imports. Veyrat's group of declared apostates claims Paul Bocuse as their pope. After all, he was the first big name to champion nouvelle cuisine. When the eight members first declared themselves, they totaled twenty-one Michelin stars among them.

The senior rank included the popular Parisian Alain Passard of Arpège, and the born-again Pierre Gagnaire, who went bankrupt with three stars in the grim city of Saint-Étienne only to regain his stars in Paris. There was also Michel Troisgros, the youngest of the Roanne clan, along with Michel Lorain of Joigny and Michel Bras of Laguiole. Two-star members are Olivier Roellinger of Cancale and Jacques Chibois of Grasse.

I was especially interested in Veyrat for historical purposes. A fine French restaurant is essentially an extension of the personality behind it. And, as chance would have it, I knew Veyrat when. It would be fun to revel with him in his success and reminisce about the old times. Perhaps I might also learn something about character development in the hallowed Michelin galaxy.

Veyrat was a regular part of my winters when I moved to France in the mid-1970's. A friend used to take me skiing with her family at a tiny spot called Croix Fry, a few wheel-spinning turns past Thones in the Alps just above Annecy. Only the tiny Veyrat family inhabited Croix Fry: a sister and a brother, who rarely spoke to one another. Marie-Ange struggled on her own to run the family's rambling, rustic lodge, established by their grandfather. Her husband had been crushed to death when a truck he was repairing slipped off the blocks. Marc, determined to make a name for himself, opened a restaurant up the road.

Going to Marc's was an undertaking of no small proportions. We had to lie to Marie-Ange about why we were missing one of her fabulous *raclettes* or fondu, which, on demi-pension, we had to pay for anyway. We always spent a fortune with Marc, although his prices were reasonable for France. The food was so good that we just waved in the general direction of the long menu and said, "Yes." Then there was the drive home in the snow, stuffed like Strasbourg geese, freezing cold, and half blind from heady local wines and Savoyard digestifs that the twenty-something chef-propriétaire lavished on us.

It was always worth it. The kid could cook, all right, but that was only part of it. The passion he brought to his kitchen was something to behold. In those early years, Marc Veyrat could barely have broken even. Regularly, he would burst from the kitchen with an elaborate experiment, one of his "surprises" that would not appear on the bill. Once it was a palate-clearing exotic fruit sorbet under an elaborate sculpture of baked spun sugar. Another time, he had figured out how to infuse bouquets of mountain herbs into everything but the napkins. He appreciated any adulation, but mostly he wanted connections. Marc, with big-time plans, was sure he lacked only a better location and financial backing.

For all the good food around him, Marc had a perpetual lean and hungry look. He greeted regulars with more relief than warmth. When the dining room was half empty, as often as not, he had time to visit. The topic was always chefdom. He had been to Paris for a course in something or other. He was competing in a young chefs' competition. Someday, he pronounced as if swearing on a biography of Brillat-Savarin, he would be a triple star.

Part of the fun was that we felt like we were supporting the arts. Here on a backwater Alpine meadow was a one-time logger and shepherd producing all the glories of the French table: colorful collages of perfectly cooked prime ingredients on fine china amid crisp snowy linen. Most chefs rose early to cruise the markets, but Marc had to add an hour and a half round-trip to visit his suppliers. He stayed at it well past midnight, helping his slim staff clean up the evening's mess. Meantime, he studied. From his enthusiastic effusions, I learned more about food than I had picked up in a lifetime of eating.

I wrote about Marc Veyrat a few times but then lost touch. We started skiing at Val d'Isère and frequented other tables. Still, I remembered him and his grand dream. He had the stuff, but France was hardly short on culinary talent, and only a hearty few diners and the odd mountain goat made it up to Croix Fry. If he did make it, I felt certain, he would be somehow ennobled by the hard road to the top.

And then in the mid-1990's, Veyrat suddenly blazed in the firmament. He had gone bankrupt in his first attempt at the big time. But there he was in the newspapers, beaming at the award of his third star, still in his signature black wide-brimmed Savoyard hat. Had I looked a little closer, I'd have noticed that the hat was several sizes bigger.

BY THE TIME I reached Veyrat's new place in 1998, I was ready for anything. No comment about him was lukewarm. At one extreme, French food lovers gushed. François Mitterrand had visited by helicopter. At the other, I'd heard his manner referred to in terms normally reserved for late-night cable television. To keep an open mind, I did little prior research. To reserve an audience, I sent him a fax.

Assuming he would not remember me, having fed a lot of people in the interim, I explained who I was and what I had in mind. Perhaps we could chat after dinner. Whatever else, I figured, the fact that any writer who was making a twelve-hour round-trip journey to taste his food and pay his prices ought to shake loose a brief encounter. After all, the place only sat sixty. A polite reply from the reservations clerk confirmed my fax but made no mention of Veyrat.

The Auberge de l'Éridan was not hard to miss. Its imposing elegance, it turned out, was one of Veyrat's wars. He had managed to circumvent a village ordinance in Veyrier-du-Lac, adding on a third story. Neighbors who found themselves looking at the chef's name in huge letters rather than their beloved blue lake ran for their lawyers. The building, nonetheless, stayed.

Inside, the place was splendid. In the eleven guest rooms, Rolex had plated faucets with gold and imbedded golden flecks in the sinks. This was another battle. Veyrat took a loan worth five million dollars and spent something closer to nine million. When the bank wanted its monthly payments, he was crushed. A classic bit of network footage from 1995 shows Veyrat in a teary sulk, threatening to close the auberge and throw a hundred people out of work if the bank did not lower his interest rates. Something was arranged.

From the trouble I had booking a table, and the cars in the lot, I guessed that Veyrat's financial troubles were behind him. If his neighbors dined elsewhere, plenty of people shot down from Geneva and the tonier resorts nearby.

An immaculately tuxed *voiturier* took the car, a de rigueur beginning to any top-class French feed. We descended in a glass elevator with a view of the wine cave and then swished through a posh parlor decorated with Savoie antiques and wooden farm tools. One glass case displayed Veyrat's cookbooks and assorted honors. Another featured a photo of the chef in his broad black hat, musing about life with a silly-looking flower in his mouth.

Our table was perfect, but almost immediately I got an unmistakable whiff of what in America I'd call attitude. For the French, of course, that would be a crude simplicity. Buying a mere morning croissant in France can lead into a thicket of innuendo and nuance where impressions are hard to miss but easy to misread. In a pretentious restaurant, these subtleties can be an impenetrable jungle. All you can do is sniff the air, read the signs, and hope for a pleasant trip down the path of least resistance.

The staff was surprisingly young, and each gave the impression of over-weening pride to be flying so close to the sun. This could be a good sign, meaning that the place prepared a regular fresh crop of apprentices to populate the future. It could also mean that even the hardiest soon decided they could not stand the heat and got out of that specific kitchen. In any case, for reasons of pure bigotry, I was a little uneasy. Surgeons, stock-brokers, and sommeliers ought to be old enough to shave.

The clientele was heavily American, especially for late September. This, again, meant nothing in itself. Plenty of foreigners appreciate good food and insist on the quality for which they are billed. But, for the same reason that Americans count trucks outside a roadside beanery, Frenchmen check the room for well-polished possible repeaters. A lack of this category suggests the place might have shifted toward the realm of uncouth Anglo-Saxon red-guide camp followers who would rave if served deer droppings in *béchamel*.

The test came soon enough with the dreaded language issue. This is always tricky ground. Speaking French, contrary to the belief of many peo-ple who speak French, is no particular accomplishment. France is full of two-year-olds who handle it fluently. Not many foreigners who flaunt their perfect French could comfortably order a meal in, say, Uighur.

But French is the language of a fine restaurant in France. Along with the tastes and aromas and sights, there are the sounds. It is the murmur of a charming old reprobate trying to put the model across the table in a mood to take her Armagnac upstairs. Or the luxuriant rise and fall of a well-told story from the next table. And if possible, dishes are best left untranslated. In French, you might find something like *ragoût de boeuf épicé aux haricots rouges*. In English, that's chili.

If you get to call a crêpe a crêpe back home, why must you call it a pancake—or pahnk-ache—in France? Images of Aunt Gertrude with her fluffy pink slippers and box of Betty Crocker mix tend to dim down the effect of Champagne.

For me, Hubert at Loiseau's La Côte d'Or is the perfect model. He is fluent and charming in English, if the diner wants it that way. But if Hubert senses a diner would prefer to speak French, even mangle French, in the interest of *luxe, calme, et volupté*, he generously obliges.

"It's the nose," Hubert explained to me once. "We call it *pif*. That's the whole secret. You must guess exactly what each person wants from the experience and then provide it. If they want you to be invisible, you disappear. If they want drama, you are the show. The language, like the mood, is theirs to choose."

Experienced waiters might start with English to offer the option. The good ones know that pressing it implies an insult that, at the very least, harks back to old French prejudices that all Americans are rich, vulgar, and monolingual.

It harks farther back than that, if one wants to poke around in the nuances of condescension which so enrich French civilization. Charles Dickens caught the sense of it in *A Tale of Two Cities*, as Madame Defarge, the dour wineseller and secret revolutionary, deftly ices an Englishman whom she suspects is spying for the king's police. Polite formulations, strained through the teeth with contrived simplicity, make the insecure outsider want to bolt for home.

Today, the meaning is clear enough: We'll serve you because you're here, and we will find a way to communicate, but don't make the mistake of feeling as if your substantial dues entitle you to membership.

At Veyrat's, someone had apparently instructed the serving staff that non-French do not get to speak French. My guest was an accomplished actress who could have faked elegant French fluency even if she had not learned the language long ago. I manage.

One young waitress in a costume revived from forgotten folklore threw herself into English, undaunted by her inability to speak it. We each replied in French. She persevered. I tossed in some Savoyard slang, a few convoluted subjunctives and my best Charles Boyer back-of-the-throat rumble. She stumbled along, returning often to the one word, bread, that she handled flawlessly.

Finally, we wore her down. Still, she had her revenge. My friend, who spends her time in the north of France, asked about *sariette*.

"It is an herb that grows in Provence," the waitress said, in French. "It is very well known," she added, pausing slightly to add the implied: by everyone but you, you stupid cow. "If it means anything, the name in English is savory."

It was that sort of evening.

Veyrat made no appearance, but he is reputed to avoid setting foot in the dining room. I gave my card to a young man whom I assumed to be the maître d'hôtel. He went off and said no more about it. When the first course arrived, however, the waiter announced, "A surprise from the chef."

The warm foie gras in fennel on the menu was accompanied by a slice of cold foie gras flavored with fig compote and bitter orange. Both were excellent. After a terrific course of a lake fish called fera, there was another surprise. The waiter produced, with a grand flourish, three tepid quail eggs in cream.

Now here was the sort of dilemma you face when a Gulf Arab host honors you with the sheep's eye at a formal dinner. Visceral hatred is too mild a term to describe my feelings for raw egg yolk, and I don't like cream. I considered leaving the gift untouched. Then I remembered Loiseau in his kitchen, peering at each returned plate to see who left what. Closing my eyes and pretending they were merely sheeps' eyes, I swallowed down the quail eggs.

This was followed by another trial, a grim gelée of fowl in sharp-flavored herbs. But then there was a wonderful purée of *rattes* with truffles. (A ratte, when I asked, was described as, "A delicately flavored, tender miniature tuber found in the hills of Haute Savoie." Another answer might be, "A small potato found almost everywhere in France.")

I was eagerly awaiting the pièce de résistance, slices of tender light and dark chicken in a flaky crust. Instead, the waiter produced yet another surprise. From the more expensive menu, he served a roasted pigeon in bitter cardamom.

By now, I was seriously confused. If Veyrat was being generous, I did not want to be ungrateful. Yet, looking around, the occasional "surprise" seemed fairly standard. And I had not chosen the chicken on the (slightly) cheaper menu to save money. I didn't want the substitution, however good it must taste to fanciers of nearly raw pigeon. But this was business.

The cheeses were well-chosen Savoie specialties, from a creamy Reblochon to pungent pellets of chèvre from Veyrat's backyard of Manigod. The desserts were at least inventive, including Veyrat's trademark cluster of five floral-infused crèmes brûlées, each to be eaten in its proper order. I had a pleasant flashback memory of the masterful frozen concoctions that used to appear at Croix Fry. That was when the flavors of mushroom sorbet arrived.

We shifted to the couches for coffee, and I asked for the bill. The amount, impressive, topped two hundred dollars a person. A humble Condrieu red that costs 123 francs at the vineyard came in at 630 francs. Each glass of *vin de paille*, which the sommelier offered with the foie gras as though it was a courtesy of the house, was 125 francs. But I wasn't there to quibble about the prices.

Before leaving, I sent yet another card to the chef. In due course, a waiter announced, at least in French, "Monsieur Veyrat is on the telephone. He will salute you on the way out at reception." Something in his tone suggested that I had choked down those quail eggs for nothing.

Fair enough. Escoffier did not mingle with the clients, either. But then neither did Escoffier encourage television cameras to film him gathering moss under forest logs.

And Veyrat was a busy man. Apart from l'Éridan, he was the highly visible technical adviser to a French food conglomerate that did everything from running tour boats on the Seine to feeding airline passengers. Also, he counseled a ubiquitous Italian restaurant chain.

I decided not to wait but nonetheless bumped into Veyrat on the way out. If the fax had reached him, it had not registered. I evoked the old days, triggering a slightly pained oh-God-another-groupie smile. He was not eager to relive his humbler beginnings.

Whether he suddenly felt an expansive wave or he detected yet more publicity, Veyrat warmed up before I beat a hurried retreat. He added wattage to his smile and led us through the swinging doors to the log cabin playhouse he had built smack in the center of his giant kitchen. It was the All-French Dream.

If American street kids escape the ghetto by learning to swish three-pointers from half court, French peasants slip their traces by whisking eggs to a tasty froth. Veyrat had cooked up an empire, and he was proud of it.

"Here, I create," he explained, waving toward a flat surface cluttered with sketches, letters, and half-evolved ideas. "Here, I educate," he added a moment later, showing off a classroom theater with banked seats and overhead mirrors where the people who turn out industrial packaged food products come to learn how to inject some of the master's magic. "Here, I relax," he said, flopping into one of the chairs he keeps for pals who spend hours helping him recycle the wine cellar, bottle by bottle.

And there, he did not say as he glanced toward the heart of the kitchen, he terrorizes. The little cabin has a commanding view of staff at work. And vice versa. Veyrat's helpers keep a sharp eye on the door lest he come storming out to deliver a blistering bollocking for a real or imagined foul-up.

"Our group of *chefs révoltés* believes that there is no such thing as hard and fast rules," he said, when we sat down to talk food. "The traditional ingredients from the mountains and forests, the old ways of preparing dishes, can all be used in new ways. Tastes evolve, and so should we."

I mentioned Loiseau, and Veyrat bunched his lips and rolled his eyes. "He's stuck in his ways, poor old guy," he said, the rebellious son giving up on a father who just won't learn. It was clearly a matter of preference, but the comment struck me as odd. Veyrat, *l'enfant terrible*, was forty-eight. Loiseau was forty-seven.

PIERRE GAGNAIRE DOES NOT wear a funny hat, and he does not seek out photographers to picture him at creation. People go to him for lunch and dinner, not a circus, and he devotes his energy to shield them from disappointment. When he stops to talk, he is rapid-fire and not particularly articulate. Not rude, just busy with thoughts elsewhere.

Gagnaire's not overly celebrated restaurant in the eighth arrondissement is frequented by the sort of French eater who knows what he likes and is in search of a pleasant new surprise.

"The world is full of rich flavors, and we look everywhere," Gagnaire said, as I digested a fabulous duck done expertly with flashes of saffron and deftly sliced Asian vegetables. "We cannot restrict ourselves only to things that someone else has done before, or to only what we find in France."

He does not borrow, however; he colonizes. Once a spice or a savory ends up in his kitchen, it is as French as couscous. Whatever the dish, it appears as an art form on a large, fine, snowy white plate, situated just so in a nest of blinding linen, glinting silver, and stemware that reflects beautiful people at the next table. At the high end of Paris, experimenting with flavors is one thing. All of the rest remains sacred.

For an enfant terrible innovator, Gagnaire is strangely doctrinaire. He does not even like foreign apprentices. "I get a lot of applications from everywhere, especially Japanese," he said, "but I've got to be careful. People come to learn our secrets, to take away our art."

In talking to Gagnaire, and then to other révoltés, I sensed that this whole debate had gotten blown all out of proportion. Marseille bouillabaisse, a terroir dish if there ever was one, depends upon saffron. The most hidebound old chef in the deepest corner of olde France uses Indonesian black pepper.

Whatever his articulated philosophy, Gagnaire is a young version of the old-style exacting, temperamental French chef who believes that cooking is as all-consuming an art as Impressionist painting. But unlike other sorts of artists, the pride is strictly personal. Once a chef d'oeuvre has been devoured, it is gone.

"Gagnaire is a sniper," a senior Michelin inspector once told me, meaning that as a high compliment. "He taught himself cooking, and he learned well. He masters the basics and yet he is willing to try anything, any idea or combination, to see if it works. If it doesn't, he'll just take another shot."

Pierre Gagnaire was the one who horrified French foodies by going out of business in spite of Michelin's ultimate seal of approval. He played and lost a shaky bet. Rather than move to a well-heeled city or charming countryside, he opened his restaurant in his hometown of Saint-Étienne. It was a gritty little industrial city with few jobs, diminishing fortunes, and a football team for culture. But if his food was good, he insisted, people would come. It was, but they didn't.

The loyal following from the old days could not afford the new prices. A few artists paid with their work, but soon the walls were full. Tourists who strayed into Saint-Étienne usually ended up lost in the one-way streets before heading elsewhere. Lyon was only an hour's drive away, but who wanted to leave Lyon at dinnertime? Gagnaire, meantime, refused to lower standards and head downmarket.

Had he capitalized on his three stars, Gagnaire would likely have been able to subsidize his restaurant and earn a handsome living. Veyrat counsels restaurant chains, among other things. Loiseau has not only his endorsements but also stockholders. Michel Bras produces a line of vaccuum-packed dishes, and he works with Lagioule knives in his remote part of central France. Alain Ducasse, even more than Bocuse before him, is a one-man conglomerate.

Gagnaire, however, is only a chef. When I asked him if this was enough, he found a burst of half-mumbled words to say that it was. The more telling part of his answer was a surreptitious glance over his shoulder at the work piling up in his kitchen. Feeling merciful, I let him go.

IF JACQUES CHIBOIS IS a rebelling iconoclast who rejects the old ways, he manages to disguise it well. His Bastide de Saint-Antoine in Grasse restores wavering faith in everything holy about the French Sunday lunch.

He may borrow methods and flavors from elsewhere, but the stars of his menu are French crustaceans and fish, served succulently in olive oil and the freshest of Provence and Côte d'Azur vegetables. When he is not hurrying to the Nice airport to accept yet another award somewhere, he can be a warm host, in the old aubergiste tradition.

I'd first met Chibois in Avignon where a group of French chefs had gathered to show some of their secrets to visiting American food writers. Clearly, he loved his work. Each knife cut was a functional flourish, elegant without an erg of wasted motion. He shifted effortlessly from luxuriant slow motion to blinding speed, depending upon the job at hand.

"Simple," he kept saying of his subtle alchemy, as he tossed about ingredients in a sauté pan with all the simplicity of a surgeon tying back-handed sutures in the dark. He joked easily and often as he worked.

In his own habitat, Chibois tends toward subdued and harried. He is after perfection, and his dining room is substantial. If a table of people in silk ties and heavy makeup want to take their meal seriously, he will oblige. For friends and low-key regulars, however, he is always ready for a laugh.

One Sunday, I asked Chibois if he thought the French leisurely lunch was in danger, with all the other options now available each weekend to busy people living modern lives.

"It is, in a way," he said, twisting his ginger mustache into a thoughtful mode. "But this is what saves it," he adding, sweeping an arm across his patio. The gesture took in rows of elegant tables and stopped at a towering bank of blazing red bougainvillea that over decades had been pruned to frame each window of the inn's three-story stone wall.

Sitting in that splendor, I felt the same rush I remembered from Les Baux-de-Provence when Raymond Thuilier served me my first great French meal. Back then, Thuilier was in his eighties, more than twice Chibois' age. But there was something ageless and timeless and Frenchly generic about a perfectly done outdoor terrace.

The food was wonderful. But food was only part of it.

IT IS IN Alain Passard's immaculate little Parisian kitchen where the metaphor comes together. Perhaps the most imaginative chef in France, and one of the most skilled, Passard manages to make it all look easy. And he puts words to it.

Passard sees the group of eight as no more than friends who share a highly personalized idea of cooking. When he lays out their philosophy, you can substitute almost any word for "cuisine" to see where an evolving France might be headed.

"We are a mix of chefs who love the old French cuisine but also a French cuisine that is eager to open up to the world, the whole world," he said. "We look for new ways to cook, to season, to buy products. That is so easy now. I travel a lot, to Japan, to Sweden, to California. Everywhere, I find things—a product, a passion—of very good quality."

France had plenty to offer, but why stop there? "After all," he continued, "what is a product? A color. A taste. A *parfum*. A shape. A light that reflects. I love the feel, the design of products, wherever they come from."

I met Passard in his cluttered office not long before he had to go cut up ducks for the evening service. A friend waited in the corner with something on his mind. The phone rang, and he gave patient instructions for feeding his kids at home. A *sous-chef* came in with a crisis. But Passard loves to talk about food almost as much as he loves to cook it. I scribbled furiously to keep up.

"What I really love, when I need inspiration, is to walk through a market. That's my source of revelation. The other day, I created something incredible. I came upon a pile of onions, beautiful white onions, almost translucent, and next to them was a small crate of dates. The two were almost winking at each other, a perfect dialogue."

Passard's friend, having forgotten what he came for, leaned forward to hear the rest.

"I took them to my kitchen and made a wonderful *fond d'oignons au beurre salé*. To that, I added little cut-up pieces of date. This I served with grilled lamb, seasoned with cumin, in a light sauce of *verveine*, mint, pepper, garlic, olive oil, a little coriander. It had the flavor of Morocco, slightly spicy. People went crazy for it. They thought they were in Marrakesh."

This was for starters. Passard might have been a composer or a painter, speaking of subtle touches and bold strokes to create something sublime. A dish must have balance and tonality, he explained. Acid is offset by a note of sugar. Each sort of bitter demands its own type of sweet. All of the flavors have to come together. You must find the right tonality.

Not long before on a market ramble, Passard came upon nasturtiums.

"I like to work with flowers," he said. "I made a *velouté* of nasturtiums, and the flavor called for something else. Iodine. So I added the coral of sea urchins, which brought out the essence of the flowers in sublime harmony. But it needed a third element. What to do? I tried a few spices, and then I hit upon saffron. Only the slightest pinch. You shouldn't be able to taste it but merely suspect that it is there."

He rhapsodized about the rich yellow color of nasturtiums. His friend, enraptured by now, blurted out: "And orange."

Passard smiled indulgently. "Only yellow," he said. "The orange loses some of its verve in cooking. But the yellow . . ."

Chefs like Passard are an endangered species. Arpège seats forty, and he has forty employees. The high-quality ingredients he demands are horribly expensive. He resists the temptation to branch out, preferring to stay in his kitchen, where he knows he is needed. Yet he is decidedly upbeat about the future.

"True, those of us in my end of the business may be the last of our kind," he said. "There is too much expense and effort compared to what comes back. But I don't think the standard of French food is dropping. Quite the contrary."

France, he said, is full of people in their twenties with fresh ideas and business sense. "Their formula works very well," he said. "It's the old bistro style: low investment, simple but good food, high quality, reasonable prices. People flock to these places."

At the same time, he said, artisans are finding ways to improve upon the old products. His latest discovery was a man in Normandy who raised superlative pork from free-range pigs.

"The basic element here is people who get their hands into the process," Passard concluded, reviving the theme that motivates Lionel Poilâne. "This pork guy is completely nuts, but he is terrific. It is wonderful to see these people at work, whether raising food or preparing it. Our quality is handmade, that's the difference. With a chef, you can tell immediately by the way he moves his fingers. If he has a heavy hand, it is deadly."

Passard could have gone on all night, but it was feeding time out front. And, by then, I was perfectly stuffed and seasoned. I left champing at the bit to get back to finding more of those products, people, and places.

A Goose
in Toulouse

———

EIGHT

A Goose in Toulouse

THERE IS SOMETHING singular about the lovely old capital of Languedoc, with its pink hues and grand parks and undercurrent of gaiety. The mood is relaxed, satisfied, yet well short of smug. Even during the World Cup, when English soccer thugs were urinating on the bushes and heaving bottles for sport, a courtly old gentleman of Toulouse simply shrugged when I drew his attention to them. "It makes for a change," he said.

During the World Cup, in fact, the city supplied visitors with "smile vouchers," which they were asked to give to "the most courteous and the nicest" local residents they encountered. Those who earned the most vouchers at the end were honored by the Association de la Courtoisie Française à Toulouse.

I put it down to all that goose fat.

What else could it be? Geese have always loomed large in Toulouse and the surrounding Musketeer territory, from Gascogne to the Landes. I knew about olive oil country and had a fair notion of butterlands. But goose grease? I decided to learn more.

In the tower of books threatening an avalanche across my desk, I found an album of rural postcards showing French peasants between 1900 and the Great War. One, from Toulouse, depicts a woman massaging the long neck of a goose as she crams yet more corn mush into a funnel stuck in its bill. This is how you make foie gras, of course. It is also the way to plump up a fowl so that it renders the fat essential to the cassoulets and confits so beloved to southwestern France.

At the Paris Agricultural Salon, I bumped into a show-stopping *oie de Toulouse*, the Toulouse goose. He was a real bruiser, with barrel chest and broad back. Fluffy feathers covered a thick neck. His head was high and proud, with a noble bill. Thick grayish-brown plumage draped enough goose flesh to brighten the Christmas of a very large family.

He was, I learned, the bigger of two sorts: the Toulouse goose with a wattle. These can top twenty-five pounds. But the smooth-necked variety breeds more enthusiastically, which means it is preferred by the producers of foie gras.

Soon afterward, I found myself at Les Jardins de l'Opéra in Toulouse, beaming happily at an earthenware crock of the restaurant's succulent signature cassoulet Toulousain. Run by a two-star master named Dominique Toulousy, Les Jardins is a temple to regional cooking. And Fructuoso Polo, the roly-poly Spanish-born chef de cuisine, gave me the first secret in a single word.

"Duck," he said.

"Duck?" I echoed.

"Duck," Polo repeated, with convincing finality. He folded ample forearms across his chest, in case I wanted to make something of it. "We don't use goose. Duck is much finer, much tastier, more flexible. You can do anything with it. And it is cheaper. For cassoulets, confits, foie gras. Not goose. Duck."

This, I soon realized, was hardly the last word. Controversy over fowl of choice rages with growing intensity among chefs and consumers. Those in the duck camp are far more numerous, and their ranks are growing. Yet plenty of traditionalists still prefer to cook a goose. The question, most likely, will never be settled. Given a choice, southwesterners prefer both.

Dinner at Les Jardins de l'Opéra makes a hell of a case for duck. Almost everywhere else, cassoulet is made from white beans cooked at length in fowl fat. Toulousy does it the old way, with tender green fava beans. An essential element is Toulouse sausage, meaty pork that is loosely packed in its skin so that it saturates with flavorful cassoulet juices. Most cooks sprinkle corn starch on top to give their cassoulet a crust on top. Toulousy uses only a layer of duck grease, crisped in a final flourish. But the crucial ingredient is *confit de canard*, duck cooked in its own fat with salt and then potted.

"It's not hard to make," assured Polo, the standard line of chefs as they toss off interlocking miracles with food and flame. "In the end, you can always tell when the duck is ready. You can pass a straw through it, right to the bone. It must be that tender."

TOULOUSY IS A duck man from goose country, reared in the nearby department of Gers. Especially on farms in the hilly Gers backcountry, purists still like the stronger goose flavor, gamey and pungent. It is an acquired taste going back more generations than anyone can remember. Long before people thought much about ducks, geese starred in local lore and literature.

From the standpoint of tradition, in fact, the case is open and shut. Geese were domesticated at least three thousand years ago, maybe even eight thousand years ago, while until only relatively recently ducks were quacking in the wilderness.

Romans stuffed geese with dried figs to fatten their livers; we have that from Pliny the Elder. Ancient Egyptian designs depict something suspiciously similar. In Egypt, sacred geese were offered to the gods. The Greeks also honored the goose, as did the Mesopotamians. Celts left food in their tombs to nourish the departed, and roast goose was a favorite meal for the transcendent journey.

In 390 B.C., Gallic hordes besieged the Roman Capitolio for more than seven months. Famine had weakened the defenders. Gauls sneaked in for a final attack, but geese about to be sacrificed in the Temple of Juno raised a squawk. The Romans, thus alerted, overpowered the Gauls. Since then, geese have been permanent residents of the Capitolio. Every year on the anniversary of the battle, geese are paraded through the streets on richly decorated litters.

After Rome conquered Gaul, herds of geese followed a sort of Chisholm Trail from Boulogne and Calais to Rome, driven by goose boys. Charlemagne ordered country domains to remain well-stocked with geese. Goose poachers were severely handled. Eventually the peacock, and then the turkey, were also thus protected.

Queen Elizabeth had just sat down to a fat roasted goose at the Château d'Amfreville on September 29, 1588, when messengers announced that

Felipe II's Invincible Armada had been blown awry in a storm. "Bring me more Burgundy," she is alleged to have cried. "I need it to toast this fine goose and the news of this wonderful day." A year later, she had the same meal and decreed that the lord mayor would be elected on that day.

Times change, alas, and I drove from Toulouse into deepest Gers to update myself on goose-duck matters. I wanted to find Toulousy's old friend, André Daguin in Auch, the legendary duke of duckdom. Daguin was the first to serve rare sliced duck breast, giving the world *magret de canard*. Years earlier, I had stopped at his Hôtel de France for a two-star lunch. The foie gras menu offered duck liver in a dozen ways, from warm *escalopes* in delicate fruits to garlic-laced pâté.

Daguin's retirement in the mid-1990's sent his devoted clientele into mourning. His daughter Ariane was comfortably packing duck products in New Jersey, running a company called D'Artagnan. His sons and second daughter were occupied elsewhere. With no one to take over the Hôtel de France, he sold it outside the family. The stars went quickly.

I had hoped to find Daguin in Auch, perhaps wearing faded blues and pottering around out in back of his home stuffing grain into ducks for old times' sake. In fact, I found him months later, in a serious suit and a large Paris office a few steps from the Élysée Palace. He commuted from the Gers for four days each week to direct the Union des Métiers et Industries Hôtellières.

Beefy and barrel-chested, with gray hair brushed back from a ruddy forehead—and hardly retiring—Daguin spoke in a broad Gascogne accent that his new surroundings did nothing to blunt.

On the duck-goose issue, he came straight to the point. "Well," he said, "figure it out. There are three hundred thousand geese in France, and there are ten million ducks. Soon there will be three hundred thousand geese and sixteen million ducks."

The sharp shift was relatively recent, he said. Fifty years ago, geese and ducks were raised in equal numbers. By 1970, however, geese leveled off at 300,000 and ducks had multipled to five million.

"Ducks are so much easier to raise and to fatten," Daguin said. "Try to stuff grain down a long, delicate goose neck. It takes a real professional to do it—and a lot more time. But ducks are so voracious, they almost stuff themselves."

Chefs prefer to work with duck livers, he said, rapidly sketching some comparative fowl anatomy on the back of a letter to make the point. Because of differently shaped lobes, duck livers are easier to steam, sauté, and scallop. When cooked in a pan, they do not reduce in size like goose livers.

"I'm not going to say that one tastes better than the other, but people have their preferences," he said. "The taste of goose liver is more compact, perhaps, and duck has a more marked flavor. All in all, I'd say duck is more popular."

The French love both kinds. Altogether, 30,000 families in southwest France, in the Strasbourg area and elsewhere across the country, make their living by force-feeding fowl to produce foie gras.

When it comes to rendering fat, geese are far superior. Ducks provide more meat, pound for pound, because so much of a goose is grease. With fat, Daguin said, there is little difference between the two. "The taste is similar, and both are chemically the same—unsaturated, so they are easy to digest and good for your heart. Just like olive oil."

Daguin explained his own success as a chef with fetching modesty. "When you invent a dish, you don't really discover something," he said, "but rather you just put together what is already there in a new way, according to circumstances." Magret de canard is his best example.

"People always knew the possibility," he said. "My grandfather used to tell me that the breast of duck was by far the best part, but that it was dangerous. Back then, and until not long ago, ducks were allowed to peck around in their own filth. You were much better off to make them into confit or at least cook the meat for a long time."

Modern breeding changed all that. Once ducks began to be raised in controlled pens and given mixed feed, the meat was free of parasites.

"That's when I got the idea of serving it very rare, sliced thin like beef," Daguin said. "I took some ribbing at first, but it seems to have caught on."

Daguin is my particular hero because of another innovation. Before him, chefs sautéed foie gras, but they served it whole. If you did not have four hungry friends at the table, it was out of the question. But he decided to slice it into escalopes for individual portions.

When Daguin began cooking, the foie gras cycle was limited and seasonal. Ducks began laying eggs in the spring, and the first ducklings were old enough to be stuffed just in time for Christmas. By fall, egg laying stopped until days got longer again. But electricity made the difference. With lights to mimic the sun, ducks now lay eggs all year long. And this, naturally, explains the spike in their population.

Fowl breeding, I remarked, seemed like a good example of how modern times were improving the way Frenchmen ate, despite so many reverses.

"Of course," he snorted, with a dismissive wave. "French cuisine would be in fine shape. What is killing it is the government tax policy. Every year, three thousand restaurants in France go bankrupt, usually to be replaced by fast-food joints." Suddenly, we were a long way from goose fat.

"It's these petty bureaucrats and their stupid tax inequities," Daguin fumed, no longer the diffident provincial ex-restaurateur but now the lobbyist defending a whole culture in peril. He punched numbers on his telephone and spoke briefly into it. Moments later, a secretary appeared with a fat dossier.

Before I found time to digest the restaurateurs' complaint, it was all over the evening news. Chefs in tall white toques gathered outside the National Assembly and pitched eggs. Police sprayed them with tear gas and carried some off to jail. Basically, restaurants had to charge sales tax of twenty percent. But fast-food joints, which served meals in paper sacks, were allowed to charge less than six percent.

Daguin was well-placed to howl. He won his two stars the hard way, and here he was with all the data in hand to look at his profession as a whole.

"If young chefs starting out can't make a decent living," he said, "what can we expect for the future? There are plenty of skilled people ready to work the long hours, to make the sacrifices, but they have to turn some profit if they are to succeed."

With him, the Big Mac attack was not ideological.

"Look, I'd rather have a sandwich at McDonald's than a *blanquette de veau* at some bistro where they don't know how to cook," he said, "but I don't want to see decent bistros dropping off the map just because of officially created false economics. At the beginning, the McDonald's people and other fast-food operators were able to convince the authorities that they were carry-out service outlets. Now they have an unfair advantage."

At the top end, Daguin said, economic pressures can be even worse.

"After a second Michelin star, it is almost impossible for a chef to make a profit from his restaurant," he explained. "The best you can hope for is to market your name as a consultant, in books, in endorsements, with a shop, a hotel. Every centime your kitchen earns goes to keeping up quality, paying staff, taxes. Especially if you're not near a large population, you have to do something else as well."

That, he added, was why Pierre Gagnaire went bust in Saint-Étienne. In Daguin's view, Gagnaire may be the best chef in France—or at least close to it. But, in the face of hard economics, that is not enough.

I asked Daguin what he thought of the purported battle between the traditionalists and the révoltés—Veyrat, Gagnaire, and the rest. He snorted again.

"That's just some invention of food writers who want something to talk about," he said. "Everyone uses exotic ingredients, and everyone tries new things. Some take it further than others, but the basic rules are the same."

Daguin stopped to laugh from somewhere deep down.

"Can you imagine French chefs getting together on anything? You put thirty or forty in a room, and they won't find a single thing to agree on. Even cooking times. They're impossible. Everyone has his own idea, his own little tricks and prejudices. And that's just how it should be. The day they start agreeing on things is when good French cooking will be finished."

"GOOSE IS COMING back into fashion," declared Régis Chiorozas, with the satisfied air of a vindicated man. "And it is about time. It is a much nobler fowl."

I had gone to Périgueux in the deepest Dordogne, not Toulouse, to find my goose lover, but he was the real McCoy. Régis, a one-star chef for fifteen years, runs the Château Reynart just outside of the Périgord capital.

Ducks overran geese some years back, he explained, because of kitchen technology. Way back when, only a third of a stuffed duck liver could be packaged as prime foie gras, and producers did not know what to do with the rest. But Rougié, a large industrial packer, found a way to make bloc de foie gras and then a mousse de foie gras, which solved that problem.

Geese were already at a disadvantage. Once the livers were extracted, there was nothing to do with the meat but make confit. Roast goose demands a different breed, which is nearly an overgrown duck, Régis said, and its liver does not stuff.

"Actually, confit is not really a recipe but rather a means of conservation," he said. "Before refrigeration it is what people did to keep meat edible during the long months when fresh birds were not killed. Geese and ducks were salted and kept in their own fat to be used whenever necessary. Nowadays, the dish is not so popular."

Big business and Brussels had muscled aside many small artisans throughout the Périgord, Régis explained. Arbitrary requirements forced an investment that only big producers could afford.

"Many of these small farmers turned out wonderful stuff, but they just barely squeezed by," he said. "Some didn't declare their production to save on taxes. Now they have to go through special laboratories, put in expensive gadgetry they don't need, all because the big guys don't want the competition. If you deal with two or three hundred ducks, you're finished. Unless you're dealing in the thousands, it doesn't pay."

Régis repeated what Daguin had said, that the basic question with foie gras is how it melts down in cooking. There followed a technical conversation that began with a glass of Champagne and went on until the last cognac, late into the night. During the course of it, Régis served me a succulent slice of foie gras with Sauternes, followed by sauteed foie gras layered with baked Granny Smith apples. The main course was his speciality confit d'oie, which is sections of the tastiest part of the wing. It came with tender cèpes and sliced garlic-laced potatoes.

A single embarrassing fact attended my perfect Périgord repast. That foie gras was duck.

"Ah, well, I much prefer to serve goose liver," Régis said. "It has a finer, firmer flavor. But I can't sell it. It is too expensive, and most of my customers don't appreciate the difference enough to want to pay extra."

The next morning, Régis took me into the medieval heart of Périgueux to the Saturday fat market. Clutching a straw basket and an umbrella, he launched his sturdy frame down the narrow cobblestones, among splendid old facades and overhangs. I followed in his wake. Every few moments, someone stopped to salute the chef. He paused often to sniff and savor, passing judgment with no more than an eyebrow wiggle.

"We must be extremely vigilant if French food is to keep its high standard," he said. "The threat is not McDonald's or fast food. That's a false problem. It's a different clientele. Everyone has to eat somewhere. But we are in danger of losing the best that we have."

As an example, he seized a handful of *mâche*, which is like a sweeter, more tender watercress. "Look at this stuff, the rich texture, the fullness of it. Big green leaves. You can chew it and really get your teeth in it." Régis was getting seriously worked up. "It makes a noise like its name: mâche, mâche. Nothing at all like limp supermarket junk."

Just then a Périgord truffle man appeared, and he took off on a different tack. "In the market at Saint-Tropez, I saw some eggs in a jar with truffles," he said. "The idea was that they were supposed to infuse the eggs with their aroma for scrambled eggs with a real truffle taste. Except that these genetically screwed up eggs aren't porous anymore. You can leave truffles in there all year, and nothing will happen."

It was early at the *marché aux gras*, but diehard vendors had set up on tables in the big striped tent in a central square. One woman offered a mound of duck skin next to containers of clarified yellow fat.

"That's what we use here for everything," Régis said. "Just like butter or olive oil. Goose or duck, the taste is the same. But that distinctive flavor you always get in southwestern cooking? The fat."

At the end of one row, an old farmer stood behind an impressive display. I explained why I was there, and he nodded in silence. I asked his name, and he waggled his chin at a large merchant's license on the table declaring him to be Rolande Leymarie of Chignac.

To his right was a pile of flat round cakes, rusty red in color. They were *sanguettes*, apéritif crackers made from dried duck blood. Next to them were slices of magret, lean cuts like beefsteak from the duck breast. Legs were piled on one tray and wings on another. Skin and clarified fat were lined up behind.

Régis pointed to a mound of tender slivers from the duck wing. "We call those demoiselles," he said. "Sometimes I use them to make 'duck suckers.' I grill them on a brochette with cumin, honey, and sesame."

I surveyed the stand and commented to Leymarie on the absence of goose. "Never touch 'em," he said. "Takes too long to stuff the damn things. Can't sell the meat. Just duck."

Régis walked away smiling, but I think I heard him grinding his teeth.

GOOSE GREASE OR NOT, I returned often to Toulouse because I like it there. The city calls itself a model for the third millennium. It might be. If anyplace now represents France and its extremes, it is Toulouse.

Polls repeatedly rank Toulouse the most liveable city in France. It is comfortably sized, rooted in its past but open to anything new. Its hyper-modern hospital in stately old buildings is among the best in Europe. For any number of reasons, it is where most Frenchmen say they would like to move.

For starters, *la ville rose* is lively and beautiful. When sunlight sets fire to the salmon-hued bricks, it is even stunning. People gather on the grass by the arched Pont Neuf, as in Paris much older than its name suggests. The Place du Capitole, a tile-and-cobblestone esplanade, throbs with music, markets, and meandering in any weather. Cafés and cabarets jam solid with university students.

The tourism office is a tower keep by leaf-shaded fountains and elegant shops off the adjacent Place Wilson. Inside, friendly people can tell you that Toulouse has 150 parks and plazas, 4,000 public benches, 160,000 trees, and 400,000 flowers.

The old center radiates from red-bricked quais on the Garonne, built in the eighteenth century by trade-minded city fathers who meant to show the world some grandeur. From the port, the Canal du Midi begins its long meander across the bottom of France toward Montpellier and the Rhône. Back from the river, the Rue de la Dalbade is lined with gorgeous old homes built by the local nobility between the fifteenth and eighteenth centuries.

Toulouse is also technology heaven. Ariane rockets are made there. The supersonic Concorde was born in Toulouse, still ahead of its time a half century later. It is Europe's Seattle, headquarters of a French-dominated Airbus consortium that builds wide-bodied planes that compete with Boeing.

Aerospatiale in Toulouse builds those heat-seeking Exocet missiles so beloved by military dictators. During the Falklands War, assembly line workers cheered with pride when Argentines used their handiwork to smoke a British warship. But in a French spirit of fair play, diplomats passed secret aim-spoiling codes on to London so that did not happen too often.

Industrial suburbs stretch away from Blagnac airfield and Aerospatiale's 500-yard-long main hangar. The city's four universities, four engineering schools, sixteen institutes, and thirty-four other schools of advanced studies are sprinkled just about everywhere.

Clearly, town planners put in some thought. You can even follow the road markings and find a place to park in the medieval part of town. For the rest, urban architects designed outskirts that were to live on in greater glory, pilot planning for the third millennium.

Le Mirail, for instance, an expanse of high-rise apartments and suburban businesses around a university campus, was supposed to house a dynamic, youthful, and convivial mix of young workaday families.

As it turned out, Le Mirail offered France a chilling example of what happens in a well-fed society when too many people find no place at the table.

Le Mirail evolved into what other sizeable towns call *la banlieue*. The word means suburbs, but the connotation is neither Grosse Pointe nor Scarsdale. It is now code for the more specific term, *"quartier sensible."* That means, essentially: a ghetto populated by immigrants, darker-hued French citizens, and white working-class French families who are not able to move elsewhere. They are no-man's-land expanses around Paris and Lyon. But Toulouse?

So I was surprised late in 1998, after a visit to France's lovely model city, to see a headline reading, "Day of Riots in Toulouse After Death of Habib, 17."

Nothing was really clear about the spark that set things off. From most accounts, a police patrol had come upon some kids breaking into a car at 3:30 A.M. on a Sunday. Officers fired but did not chase the fleeing kids. At dawn, someone walking his dog found Habib Ould dead with a 7.65 caliber police bullet in him. He had run a hundred yards from the scene and collapsed. By noon, when the news circulated, crowds gathered in the tough La Reynerie section from all over Le Mirail.

By nightfall, cars were aflame. Rocks rained down on the besieged police. Outnumbered, faced with something new, the riot troops fired plumes of tear gas. Molotov cocktails flew back in riposte. At least six officers were injured in the first clash, and sporadic pitched battles went on for most of a week. Meanwhile, thousands marched through Toulouse holding aloft photos of a smiling Habib and banners in French and Arabic that read, "They murdered Pipo."

The story had the familiar buzz words evoking an underlying malaise that was troubling all of France: "integration" and "assimilation." What they meant was that after centuries of absorbing new immigrant groups, Frenchmen of the old sort saw themselves faced with a people who prefer a different sort of Sunday lunch, which they would rather eat on Friday.

For years, occasional flare-ups drew attention to the "sensitive neighborhoods," usually around Paris or Lyon. The film *La Haine*, "Hate," traced the patterns of frustrated, youthful exuberance to final gunplay. But the

Toulouse spark ignited hot spots smouldering all across France. Habib was shot in mid-December. Over the Christmas holidays, shops and cars burned in Lyon, Saint-Étienne, Lille, Paris, Longwy. Tranquil Strasbourg saw the worst. In a single weekend, twenty cars were torched and city buses were stoned.

Vehicule flambé was a favorite dish. In Grenoble, for instance, kids stopped a bus and flung a firebomb under the seats. The driver crashed into a tree and escaped, with his passengers, before the bus exploded.

Across France as a whole, no one kept careful count.

In less likely places than Toulouse, frustrated ghetto youngsters tried their hand at the violence they watched nightly on television. Arles caught the fever, among other tranquil southern cities. And often the police, overwhelmed or fearful of criticism if they overreacted, simply stood back and watched.

By the time 1999 got started, French society had a new classification: *les sauvageons* were disaffected youths capable of violence just for the hell of it. Magazines scoured their Rolodexes for sociologists, who came up with conflicting analyses and forecasts. Clearly, this was something to watch between meals.

In a thorough post-mortem, Le Monde wrote, "Riots in parts of Le Mirail were no worse than elsewhere, but because they happened in the 'the city where Frenchmen most prefer to live,' according to all the polls, they showed the depth of the social crisis in France."

Sociologists had explanations. Sophie Body-Gendrot, a friend who loves dark chocolate, drafted a study for the prime minister's office. In short, she said, an excluded class of kids do not feel connected to the same institutions and values of those around them. Repression, the usual answer, only makes it worse. And neither tolerance nor understanding can be enforced. Certainly not at any individual level.

"It is easy to single out suburban kids, or National Front voters, but it's much more widespread than that," Sophie had explained in Paris. "Whole segments of society are rejecting authority, not paying rent, refusing the old norms of civility. It's getting worse, and I don't see solutions."

The predominant reaction in the government, she said, was to tighten the screws, putting out more police and imposing more severe sentences in courts. That would likely make things worse. "We need much more dialogue," she concluded, "but the French don't know how to engage in dialogue."

When I returned to Toulouse a few months after the riots, I walked around the old center to sniff out sentiments. Near the Garonne quai, I stopped at a small news and stationery shop owned by a slim woman of a certain age, with severely angled clear-framed glasses and a fussy but not unfriendly manner. She was straight out of the manual: shopkeeper, mother, petit bourgeoise, who ruled her small domain.

Yes, she explained, the problem was down in the banlieue. Police killed an Algerian, or something. But a lot of them marched into town to demonstrate.

"That makes you afraid, you know," she said, with a little shudder. "Mind you, it's not that I have anything against 'les Arabes,' but they come here and don't fit in with our way and yet expect everything for free from us."

"Les Arabes," in this context, has nothing to do with the Middle East. It is a semi-polite term—there are much worse—for North Africans from Algeria, Tunisia, or Morocco, three former French territories. Many of these "immigrants" are second or third generation descendants of French citizens who as soldiers died defending France. Others include Zinedine Zidane, the French-born son of an Algerian night watchman from Marseille, who did the most to help France win the 1998 World Cup.

The stationery store lady warmed to her theme. She was no racist, she assured me, as I paid for my papers and turned to leave. "You just have to understand," she concluded, "*ces gens-là . . .*" That translated to: those people. Everyone knows roughly who is included in that collective reference, but the connotations vary slightly as you move around France. In Toulouse, it means olive-hued, Allah-fearing people who would rather eat lamb on a spit than duck or goose.

MONTPELLIER, JUST OFF the coast at the Provence end of Languedoc, is one of those underappreciated French places which too many travelers flash past on their way to somewhere else. It is a mere thousand years old, nothing compared to the Greek and Roman cities nearby that had risen and fallen and risen again before it was even built. The university medical school may be the world's oldest, true enough. Rabelais studied there. But

Montpellier flourished as a place of passage back when autoroutes did not allow traffic to bypass it at ninety miles an hour. If pleasant, it is not compelling.

During the 1990's, however, two shy twin brothers put Montpellier back on the map in the usual French way. Aromas wafted from the kitchen of their Jardin des Sens, and Michelin came running. Everyone else soon followed. Dye does not disperse in water faster than word circulates in France about a good new restaurant. I happened to be in a remote village near Lyon and someone mentioned that he'd heard of a terrific spot to eat. It was in Montpellier. By chance, if not the natural order of things, I was just on my way there.

Not to put too fine a point on it, I had what may have been the most memorable lunch of my life.

Senator Marcel Vidal of l'Hérault Département, a member of the Senate Cultural Affairs Committee, had invited me down. He wanted me to see how olive oil producers and vintners were trying to save the stricken region from its dubious distinction as the poorest in all of Europe. Its winemakers had spent decades turning out lakes of low-cost plonk, but this was changing. Also, Vidal was an organ fanatic; we would not miss the ancient instrument he had brought back to life at his favorite church in Clermont-l'Hérault.

But the program, naturally, began with lunch. We were greeted at the restaurant by a balding young man of almost painful diffidence. He quickly delivered us to a nattily dressed ball of fire I recognized as Olivier, the maître d' and manager on whom all reviewers seemed to comment. Our initial escort bowed a little awkwardly before melting away. Later, I went back to sneak a look at the name scripted across the shy host's white tunic: Jacques Pourcel.

The Pourcel twins, Jacques and Laurent, already had a reputation for being somewhat eccentric, which in haute cuisine code usually means imperious. But the comments I'd seen had gotten it wrong. The Pourcels semed bashful, overwhelmed with their success, and anxious that somehow it might all go away. It was only natural that French food critics, having sampled their work, might think such genuine humility to be suspect.

We sat down before one o'clock, and it was nearly six before our small party floated out on a cloud of cigar smoke and Armagnac fumes. It was difficult to count the courses because a half dozen arrived before the meal even started. At the end, when dessert followed dessert, no one was in any condition to count.

The Jardin des Sens, or garden of the senses, pleasantly deposed old notions about what makes a French restaurant elegant. It was carved out of a so-so hotel in a nondescript part of town. The parking lot made one happy that a *voiturier* was on hand to keep an eye on things. Inside, architects and decorators had gone wild.

Tables at different levels overlooked a glass wall onto the lush garden around an olive tree. Decor was unabashedly futuristic, sumptuous yet simple, comfortable and classy. The linen was Porthault, and the china, Bernardaud. No one was pretending that this used to be some Renaissance king's hunting lodge. It looked more like the Jedis' senior officers mess.

The food was equally modern, fit artfully into tradition. From an assortment of *amuse-gueules*, I plucked tiny octopus lightly deep fried in batter with a savory sauce, a refined and miniaturized version of the Sète speciality, *thiel*. Entrées began with a deep-fried fat breaded Mediterranean oyster replaced in its shell with a succulent tomato and fennel coulis. There were three other entrées.

A purée of *potimarron* (this is a delicate French pumpkin with a chestnut flavor) laced with truffles was served in a small soufflé ramekin. Little rougets, red mullet, came with asparagus cannelloni. And, to a chorus of noisy, appreciative sounds, came the Pourcels' show-stopper. An escalope de foie gras, just seized to delicate crunchiness in a hot pan, was laid atop spice bread in a baby spinach leaf nest, dribbled with sweet Banyuls wine, and served with poached apple.

After that, lunch started: *loup de mer* (sea bass) with a purée of Niçoise coco beans *à la vanille* and the tiniest sliced deep-fried onions; a gigot d'agneau of a tenderness I did not think was possible in a sauce I was, by then, too wine-addled to describe; a cheese platter large enough to accommodate a helicopter; endless desserts of chocolates, homemade ice creams, fancy sugar designs, and fruit coulis.

It was an astounding tour de force. The brothers had come up the usual hard road. Jacques trained with Michel Trama, Pierre Gagnaire, and Marc Meneau. Laurent worked under Alain Chapel and Michel Bras. Together, they managed a perfect balance. Complex dishes blended seemingly clashing flavors with breathtaking precision.

This, for me, was the height of modern French cuisine. At superior tables in America, where chefs try daring experiments on classic themes, I usually end up disappointed. A shade too much of one thing or another, and something overpowers; the whole is lost. But the Pourcels, like the best French chefs, do not play with their food. They understand every nuance. Proportions are perfect. It is certainly in the training. Maybe it is also in the genes.

In between appreciative moans and gasps, I spoke to Vidal's aide, Françoise Pouget. She is one of those women France produces so well, stylish in an effortless way, quick to smile but capable of repelling a pirate attack with a glance of profound displeasure. She had gone to sea in the merchant marine, in love with a ship captain. Then she ran a small restaurant. She sold fine groceries in the Montpellier market until she opened a homemade pasta shop. Among other things.

Françoise was a legislative assistant, but her favorite job was president of the République d'Olive. This was a loosely defined country that existed only in her head, and her press release, but she had a purpose. The world was ready to appreciate olive products, she felt, and she was there to show the world how.

Not surprisingly, our conversation involved food.

"The quality of food in France is dropping fast," Françoise said, "and that's maybe the worst problem we now face." One could still find a decent meal, she allowed, as we each applied scalpel-sharp Laguiole knives to juicy, red lamb we could have cut with Popsicle sticks. But a whole new generation was on its way to parenthood with warped culinary values.

"These poor children are suffering from all this frozen, industrial supermarket junk they get fed," she said. "They don't know any better, and unless their parents teach them, how will they learn? McDonald's! Okay, once in a while. You can't make something like that forbidden fruit, or kids will obsess about it. Like the jam jar on top of the cabinet. *Quand même!* You have to make that an exception."

Françoise, with no kids of her own, struck me as very good mother material. She liked children, at least, and was not without opinions on the subject.

"It's ridiculous for mothers to say they no longer have time to cook properly, to make a decent meal for their family when they get home from work," she said. "That's a flat lie. It takes no more time to prepare something decent than to make junk."

By this time, her voice was rising above the click of cutlery, and her last piece of gigot had begun to congeal. "A mother who can't work up the motivation to peel a carrot for her children so they can eat properly ought to have her kids taken away as a bad mother. Just like that, by a special court! Banished from motherhood!"

Françoise laughed at this. She may have been joking.

NINE

Right Turn at Toulon

BACK IN THE Scott and Zelda days, Mediterranean breezes off the port of Toulon were scented with lemon blossoms and grilled fish in fennel. It was neither glitzy like Nice down the coast, nor raw-boned and rowdy like Marseille, in the other direction. Not far from the rich vines at Bandol, Toulon was a pleasant mix of biggish city, backcountry, and the beach.

People lingered over lunch, speaking Provençal as much as French. Their favorite dish was *revesset*, a Toulon speciality dating back to the Middle Ages. This was a fish stew featuring the more noble Mediterranean species, rather than leftovers of the catch as in Marseillais bouillabaise or chunks of white fish as in Niçois bourride. Unlike its cousins, revesset was based on vegetables: Swiss chard, spinach, sorrel. It leaned heavily on Provence herbs and, of course, olive oil. Doing it justice required happy spirits and most of the afternoon.

These days, revesset is hard to find and so, in fact, is the Mediterranean. The port is mostly a naval base, all business and military, set behind an urban cluster with only traces of its former charm and not much time for lunch. It is the only city in southern France where a drive along the port offers no view of water. And that occasional whiff of social tension I sensed in Toulouse is the pervading odor in Toulon.

In 1995, a National Front candidate named Jean-Marie Le Chevallier was elected mayor of Toulon. A professional politician, oiled and polished with wire-framed glasses, a doughy face, and silk ties, he won a convincing 37.02 percent of all votes cast.

That the far right did well in Toulon surprised no one. It has been that sort of place since the late 1950's when vituperative French settlers, *pieds noirs*, fled north after losing the war for Algeria. In the 1980's, the Maison des Paras, a social club with fascist insignia and weaponry on its walls, was closed after several members blew themselves up on their way to plant a bomb. But the landslide shocked all of France.

Core support came from a class of people like those who were known as the when-we tribe after Zimbabwe won its independence. (As in, "When we were in Rhodesia . . .") They found followers among ordinary French families who feared their Sunday morning church bells would be replaced by the Friday wail of a muezzin. As crime rates rose and employment dropped, people blamed Arab immigrants and voted the far right.

Corruption among incumbent Socialist city officials did not help. Le Chevallier campaigned on a promise to wipe out backroom payments and bring unquestioned decency and morality to municipal government.

"Toulon will be the laboratory-city for the National Front," party leader Jean-Marie Le Pen crowed, as his people moved into the thirteenth largest city hall in France, capital of the Var. And it turned out to be, right up until the whole National Front movement imploded like a lab test gone badly wrong.

Toulon was neither the National Front's birthplace nor its most resounding victory in a campaign to seize power at municipal levels. The party first surfaced in Dreux, a hard-edged town on the periphery of Paris. It spread most rapidly in southern towns, including white working-class suburbs of Marseille. It did well in the old Roman city of Orange because of local issues in the balance. But Toulon, a real city, a major port and naval center, was where it mattered.

Le Chevallier wasted no time making headlines. His wife and City Hall aide, Cendrine, a hard-boiled blonde with a shrill voice, set up the controversial Toulon Youth project. Critics said she took funds from poor kids in desperate need to design programs for the petit bourgeois. Soon after, she was prosecuted for hiring only National Front supporters. Another chief aide, a former Foreign Legion officer who cruised the gay bars, was murdered in a crime of passion. And then a half-dozen officials, including Le Chevallier himself, were investigated when a businessman said he bribed City Hall for the Toulon school lunch contract.

By the end of 1999, the National Front showcase was shattered beyond any repair. Le Pen had split, furiously and brutally, with his more housebroken second-in-command, Bruno Mégret. Cendrine Le Chevallier shifted her alliance to Mégret's new National Movement, but the mayor stayed loyal to his old comrade, Le Pen. Finally, he also delivered an emotional farewell to the National Front. Le Pen's response was characteristic: "I was bothered more by the loss of my cat, who disappeared last night."

The organized far right, by then, was skidding fast into folklore. What had scared so many Frenchmen was turning into a bad joke. In elections for the European Parliament, the two factions totaled fewer than ten percent of the vote, less than half of those cast for the French hunters' rights party.

But if the extreme right leadership was in disarray, the sentiment behind its initial success had hardly gone away.

To cruise Toulon properly, you need a boat. I hopped on a tourist launch which takes an hour to circumnavigate the huge natural harbor. From the sea, it is suddenly attractive, an old city that stretches for miles, "*tout-long*" its curving beach.

In the French naval shipyard, workers refitted the U.S. Sixth Fleet flagship. French aircraft carriers and nuclear-missile ships attest to a significant presence. Old fortresses, strengthened further by Napoléon, bore witness to an impressive history. But our boat captain's commentary recalled a more recent shameful past.

"It was here on a November morning at five A.M., in 1942, that sixty-five warships were scuttled and went to the bottom," the captain said, as we approached the breakwater protecting the port. He must have made that announcement a thousand times, but his voice still caught a little. "Only two submarines slipped away through that passage to join the Free French Forces."

As German troops knifed through France toward the south, General de Gaulle's loyalists in North Africa pleaded with the Vichy government to evacuate the navy. A fleet of warships might turn the tide against

Hitler's faltering campaigns. Vichy officials dithered. Admirals in Toulon, divided in their sympathies, took no action on their own. By the time they decided to move, it was too late. They sunk their own ships, depriving not only Hitler but also the Allies of a powerful navy.

Retribution was horrendous. Allied bombing left the old port and the city around it a pile of smoking rubble. And Toulon has suffered ever since. When it was rebuilt, towering apartment blocks lined the port. Today, seedy and hideous like some sort of Stalinist nightmare, no one can afford to tear them down.

"You don't have to tell us how ugly our city is," lamented Odette Casanova, deputy for Toulon in the National Assembly, whose mission is to persuade outside investors to bring jobs to Toulon. "We see it every time we look toward the water."

Madame Casanova, a Socialist who defeated a National Front candidate, thus taking away the only far-right seat in the National Assembly, suffers from her insistence on saying what she believes is true. This makes it difficult for her to cheerlead for Toulon.

"We have no cultural activity in this city," she told me. "Zero. Even the little nearby town of Sanary has a theater." She blames the National Front for crushing what little creativity there was by cutting funds and banning cultural expression it did not like. But that is only part of it.

"Even around the university, there are no cafés," she said. "If students want to hang out and have a drink, they get in their cars and go somewhere else."

I had noticed this the night before. Toulon had no shortage of *"bars américains,"* which seemed to be defined as any place where a haggard blonde with a minimum of trashy attire leans in the doorway.

"The National Front gave us a terrible reputation which we will not soon shake," Madame Casanova said. "Who wants to come here to invest money? It was hard enough before, but now . . ."

When I asked if Toulon was a racist city, she paused a few moments. She wanted to say it wasn't. But she did not want to lie.

"There are racists here," she finally answered, which seemed fair enough. There are racists just about everywhere. "Still, you don't see any conflict between ethnic communities. We don't have trouble in the streets, the way they do in other cities. People get along."

This was the same answer I had gotten from Henri Couillon, the center-right regional councilman, and other solid citizens. It was true, in its way. Overt racial incidents, the sort you'd hear about, were rare.

That night, I dived happily into a plate of chicken yassa at a Senegalese restaurant called the Baobab. Patrice Amsi, the owner, guffawed when I asked whether the National Front caused him any problems.

"Hey," he said, "they're not dumb. When Cendrine Le Chevallier ran for the Assembly, she had her campaign workers party here. They rented out the whole place. I'm the only one on the Place d'Armes with a permit for outside tables. That's not because they love me. They just want to say that they gave the black guy a permit and not the white guys."

In neighboring Hyères, run by a center-right mainstream party, his experience was different. "I applied for a disco license," he said, "and they told me to beat it. 'We don't want any mumbo-jumbo music around here,' they said. Straight out."

But the problem seemed less the National Front itself than the undercurrent of ethnic fear that brought it to power. As I sniffed the air around Toulon, it was unmistakable.

"Tough, tough, tough," a gray-grizzled Algerian said through missing teeth when I brought up the subject. This was twenty minutes after I sat near him on a park bench. During that time, we worked ourselves from intense mistrust to simple mistrust. When I first asked about the National Front, he assumed I was a member. Eventually he opened up, but our conversation did not last long.

His name was Fahti. He had come to France early in the Algerian War, a clear sign of his sympathies. His father had fought for France in World War II, as so many Arabs, Asians, and Africans did. As the war began going badly, tensions increased. When the pieds noirs came home after it was over, Fahti was no longer an Algerian-born Frenchman who helped spice the melting pot. He was one of "them," and he has been one of them ever since.

As I talked to others like him, the picture seemed clear. In places like Toulon, there is no need for racial assaults. The "immigrants" know their place, even if their fathers did happen to die for France. If the conversation gets uncomfortable, they drift away.

This is not the kind of Archie Bunker racial hatred that regards all members of a different race as inferior. It is a class division. Individuals can cross the line.

In fact, on any given Sunday, you are likely to find white-bread French-men and Arabs, assimilated or not, enjoying together what has become Toulon's new popular dish: a North African *mechoui*.

MARSEILLE, WHERE THE first mixed marriage dates back 2,600 years, is a different story altogether. Protis, commander of a Greek expeditionary fleet from Phocaea, proposed to Gyptis, the daughter of Nann who was chief of what in politically correct terminology might be referred to as the local Native Frenchmen. In fact, Nann's people were Ligurians from down the coast in Italy. So goes the Marseille bloodline.

The Phocaeans and Ligurians together built Massalia, later Marseille, which managed to digest unlikely blends of disparate communities ever since. Something about the great old city captured French imaginations. When Aix-en-Provence threatened its prominence, Louis XIV built the Cours Belsunce to assert Marseille's grandeur. After the Revolution, it was only natural that the stirring, and bloodthirsty, national anthem be called "La Marseillaise."

Protis landed at the mouth of the Lacydon, a pristine rivulet of mystical powers which met the Mediterranean at the top of the Old Port, today's Quai des Belges. Its ancient course lies under the Canebière, once a posh Champs-Élysées South and now a traffic-choked boulevard of faded glory that runs from a McDonald's by the train station to a Quick at the port.

A bronze plaque set flat into the smooth paving stones of the quai des Belges proclaims:

ICI vers l'an 600 avant J. C. des marins grecs ont abordé venant de Phocée. Ils fonderent Marseille d'où rayonna en occident la civilisation. Here in about 600 B.C., Greek sailors landed from Phocaea. They founded Marseille, from where civilization beamed to the Western World.

A few steps from the plaque, under a rich blue umbrella, Nana the fishwife looks timeless enough to have been there when Protis landed. In fact, she has been selling her husband's daily catch at her market spot for only fifty-five years.

With short iron curls around a handsome face of saddle leather, in a threadbare blue apron and sturdy shoes under sturdier ankles, La Nana is a metaphor for Marseille. And with gestures straight out of a Marcel Carné black-and-white film—the full-body shrug, the devastating eye roll, the bent-fingers hand language—she personifies a greater storybook France beyond.

"Where are we going in this world?" she said, repeating my question in a raspy voice that carried halfway to Lyon. "I'll tell you, *mon beau*, we're headed toward perdition. These women today, they don't cook fish for their families. They buy Findus." The mention of this popular frozen-fish brand brought her mouth into a twist, as if she was tasting something awful. "Or they go to that McDo over there," Nana continued, the scowl deepening as she swept an arm toward discreet but plainly visible golden arches.

Her husband, Michel, had been lurking in the background, listening. Suddenly, he was on fire.

"People nowadays eat crap!" he pronounced, with such heat that the brim of his wool cap vibrated about his wizened face. "Crap! They eat chicken poisoned with dioxins, mad-cow beef, cardboard sandwiches, industrial garbage. And no fish. Used to be, we'd sell four hundred kilos a day. Now we're damned lucky to unload thirty kilos."

Bad weather and cross currents had limited the catch that morning, but Michel had plenty of a fish I offended him greatly by calling a sardine.

"Hah!" he said. "That's no sardine. It's a *jarret*. An ugly little sucker, I'll admit, but it is delicious grilled in olive oil. This is a Marseille specialty, but not enough people still appreciate it."

During a lull in customers, I went back to Nana for some broader philosophy about life in general. She had spent nearly every morning for more than a century at the heart of France's oldest city, happily insulting pompous Parisians, passing the time with tourists from Kansas City to Kyoto, watching the world evolve.

When you think back, I asked her, what is the biggest difference between then and now?

Nana fixed me with her best 2,600-year stare.

"I already told you, *mon beau*. People aren't eating fresh fish."

I HAD GONE to the Quai des Belges fish market because of dark reports that bouillabaisse was in dire straits. Overfishing by trawlers had depleted stocks. Rock fish were getting scarce as the coral they fed on died off. Marseille had finally begun to treat the rivers of sewage it dumped in the Mediterranean, which, coincidentally, killed the tasty filth that fish loved.

Nana and Michel notwithstanding, the news was good.

"No problem," declared Jean-Michel Minguella, who ought to know. "It's expensive, all right, but you find the fish. New reserves off the coast are building up stocks. They're controlling the trawlers better. Old fishing families are still going out in boats. If you've got money, you can get bouillabaisse."

Minguella and his brother, Pierre, opened the Miramar restaurant in 1965. Nearly every morning since then, he has walked down the quai to shop for the day's fish. Honest bouillabaisse must contain at least four of nine species of Mediterranean rock fish.

"I always find them," he said. "If they're not here, then they are down the coast a little ways at other small ports. No problem."

It was Minguella's Michelin star that had brought me to see him. But I soon realized our mutual history predated his restaurant. Back in the 1960's, when I first learned what a Frenchman could do to a fish, I was living in Lagos, Nigeria. A mere four hours on an awful road took me to Cotonou, capital of the former French colony of Dahomey (now Benin), and the Hôtel de la Plage. The food was like nothing I had ever tasted. And the chef, whom I never met, was Minguella.

"I spent four years in Africa and thought about going to New York," he said. "Then my brother and I decided to open up here. I still love to travel. At least once a year, I go somewhere for a week to work."

Memorabilia upstairs adds detail. The French ambassador to Saudi Arabia flew him over to make bouillabaisse as the main course of a state dinner. Minguella has gone all over the Gulf. For major gigs in San Francisco and New York, he had rock fish flown fresh from Marseille. He never bothered to learn English. He speaks cuisine.

Minguella is friendly in a gruff way, bear-sized and solid jawed. His accent is all Marseille, full of swallowed, scratchily rolled r's and clanging final g's after words that ought to end with n's. He is proud of his eighty-seat empire near the Hôtel de Ville, but no one gets into the tiny kitchen, stacked high with battered stock pots, when mealtimes approach.

As we chatted at a terrace table by the yachts and workaday craft in the Old Port, a woman sidled up with a blue plastic sack. Minguella peered inside to inspect some lovely rouget. He nodded and made a mark in the little school notebook she carried. Moments later, a man came up with a white sack containing a regal loup. He glanced around nervously, as if he were offering Marseille-cooked heroin. Minguella inspected the rich red of gills and the clear eyes. Another nod and another mark in a notebook.

"I've got a few retired people out scouting for me," he explained. "If there's good fish around, I'll find it. There is no mystery to bouillabaisse. You have to have top-quality fresh fish. When you see restaurants advertising it for eighty francs, forget it. You know it is impossible."

Perhaps eighty percent of restaurants around the Old Port offer cheap bouillabaisse, made from a few sorts of frozen fish. To combat this, Minguella and a handful of other restaurateurs imposed the Bouillabaisse Charter, a sort of appellation d'origine contrôlée to assure the wary diner.

At the Miramar, bouillabaisse costs 250 francs per person for a minimum of two people. Minguella's recipe is available on his website, www.bouillabaisse.com, but the Internet cannot help locate a quivering *rascasse* fresh from a Mediterranean reef.

The simplest and most effective recipe requires only one ingredient: a plane ticket to Marseille. And Minguella assures that there is no hurry.

"Old guys like us will retire, but there are plenty of young chefs who can take over," he said. "Bouillabaisse is not exactly complicated."

The dish started out like so many European specialities, a poor workman's lunch from the easiest ingredients available. Fisherman made a stock and tossed in the broken bits of their catch which the market did not want. After World War II, it grew fashionable. And then it got fancy.

Bouillabaisse starts with a stock of olive oil, garlic, onion, tomatoes, fresh fennel and fennel seeds, sea bass in chunks, and—at the Miramar—a splash of pastis. Once the ingredients are cooked and stirred to a thick paste, they are covered in hot water over high heat. When the pot boils, the fire is lowered. Hence, *bouilla* (boil) and *baisse* (reduce). After twenty minutes, the stock is strained with a food mill.

Croutons are toasted baguettes rubbed with garlic. *Rouille*—the word means rust—is made from yet more garlic, red pepper flakes, salt and black pepper, egg yolks, olive oil, and saffron.

To put this all together, you add saffron to the stock. Potatoes are an option. If you have rascasse (sea robin), that goes in first and cooks two minutes. Then the Saint Pierre (John Dory), for two minutes. Lotte (monkfish) and congre (conger eel) take five more minutes. *Galinette* (gunard) and *vive* (spotted weever), cook another five minutes. Mussels and soft-shelled crabs go in at the end. When the mussels open, in about three minutes, all the fish is removed with a slotted spoon.

At the Miramar, bouillabaisse arrives in still life in an earthenware crock, with a large rascasse perched atop a mound of other carefully arranged fish chunks and potatoes. Mussels and crabs line the edges. A first course of rich, ochre-hued soup is eaten with spicy rouille and croutons. A second serving of soup is loaded generously with the other ingredients. And servings continue until the white wine from Cassis runs out, or all diners are immobile.

While Jean-Michel cooks, Pierre works the room. He is the perfect out-front patron, elegant yet rustic in a double-breasted suit. He offers up a pastis a l'ancienne, explaining the old way of pounding fifty-two herbs into a powder along with grain alcohol to make a licorice drink so strong even the French banned it.

He cruises the salle, slapping the backs of old friends and patiently explaining to tourists how to make submarines by rubbing a garlic clove onto a crouton and piling on the rouille. All in all, he looks like a man born to fish stew.

As we left the lunch table, Jeannette asked Pierre how often he ate bouillabaisse each week.

"Maybe once or twice a year," he replied, raising an amused eyebrow. Just in case we missed it, he repeated: "A year."

MY NEXT BOUILLABAISSE WAS at dinner that same night. An old pal had come to town with a large party in tow, and he had his heart set on Marseille's specialty dish. Weeks earlier, he had messaged to ask where to reserve. I told him the Miramar. But family friends had steered him to the New York. Then he saw a piece on Marseille in an American travel magazine which claimed the New York served the best bouillabaisse in town. That somehow sounded fishy.

I had other reasons for trying the old New York. Some of the best writing on Marseille this century has been M. F. K. Fisher's. Against all odds, she loved the place. And among her fondest memories was the fresh shellfish cart outside the New York. A Corsican family opened the restaurant in 1932 and soon it was a southern France landmark. It opened onto the Quai des Belges, and Marseille's fanciest people flocked here.

In 1982, long after Fisher's last visit, the old Corsican's daughter-in-law decided to make the place what it originally was, a brasserie like the

Coupole or Lipp in Paris. The chef stayed on, and he kept bouillabaisse on the menu.

The first sign was unsettling. At Miramar, the amuse-gueule was a tasty breaded shrimp on a bed of peppers in olive oil. With the aperitif, the New York serves some unidentifiable substance in aged grease.

When the bouillabaisse arrived, the fish was splayed out on a platter in small pieces. Prompted, the waiter picked out the night's offering: five sorts of fish, but no Saint Pierre. The soup was so pale and watery I wondered if somehow dishwater had gotten into the wrong pot. Olive oil and saffron appeared in trace quantities. The fish, overboiled amid cold potatoes, was served on a dish at the same time rather than in a second round of soup. Rather than rouille, there was a kickless aïoli. M. F. K. would have hated it.

A lot of Marseille has changed drastically since Fisher last visited. Already, in her time, the Canebière had a depressing shabbiness. Now it looked more apt for an impoverished Third World backwater. The Grand Hôtel Noailles, long abandoned, had turned a filthy black beyond battered steel panels covered in artless graffiti. Beggars dotted the streets, flopped down among piles of dirt and garbage. On one corner, a Superdrug, owned by the German chain Schlecker, sold cheap merchandise under the gaze of security cameras. On another, McDonald's sold the usual.

Much of Fisher's beloved Hôtel Beauvau has been converted to a Quick fast-food joint. Quick's two upper floors overlooking the Old Port are sealed off in glass and ugly aluminum sashes. The windows are locked, keeping out Marseille's wonderful port smells and locking in the stench of old grease. Throughout, bad elevator rock throbs from speakers.

The Canebière divides Marseille like an international border. Above, up the Cours Belsunce to the Porte d'Aix and on into seething slums, is what seems like a North African city which happens to have ended up on the wrong side of the Mediterranean. Arabic is the street language, and French, when spoken, has the colorful but hard-edged lilt of black Africa.

Men in skullcaps sit in cafes and on outdoor benches, talking quietly among themselves. Women, mostly, are well-covered and well-watched by families.

Below the Canebière, a lighter shade of Marseillais lives a different life. On beaches by the Prado, young women wear nearly nothing, dancing late with youths who blast up and down in sporty convertibles. Old-style couples stroll, shop, and devote much of their lives to keeping track of the Marseille soccer team.

If cultures tend to keep to themselves, they mix with far fewer problems than in any big city in France. Tolerance in Marseille goes back twenty-six centuries. Solid citizens come in all colors. And Marseille's mafias, gangs, freelance criminals, and petty larcenists are as mixed as the general population.

The police, when agitated, practice equal opportunity brutality. Before the Tunisia-England World Cup match, Froggy and I watched heavily armed posses try to break up running street battles between local North African toughs and visiting hooligans. As riot police charged the drunken English fans, Tunisian kids advanced behind them, throwing bottles over the cops' heads. After all, they were locals.

Police charged down one street and left a young man crumpled and bleeding on the sidewalk. When we stopped one officer and asked him to call for help, he scowled. "That's the firemen's job," and he hurried on. And the kid was white.

Over the years, Marseille has gotten a bad rap. That was Fisher's favorite theme. As base of the French Connection, it was depicted as the most drug-corrupted city on earth. Visitors are routinely warned not to venture out after dark without a minor army.

Heading for that last bouillabaisse dinner, I had a rental car and decided to give Marseille the benefit of the doubt. I found a parking spot on a well-lit street a block from the port, just down a street full of bars in front of which women stood in their underwear and made lewd invitations to passersby. At the New York, I chuckled when a well-dressed man told his friend they had a terrific seat because they could watch their car while eating.

Two hours later, I returned to find my hired car parked exactly where I left it. The only problem was that someone had pried open the door with a crowbar.

Marseille was never a place you could take for granted. It has long been a hotbed of many things, and civilization is not always what first springs to mind. If Paris is the heart and belly of France, Marseille is down there closer to the nasty bits.

But then again, it is one hell of a place. Over recent centuries, as explorers and colonizers set sail from the ancient port, French civilization was beamed everywhere else in the world. At the very least, if you know where you're going, you can still get a decent bouillabaisse, and perhaps you always will.

If M. F. K. Fisher were to write her classic work today, with all the changes since she last left, the title would be the same: *A Considerable Town*.

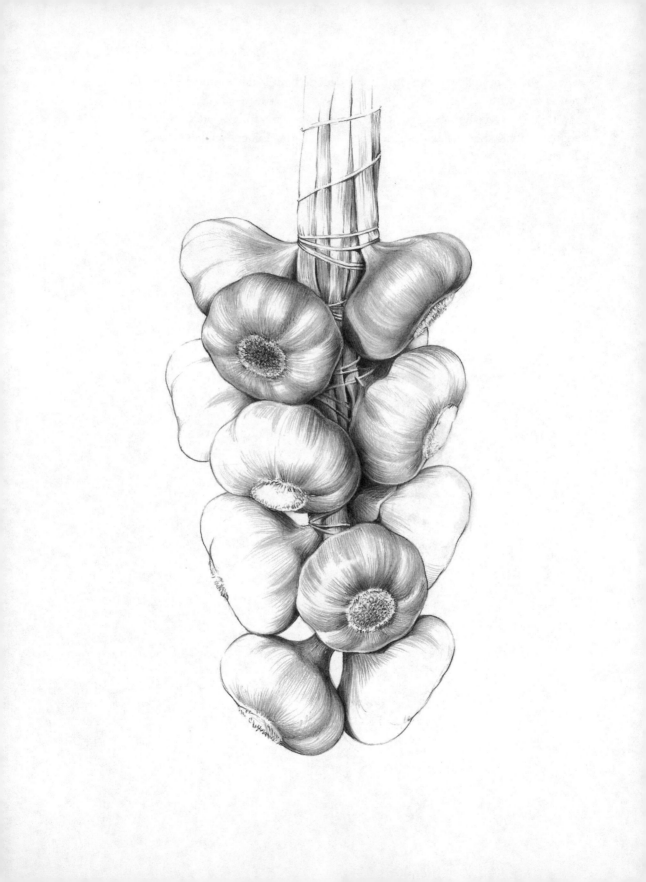

◄──◆◆◇►──

TEN

Artuby or Nartuby

EVERY FRENCH VILLAGE has its *salle polyvalente,* an all-purpose hall meant for town meetings, school plays, and, when the gods are at home in France, general good times. As Madame Collet dragged herself into the salle at Ampus on an August afternoon, it was evident that this was not one of those happy moments.

"Look at this," Madame Collet said to a knot of farmers, their own faces no happier. From a plastic sack, she extracted a brown, withered sprig and thrust it at them as if casting a spell. They all recognized it. In better times, that would be one of Madame Collet's famous bean plants, the source of *haricots verts* in olive oil that were the talk of Ampus.

The farmers had gathered to discuss why their backup irrigation canal had fallen into ruin. In most years, their small cooperative met amid easy-going banter. This time, a life-and-death pallor hung over them. Scientists in Paris and beyond could argue about formal data until they turned purple. Madame Collet alone had seen eighty Ampus summers, and the others knew their weather. Something was dreadfully wrong. Drought had always come and gone, but this was different. The Nartuby was dying. Was the Artuby next?

When I'm in Paris, I live on the Seine, possibly the most romantic river in the world, with a rich history back to the Romans. In Ampus, my river is the Nartuby. If it exudes only limited romance, it did lay in the path of those Romans who settled on the Seine. They had to build great stone bridges to cross it.

The Nartuby springs from rocks beyond Roger Martin's truffle oaks by Ampus. It drops and dribbles past placid hamlets, on through Draguignan, and widens at the old village of Trans. In summer, it freshens backcountry forests and ancient olive orchards. With the winter rains, it often swells to flood proportions, menacing Gypsy camps perched on its banks.

In fact, only a few months after Madame Collet and the boys wrung their hands over drought, winter rains hammered down for weeks on end. The Nartuby surged and roared under the bridges across it like Niagara Falls on a tear. Come summer, it would be trickling again. Ozone holes or not, that is just the way it is.

Farther north, there is the Artuby. This is an even shorter waterway, but it rushes full force from the Gorges du Verdon, France's Grand Canyon, and falls furiously southward. The two similarly named rivers are neither linked nor geologically related. All they have in common, in fact, is that they water remote and wild parts of old Provence. Deepest France depends on thousands of waterways like them. On the banks—if you switch off the TV, unlink your computer, and ignore fancy cars that occasionally flash past—you might be back in those elusive good old days.

"Paris? *Bofff*," replied Claude Teisseire, when I asked him when he last left his rural redoubt for the bright lights and big city. Teisseire, who at sixty-one looks like a well-preserved eighty, was born on the Nartuby in Ampus, with the nearest doctor a good hour's drive away. Now he repairs small tractors and weed whackers at a tumbledown junkyard of a workshop by the Nartuby outside of Draguignan.

"You can still live a reasonable life here without all the craziness of [grimace] Paris," Teisseire told me one morning, when he delivered a rototiller and spent an hour over coffee before hurrying off for his next urgent errand. "But changes? Yup."

In the real good old days, he used to catch *ecrevisse*, those delicate tasting fresh-water crayfish chefs love to put in salads, sauces, and stocks.

"We'd put out traps and catch them by the bucketful," he said. He stopped for a moment to muse, and his little mustache bristled over a grin. "Sweet, fat. They were wonderful. You can't imagine how many we caught."

That was in the 1950's, when the pure water of the Nartuby still turned the big wheel at the now abandoned olive oil mill in Ampus.

"I caught some in 1960, but those were the last," Teisseire recalled. "When they blacktopped the road to the old mill, that was it. I think the asphalt must have got in the water and mucked up the breeding grounds. Then all manner of pollution set in."

And it wasn't just the crayfish.

"Twenty years ago, no one sprayed their olive trees," he said. "We didn't even think about it. Now if you don't spray, you get nothing. Olive fly, *fumagine* (black scale). You name it, it ruins your olives. What a stupid cycle! The more you treat, the more you have to treat."

Teisseire's place, Dragui Motoculture, could be straight out of a Fernandel film. Rusted hulks littered about amount to an agricultural museum. Half-repaired contraptions spill out of the old hangar, next to a mound of unclaimed tillers. The sagging gate out front swings shut at noon, shortly before amazing aromas waft from the compound's kitchen. At pastis time, work stops promptly and definitively.

First-time customers wonder how he gets by. I tried to buy a shiny new Honda monster to dig up around my trees, but Teisseire shook his head. "Too many rocks up around your place," he said. He had never seen me before but he knew my land far better than I did. "Take this one. It's sturdier and costs half as much." Later, when I asked the price of a generator, he refused to let me consider it. "Too expensive," he said. "You can get by without it."

After a while, we outsiders understand the system. Customer relations can date back half a century or longer. True, I can usually find something cheaper than at Teisseire's if I shop around the discount malls springing up like brambles around every sizeable town. But the kid at the register who rings it up won't drive ten miles up my impossible road to adjust a set screw.

The generation shift seems assured. Teisseire's sons are stepping into their old man's shoes, shuffling comfortably around in his style of life. And they have plenty of contemporaries. If the Teisseire boys run across a banged-up Toyota half-ton, with rust holes on the doors, for instance, that would be Madame Collet's son, Gilles. Well-read and hip-looking in a ponytail and gold wire-rim glasses, Gilles stays in Ampus because he loves it. He fixes cars and works the land. When I asked what he thought of Paris, he said he hated it. At least he thinks so; he's never been there.

When you get behind Gilles or the battered little Dragui Motoculture truck in the remote hills, you can't tell whether you're following the past or the future.

There is, however, a significant difference.

LET US SAY you pass a typical old stone house on the Teisseires' rounds and hear it exuding sounds from a television set, maybe a raspy voice that could be Fernandel or another stalwart of the Pagnol epoch. If you stick your head in the window, however, chances are better you'll see a goofy American talking into his shoe, saying "Allo, chef, ici Maxwell Smart."

Frenchmen, however far up the Nartuby or Artuby they might live, watched Bobby Simone say his dying words in English, French, and German. A little channel surfing (the French term is *surfing*) will locate reruns featuring not only Bobby, but Jimmy before him and Danny, his replacement. Bobby of *The Practice* is even more popular and, on occasion, there's an old Bobby from *Dallas*.

When *Seinfeld* went off the air, a French satellite channel called Jimmy devoted an evening to it. Some evenings these days, the popular Canal Plus shows four *Seinfeld* episodes back to back, in the original, with no commercial breaks.

For better or worse, satellite television is the great leveler. Old-style transmissions across the Berlin Wall were instrumental in bringing down Communism. Now anyone with several hundred dollars available can receive hundreds of channels from just about anywhere in the world.

Ally McBeal is not bad dubbed in French, but many Frenchmen prefer it in English. Likewise, Buffy and her vampires, the *X-Files* duo, *Star Trek* crews of every generation. There is *Hogan's Heros*, with Colonel Klink speaking German. Depending upon which dish one owns, and where it is pointed, four separate episodes of *Friends* are available each night. A web-based Canal Jimmy shop sells *Friends* coffee mugs and carries the scripts.

My Nartuby neighbors may miss the New York humor in *Spin City*, dubbed or not, but they watch it. *Dingue de Toi*, as in *Mad About You*, is another favorite, particularly the episodes in which Helen Hunt cooks.

Bombed pilots and banished series all manage to show up on French screens, some with baffling success.

Sociologists who worry about American television are probably right. Effects have been obvious for years. Paris police ditched their silly but distinctive *képis* after a regular diet of "*Starsky et Hutch*." Who knows what *Law & Order* is doing to the old Napoléonic court system?

In the heavy doses the French prefer, television series can be addicting. Since they blow away commercials, hour-long episodes melt down to forty-five minutes. Often, stations run two or three episodes back to back. Cable and satellite stations repeat the same program at different times throughout the week. This lets the seriously afflicted memorize every word.

And then, of course, there are the movies. Turner and Disney channels run nonstop in the original. A dozen others offer everything from ancient turkeys howled out of American cinemas years ago to major recent releases. Special events—the Oscars, the Emmys, the country and western awards—are all there. As soon as Wall Street closes at 4:00 P.M. New York time, CNBC relays the previous night's Jay Leno after a short spiel in German to summarize his monologue.

The French respond with home-grown series. *PJ,* for Police Judiciaire, was liberally inspired by *NYPD Blue*.

In New York, a low-life perp generally mutilates a murder victim. On a recent *PJ,* the criminal was a pathetic old bourgeoise woman who had fallen on hard times. She illegally rented her basement storage cave to her maid, and a fire nearly injured the maid's daughter. *NYPD Blue* detectives might end up in bed, with flashes of skin. On *PJ,* an amorous pair of detectives made love explicitly on a precinct desk. Their captain walked in and chatted with them, either too drunk or too French to make a comment. He left; they giggled.

One series pokes fun at the integration, or not, of North Africans into the French mainstream. Another, a cute-couple sitcom, is too mindlessly peurile for even my low standard.

French television has different traditions, and a lot less money to throw around. It distinguishes itself with biting humor. The wildly popular puppet face, Les Guignols, skewers everyone, particularly the president.

Viewers have far more patience than Americans for serious fare. Large audiences watch with rapt attention for hours at a time as cameras show talking heads pick apart each others' books.

But the level can dip deeply, leaving room for all of the imported programming that spreads omniculture into the farthest reaches of France. The satirical weekly *Le Canard Enchaîné,* for example, blew the whistle on a curly-haired and unctuous host named Michel Drucker. In his New Year's Eve broadcast, he effusively thanked a singer for leaving his dinner to join the show. Later, he counted down and welcomed 1999. The show had been taped two weeks earlier.

This scoop made little impact. The feeling seemed to be that truth in broadcasting is no match for a New Year's Eve réveillon.

FOREIGN INFLUENCES ARRIVE up the Nartuby and Artuby not only by television signal but also in the presence of foreigners themselves. No one has yet scrawled "Yankee Go Home" on my mailbox. With uncommon luck, I have fallen in among wonderful neighbors. But I was careful to change the license plates on my car from 75, denoting Paris, to the local 83. Of all shades of foreigners, Parisians are among the least welcome.

Down the road toward Tourtour, Germans have invaded in force. The English long ago occupied Bargemon, and now they have colonized Cotignac. Various Nordics and Netherlanders have settled the interstices, finding their way up the narrowest roads.

Some of us foreigners have come with the idea of melting in as best we can, taking things on local terms in hopes of appreciating what authenticity remains. Others of us simply transplanted ourselves, cultural baggage and all, in search of a familiar all-comforts, no-surprises "civilization" in a bucolic setting.

This second category can be a sight to see. Few shades in nature go redder than the face of a retired Düsseldorfer in a hurry, stalled on the narrow road from Ampus to Tourtour while a flock of one thousand sheep brush their twig-flecked wool coats against his Mercedes.

But it can also throw complex social structures on their ear. With the European Union now functioning, in theory and in practice, that German from Düsseldorf had never left his own country. He flashed across the border without a pause. His Euro checkbook printed in German could pay for a lawnmower at Teisseire's. Why should he put up with lambchops on the hoof blocking the roadway?

When even Pierre Jugy is stymied by culture shock on his doorstep, however, something unsettling is afoot.

Jugy was born in Tourtour, a hilltop town of compelling charm and breath-catching views. He inherited his father's little hotel, tucked in the woods near town. With an easy laugh, an exotic Italian wife, and hard labor, Pierre has become the *aubergiste* tourists remember after a long string of stops in other places. He likes people, of any description.

When in a good mood, which is often, Pierre is apt to entertain guests with Provençal pipe and drum. Late into the night, he shares treasures from his singular cellar.

He is just as apt to let his guests entertain him. One day, driving into Tourtour, I found the village getting ready for a concert by Charlie McCoy. A long time back, I used to love McCoy's eccentric sort of country rock-esque blue grass, and I always wondered what had become of him. Tourtour found him. He came often, each time staying up all night eating Pierre's food and teaching him how to wail "Rollin' in My Sweet Baby's Arms."

Pierre's passion is flying helicopters, a skill he learned in the navy. After years of saving extra centimes, he bought a chopper. He had grand plans. He could lift visitors above the most dramatic sights of the Gorges du Verdon, unseeable any other way. In extremis, he could offer Tourtour a fast ride to Nice Airport, or the hospital at Draguignan. He had enough land to come and go without bothering anyone. Besides, this was Pierre. No one in Tourtour objected.

No sooner had the helicopter appeared than a German neighbor filed a complaint. Pierre invited the man for dinner. He offered every concession he could think of. One takeoff a week, not before midmorning. Flights only with prior approval of the neighbor. Or maybe only when the man was in Germany. The neighbor insisted on his rights, and Pierre sold his dream.

The German had a reasonable argument. He had come to the country for absolute peace. Of course, the country he had come to had existed for some time without a sprawling community of new chalets that were better suited to Bavaria. The restaurants were friendly fireside front rooms, without unlikely entrées explained on menus in three languages.

In the summer months, when outsider hordes join the normal trickle of traffic, winding roads off the Nartuby can get crowded. Road engineers have responded by overkill. Rond-points are erupting in lovely corners of old countryside.

Once rattletrap vehicles like Tesseire's truck simply blinked a signal and turned left or right. Now they are likely to embark on a large circle cut into forest and field as if spinning off toward San Diego or Ventura.

The power lines are another curse. New summer homes equipped with appliances and swimming pool heaters need the amps. Concrete pylons are cheaper than natural wood, and industrial gray is the hue of least resistance. Communities whose tax bases benefit little from so many outsiders can hardly afford to bury utility lines. And this is not supposed to be suburbia.

But, as always, then again, for people who love their old ways as much as neighbors in the Haut Var, it will take more than *Seinfeld* or a grumpy Prussian to endanger old roots.

AT THE CAFÉ DU COURS in Aups, the television shows a soccer game, if it is on at all. Old pals slap grimy cards onto a table from their first afternoon pastis until they are sure dinner is ready at home.

During the winter months, they are just back from wild-boar hunting. Most go to sleep early. In the morning, a collapsed wall or an ailing fruit tree or a job down in Draguignan will demand their attention.

All through the back country, people follow the seasons as their grandparents did. With the warmth of spring, there are wild greens to collect, especially the tender thin asparagus shoots that grow among the olive trees. The berries ripen and get fatter until it is mushroom time. In winter, truffles appear.

Full-time farmers are growing scarce. But almost everyone tends something that the term garden is too feeble to describe. The ambitious keep chickens and rabbits. Olives, fruit trees, and grapevines are standard. So are tomatoes.

And the old ways of life, linked from the heart straight to the stomach, are firmly implanted.

The phenomenon of Halloween hit France in the mid-1990's, and penetrated up the Nartuby almost as fast as it haunted Paris. McDonald's helped, with its orange and black decorations and special menus. Television did its part.

Within a year, the French had reinvented Halloween and made it their own. An American colleague interviewed kids in Paris, asking why they all dressed as witches, ghosts, or hobgoblins. Why didn't some dress up as, say, rock stars, or pirates and cowboys, or—that year—Monica Lewinsky, as they did in the United States? "But that's not Halloween," a French youngster told her solemnly. "That's a costume party."

Jeannette and I were out one October 31 in the village of Les Arcs.

The Café du Centre had done itself proud, decorating its windows and counters with carved jack-o'-lanterns. At dark, kids began to arrive. With no handy translation for "trick or treat," and not sure what else to say, each group chimed in unison: " *'Alloween, 'Alloween.*" Generous treats were produced.

Three gentlemen of Les Arcs watched this spectacle from the bar with mounting interest. Their attention settled on the pumpkins.

"You ever seen one of them things carved like that?" one man asked. That prompted a brief discussion of the knives and techniques necessary to pumpkin cutting.

Then another got to the heart of things.

"How do you eat your pumpkin?"

There followed a forty-five minute conversation that covered every nuance of squash/pumpkin family flesh: steamed, boiled, scraped, raw, candied, dried. Each related variety of pumpkin-like vegetable was covered, down to its roasted, salted seeds.

After all, Halloween may be Halloween, but France is France.

———◆———

ELEVEN

Yves and His Goats

YVES VANWEDDINGEN EARNED his master's degree in economics, acquired a closetful of suits, and went to work as a Parker Pen executive in Brussels. That, he figures, are qualifications enough to be a hardscrabble goat farmer in the south of France.

One morning in 1977, he had enough of the office. He drove down to a piece of backwoods his father owned just outside of Ampus, and he looked around for some way to make a living.

Yves decided to farm crayfish. His land had a rich natural spring just off the Nartuby. The French couldn't get enough freshwater écrevisse. Most of his neighbors tended trees: olives, almonds, cherries. But in his own private corner of paradise, Yves decided, money would grow on pond scum. He should have talked to Claude Teisseire about that pollution first.

"In theory, it worked perfectly," he explained, rattling off a complex formula of eggs per female, flow rates of water, growth cycles, and harvesting. "In practice, ah, well . . ."

While waiting for the crayfish to get around to reproducing, Yves bought a few goats. At least he could sell milk to keep up a meager cash flow. He discovered a passion for making rich, creamy chèvre. Shellfish suddenly lost their allure.

Yves, into his fifties, looks nothing like a Belgian pen salesman. Short and wiry, he moves around in turbo bursts of energy. Amused eyes peer out from behind a wild mop of brown curls and a bushy mustache. His face has the ruddy glow of someone who, winter and summer, cannot go more than twelve hours before bustling out to milk thirty goats.

"You could say that I love my goats," Yves said, pausing a beat for a surreptitious side glance to be sure I'd not heard that in any biblical way. They clearly appreciated him in return, thus making sense of that old Carnation slogan about milk from contented cows.

Pampered French goats, like those well-tended sheep near Roquefort, seem to somehow know what is expected of them. They are raised that way. As he showed me around, Yves opened the barn to reveal stacks of hay trucked hundreds of miles from the plains of La Crau, near the Camargue. It was one more detail and one more expense. Perfectly good hay grew nearby, but it was not the finest France had.

Yves explained it in the same terms I had come to hear often and would hear again and again: If you put in the best, then you get the best.

"Sure, it was hard at first, but I never regretted it for a minute," Yves said. "My first wife came with me from Brussels, but she couldn't speak a word of French. She was American, from Ohio. Is there some place called A-kron?"

After two years, it was just Yves and his goats. He built up his cheese business, with customers spread out between Aix-en-Provence and Cannes, and then he scared himself again.

"Every two days, I was in my car, delivering here and there, selling, moving, doing business," he recalled, displaying mock horror with spread fingers. "I would have been better off to have stayed in Brussels."

By now, he has it down: thirty milk goats, a French wife with a job in town, two young children, regular customers who love his product. If the European Union regulators do not get out of hand, he expects to make his small white cheeses forever.

"People like my chèvre, and I like making it," he said, with a little shrug.

We walked up the hill from Yves' barn, past the raspberry fields and herb-scented juniper forest that doubled as his front yard until we reached a handsome, rambling ranch house he had built himself. We flopped into chairs on a terrace overlooking my own modest mountainside and the valley below, with a clear-day view damn near to Corsica. "Now you see why I put up with those goats," he said, pouring fresh coffee. "Would you rather be here or in some Brussels traffic jam with a tie choking you?"

Yves' craft amounts to a bellwether of the old ways. In Provence, fewer than a hundred hearty individuals make artisanal goat cheese like he does. Others sell goat milk to larger producers. More and more, the big guys are moving into the market. Across France, with its hundreds of cheeses, there are a great deal of variations but they follow the same themes.

The chèvre process, deceptively simple, is precise. A fermenting starter helps the milk curdle. The milk is heated then cooled, and laced with a small amount of rennet. When it all reaches the right consistency, curd is ladled into molds, pierced with tiny holes so the whey runs off. Cheeses dry on racks in a cool, well-aired room.

"You have to want very much to do this," Yves explained. For ten months a year, only the most dire emergency takes him beyond twelve hours without milking his goats, and then only after finding a goatsitter.

Step by step, over a minimum of a week's time, he makes each cheese. Every day, he carefully inspects each little white disk; a small-timer can afford to do that. If satisfied, he trucks a batch to the Draguignan market and delivers another to grateful local restaurateurs.

Yves makes *pâte molle*, creamy chèvre. Others age it longer, for a harder texture. But all small producers worry about those European Union bureaucrats stuck in Brussels traffic, choked by ties.

"They try to legislate against any possible eventuality in a silly way," Yves says. Needless precautions entail ruinous investments. So far, his cash flow is positive. Who knows about the future?

When I told him about Odile Arnal and her slippery tiles in Rieisse, Yves chuckled ruefully.

"That's true," he said. "They made everyone tile their concrete floors. Then people started having accidents when the tiles got icy, so they made a new rule. The tiles had to have a nonslip surface. But that is even harder to clean than the old concrete. Two times people had to spend money, and they're worse off than when they started."

Yves' son was not yet in grade school but the question of succession would eventually arise.

"He may want to take over some day, but not without trying something else first," Yves said. "This is not a business anyone wants to go into until he is fed up with whatever he was doing before."

During the week, you have to find Yves by winding up a long, rutted dirt road. An unfortunate wrong turn places you in range of the Troll Lady, a neighbor who remains undeterred by the fortunes in fines she has had to pay for creating obstructions to public access. She is still likely to plant herself in the path of oncoming vehicles and shriek unpleasant epithets related to her disturbed peace.

On Saturday mornings, however, Yves is at the heart of the Draguignan market, right next to his friend Jeannot Romana, who sells homegrown potatoes, garbanzo beans, vegetables, and some of the best olive oil in Provence. Chatting with him there takes patience, however. Customers line up early.

"Same old, same old," Yves greeted me one morning, with a wide, relaxed smile. "Oh, wait, no," he added, remembering something that dimmed his lights. "There is a new rule from Brussels. They want display cases like mine to be refrigerated to fourteen degrees," he said. "It means nothing in terms of keeping things healthy, but it destroys the flavor. I can't sell cheese like that."

For the last several generations, people like Yves made simple wood and glass cases for displaying goat cheese while keeping it safe from anything flying or floating by. Yves' handsome old boxes were propped on saw horses, easily assembled and broken down.

But life was no longer so simple. European Union funds went to spruce up local markets, along with lists of rules devised by those bored bureaucrats. And municipalities, suddenly equipped with power points and underground water pipes, looked for useless new uses.

It was not just the cheese people. Anyone with products that might be considered slightly perishable was grappling with the issue. Those huge tubs of paella and couscous cooked out in the open were an obvious target.

"Who knows?" Yves concluded with a shrug I was beginning to know well. This was still the south of France, and Brussels was not known for speed. Maybe that was something his son would have to worry about.

A FEW STEPS AWAY from Yves' minuscule stand, André Bernard and his son sell a wide range of cheeses in the rolling shop they drive across the

Var, from market to market, all week long. The open-sided truck is stuffed with enough wares to rival a full-blown Paris creamery.

"Me, I love cheese, good wine, and women," André declaims just about every time I see him.

"In that order?" I asked the first time.

"Of course," he said. "If I weren't selling my cheese, how could I afford the other two?"

André is short and feisty, with thick wire-rim glasses, silvery hair and a Dennis the Menace impish grin. His memory is prodigious. Every customer in a half dozen markets is filed away in his human hard drive. As each approaches, he knows whom to tease with rude jokes and whom to treat with elaborate *politesse*. He asks about people's children with real interest. Mostly, he knows their lactic habits.

No one has codified the hierarchy, but André seems to know a good cheese man has a particular role in life. It makes perfect sense.

When you watch a French market long enough, you realize that people tend to shop the way they design and serve a meal. The first course is quickly dispensed with: slices of smoked salmon or raw ham; a *traiteur's* seafood panache on a shell; mushrooms to sauté in garlic and parsley. Vegetables and fruits take longer, involving an inspection tour of what is available and a sidelong glance at the prices. Fish, fowl, and meat require conversation, sometimes protracted, with the person behind the counter.

The cheese comes after. Buying it is a pleasure related to enjoying it at the table. No rush.

"*Goûtez-moi ça,*" André commands, slicing off a generous sliver of his latest discovery. It may be a Sicilian wheel with black peppercorns imbedded in it or a creamy tomme from some backcountry village in his native Savoie. Some cheeses he gets from wholesalers. His treasures, however, are selected personally on regular round-trips over the Alps to Savoie farms.

The mention of Brussels is one of the few things that dims his fire.

"They're trying to make everything uniform," André said. "It's crazy. With a good cheese, you risk nothing. Tell me, how many people have I killed in all the years I've been selling cheese?"

That was a tough one to answer, of course, but I'd bet it wasn't too many.

To make his point, André flashed his blade with Zorro speed. "This is from pasteurized milk, an industrial job," he said, passing over a slice of

Saint Albray. "This," he said, handing me another, "is something else entirely."

This process took most of an hour. Each time a new customer approached, I melted away to let André work his magic. He could have charged admission for the pleasure of watching him.

"Ah, Madame Dupont . . . ," he began at the approach of a hefty woman wheeling a shopping cart. By the time he finished producing samples and rhapsodizing about the happy mountain cows responsible for a particular nuance in his best reblochon, Madame Dupont walked away with far more cheese than she had intended to buy.

"*Alors, Monsieur Machin, je vous présente l'Américain,*" he told his next customer, working me into his spiel. I was an adopted son of the soil, he explained, who thought that little part of France was the greatest place in the world. "Ah, yes," I added, playing along; he wasn't far off. "God's quartier-général." Monsieur Machin beamed.

Some old pals of André's appeared, and the jokes flew fast.

"Ah, but life is beautiful," André said, with a theatrical flourish. "A glass of wine, a good cheese. What more can the people want?"

I left him on his usual upbeat note. True enough, there were ominous rumblings on the horizon. But this was, after all, France. As long as there were farmers committed to the old way, and customers who demanded the taste they had grown up to appreciate, it would take more than distant bureaucrats to spoil the fun.

"Let them try to ban raw cheese," he concluded. "We'll sell it under the table. Black-market cheese! Like during the war. Like during American prohibition. Hah!"

COLOR ASIDE, these are serious goings on. Anything that threatens the Yves and Andrés of France risks to erode the underpinnings of a way of life dating back two thousand years. And this is no hyperbole.

The superstructure of workaday French society, beyond the big cities, is still the marketplace. It is only peripherally about buying the family's food. As in Roman times, people gather there to catch up on what is important.

The smallest village has at least a mobile market of trucks that pass through at a fixed time. Towns have their weekly markets, and they attract people from miles around. And bigger markets are a regular event. On

Tuesdays and Saturdays, even off season, Saint-Tropez is packed with people seeking fabrics, antiques, flowers, and furniture, along with the usual fresh food and edible delicacies.

For me, the Draguignan market on Wednesdays and Saturdays is my link to a sort of reality I have grown to love.

When my well is acting funny, I run into René the water pump man, perhaps between the cucumbers and courgettes, and get him to do something about it. At the Café du Marché, I learn from Paul Bousquet about some horrible threat to pave our beloved rutted dirt road. With Pibe el Criollo, the Argentine heartthrob who sells beautiful out-of-season cherries and plums for big money, I chatter happily in Buenos Aires slang about the state of the wider world.

Jeannot Romana tells me about his mother's injured hip. His sister, Lucie, rummages around for a fat truffle she has put aside. Jeannette helps support a presumably homeless man who sits on the ground at the northeast corner. He seems an able-bodied sort, but she feels it is good karma. I prefer to help the hungry-looking accordion player with the cat on his shoulder.

I always dawdle over spices with the Habbars—father, mother, and two daughters. Row upon row of open sacks offer bright yellow curcuma, rich green cumin, chilies in a score of reds. One section displays grains: couscous, the richest of rice, tiny orange lentils. Dried fruits and nuts rise high behind the Turkish delight. Cinnamon sticks are bundled near the vanilla.

The Habbars' supplier near Marseille imports exotic ingredients from every country that cooks. The uncounted hundreds of items they carry are at least a sampling. And Draguignan housewives buy something of everything.

"This is my favorite market, and I do a lot of markets," Zorha Habbar told me. She and her husband came from Algeria forty years ago and have been selling spices ever since. "Here you always see a lot of people who sell their own produce, old families who've been at it a long time but also young people who are starting out as farmers, artisans, producers. It is a good sign."

The Corradinos buy their fruits and vegetables wholesale, but they know the lineage of every item they sell. One Saturday, Madame Corradino spent a half hour instructing me in the fine points of ratatouille. Several women waited patiently for her to finish, speaking up only to add pointers on the eggplant technology.

And for laughs, there is the Yeller. He is easy to find. The man has lungs like Scottish bagpipes. You simply listen for a rasping boom: *"Des melons superbs, dix francs le kilo."*

My first season in Draguignan, we exchanged nods. The next, he'd bellow, *"Oh, California."* And then his geography improved when his brother moved to Arizona, to my hometown of Tucson. One week, I teased him: "Hey, I heard you from Tourtour." The next week it was Paris, and then Berlin. By the time I got to Tokyo, we were pretty good buddies.

The Yeller, Michel Berberian, is Armenian like my friend Robert, the butcher with the bedside manner. Though born in Lyon, he has been selling fruits and vegetables in the Draguignan market for forty years. From the sound of it, he may be around for another forty, if the market is.

CHRISTMAS IS WHEN French markets are at their best. I made sure I was in Draguignan for the last of the millennium. Yves was not around. In December, his goats give no milk, and he gets to take a break.

After catching up with the Romanas, I headed straight for Robert's meat locker.

The place was jammed, so I got his attention by yelling from the door, "Hey, I smuggled in that cheap British beef you wanted." He laughed pretty hard, and anguished looks faded from several faces. The others, Robert regulars, also laughed; they knew enough to expect anything from that doorway.

Eventually, he had a minute to talk. I had not asked him about the economy of meat since our first conversation. Then, early in 1998, France's economy was looking bleak. It had improved.

"Things haven't changed for us," Robert said. "It is a simple matter of buying power. Say someone has a big family and tight income. He can spend sixty francs at a butcher or thirty francs at Continent. What's he going to do?

"But the difference in quality is not just disgusting, it is *affreux.*" That is one of those French words. You might say awful, or perhaps terrifying, but that would fall short. "And we're going more and more in that direction so that people are losing their taste for quality."

Robert looked stricken, and it was not about his own bank account. This was his life. However, he brightened up as soon as I got to the main purpose of my visit.

"*Voilá*, your bird," Robert said, returning from his cold room with a richly yellow Bresse capon trussed neatly in strips of fat.

"Okay, Mort, listen!" he said, making sure that I was. "You take a pan and put a little oil [he did not have to specify olive], water, salt, and pepper in the bottom. Then you heat the oven, two hundred degrees [Centigrade]. Cover the bird with butter and roast it for two hours."

He stopped a minute to be sure I was with him.

"But, Mort, listen! All the time, you keep dousing the bird with the drippings from the pan."

Fingers to his lips, kissed and then fanned heavenward, suggested the result.

With that, Robert seized his big orange notepad, found us among the Capon People, and put a check by our name. If those other fifty-nine families followed his instructions, they all had a very enjoyable Christmas dinner.

I made another stop. Markets support a thriving periphery of other businesses, and Henri Tardieu runs a proper cheese shop near Robert's. His customers had not started to pour in, and we had a chance to talk.

Tardieu seconds André's view on the primacy of cheese in the general scheme of things. His wares are carefully selected. The Roquefort is from Carle, a small old-style artisanal producer, which gourmets much prefer to Société. He carries the English cheddar I need for tacos, an unpatriotic travesty André refuses to commit. Tardieu is not dogmatic. If it sold, he'd carry Velveeta.

He sympathized with the butchers' plight, but in his domain he saw a different sort of evolution. The price difference between quality and industrial stuff was substantial, but the quantities involved were less. And the difference in taste could hardly be compared.

"I don't see any decline in eating cheese in France," Tardieu said. He contradicted some other witnesses but was clearly convinced of his opinion. "It is an economic problem more than anything else. When people don't have as much money, they cut down on the luxuries. Maybe they'll buy less cheese, or go to less expensive supermarket brands. We felt it when the crisis hit hard a few years ago. But the minute they have a few spare francs in their pocket, they're back here again. After all, we're talking about cheese."

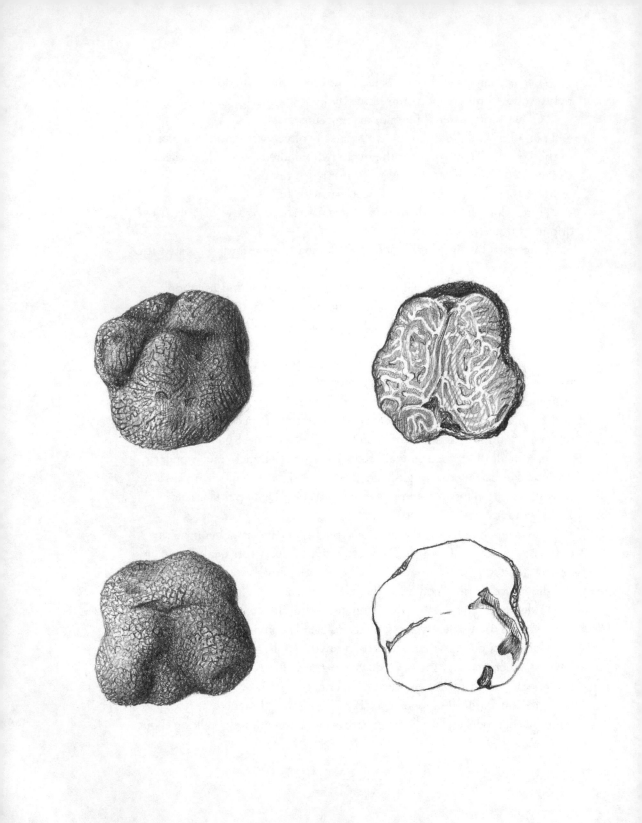

TWELVE

Bruno the Truffle King

IN THE MINUTES BEFORE 10:30 A.M. every Thursday throughout the winter, a milling cluster of people in mud-stained wool caps or perfumed fox fur stamp feet against the damp cold to wait for the opening bell. At some point, a mustachioed man with a self-important air and a long key arrives to unlock the salle polyvalente, at the north end of the boule court. The crowd shoulders its way inside. Sellers occupy a horseshoe of trestle tables. Buyers and spectators wait behind the extended arms of the man with the mustache.

Suddenly, there is frenzy. Buyers rush forward, elbowing aside old friends to jockey for position. With hand gestures, furious scribbling on scraps of paper, and determined shakes of the head—up and down, or side to side—a complex process fixes prices. The Aups Truffle Market has commenced. It is sort of like the Nasdaq stock exchange, only smaller.

Each sales position is no more than a single person standing behind what looks like an Easter-egg basket full of dirt clods. What is unmistakable, however, is the aroma. Within minutes, the odors of a ripe crowd are masked by an earthy scent unmatched by anything else in nature. It pervades the large room, and the few uninitiated sniff in wonder. Everyone else pauses to breathe in deeply and smile.

Of all the delicacies in a nation that loves exotic edibles, there is nothing like a truffle. When brushed clean of the dirt that usually cakes it, it is not much to look at. Debbie Seward, a reporter friend, once described it as looking like a cross between a shriveled human brain and a lump of coal. Neither she nor anyone else has ever found words to convey the taste, let alone the heady aroma.

Altogether, at least thirty-five varieties of fungus are properly known as truffles, ranging from small jet black tubers peculiar to French oaks to the large white tartufo bianco that Tuscans love to slice thinly over steaming tagliolini. In France, however, the term refers mainly to the "black diamond," *Tuber melanosporum*, known as the Périgord truffle, although it is found more often in Provence, Italy, and Spain.

The largest, most famous truffle market is at Richerenches, near Jean-Pierre Delay's place in the Drôme. Every Saturday morning, between mid-November and early March, an open space near the old town hall roils with strictly controlled trading. Richerenches might handle ten tons a season. But you seldom see truffles. Brokers strike deals from samples, and delivery follows.

Smaller markets are scattered around southern France, and my favorite happens to be up the road from Wild Olives, in the old Roman crossroads town of Aups. If the rains fall at the right time, the summer is not too hot, and the wild pigs find enough to eat after the first freeze, the Aups market takes on the air of a New York trading floor.

A loose reference price is determined by supply and demand. After that, there is bid and ask. Buyers scrawl offers on bits of paper and push them into diffident sellers' hands. Low-ball bids are rejected with a disgusted pursing of the lips. Successful deals rate the curt nod of a poker face.

In times of plenty, truffles may drop below 1,500 francs a kilo. More likely, they soar above 3,000. Producers prefer to deal in bulk, selling their entire baskets to a restaurateur or a well-heeled individual with a large appetite and a larger freezer.

Outside, independents sell truffles one by one. A few use rickety tables and ancient brass balances, counting change from a filthy cardboard box. One woman operates from the trunk of her BMW, weighing aromatic lumps on a fancy electronic scale. Retailers can be expensive. They are wary of questions and reluctant to give names; taxmen persist in an uphill battle to claim their cut.

I buy my truffles the way one might score crack in South Boston. My supplier, Monsieur C from nearby Tourtour, slips me a few at wholesale rates before the official flurry.

"I go out when I feel like it, and if I'm lucky, I'll find a kilo in a weekend," Monsieur C told me. That keeps him in parts for his ancient motorcycle collection and subsidizes his pottery business. "If I'm not lucky, I dig out a few truffles and then I just put them in the refrigerator for dinner."

Monsieur C uses a dog, like almost every truffle hunter in France. Pigs are far more efficient, but it is not easy to haul around a 400-pound snuffling sow in the backseat of your old Renault.

Each truffle hunter has a private reserve of oak forest, land belonging to family or friends. For reasons no one can determine clearly, the roots of certain oaks develop truffles, welcome parasites, just below the surface.

Elsewhere in France, large groves of truffle oaks and filberts are methodically harvested. Eighty percent of French truffles come from plantations. But around Aups, Tourtour, and Ampus, hunters work their favorite wild oaks. Truffle trees are easy enough to spot. Nothing else grows within a wide radius around the trunk.

The Aups Thursday market is a no-nonsense gathering of professionals, amusing to watch but quickly finished after the first frenzy. The real action is early in January, when black diamonds ripen to the aroma of full maturity, and it is time for the Aups Truffle Fair.

Posters for a recent Aups fair proclaimed: "Truffle Hunting Contest. Demonstration by a Pig." I'd seen that promise for years and the pig had yet to show. But I never miss the fair.

On a large stage, local chefs demonstrated their favorite recipes in between a running rap by the master of ceremonies. Films and displays in the town meeting hall explained subtleties of the prized fungus. A nursery sold truffle oak seedlings, the roots of which might potentially produce happy surprises in a dozen years.

As usual, the huge open space by Aups' main stone gate was alive with characters from another time. A red-faced man in a stocking cap blew rank smoke from his hand-rolled cigar, and his friends wore sweaters they had not washed since Charles de Gaulle died. But the only aroma was crisp air and truffle. Sturdy women stood behind their muddy black blobs, any one of them a match for the toughest Marseille fishwife. Tourists in bright ski jackets snapped photos of grizzled faces that stared warily into their lenses.

I watched a small man with rat-like eyes that swept the surroundings for lurking tax agents. He wore a shapeless wool cap, a streaked green field jacket and gum boots. His thin features were drawn into that sort of peasant-cunning look which Victor Hugo so dearly loved.

A better-fed truffle man next to him, Yves Richard, was happy to talk. He was fifty-five and had been working the same five hundred acres of oak woods north of Aups since he was fifteen. In the old days, he kept three pigs. Now he uses only dogs.

"*Oouuf,*" Richard replied when I asked him how his season had been. In a good year, he digs up 400 kilos, a half a ton of truffles. This was not a good year. "It was awful, and it's getting worse. We don't get rain like we used to. And then there are all those damned sangliers."

Drought is deadly to truffle growth. If rains don't fall in late summer, fungus on the roots withers away. Rainfall has grown scarce across southern France. During the 1998–1999 season, French production fell to twenty tons, one-quarter of what it was two years earlier.

But whether rain fell or not was up to the Bon Dieu. Richard reserved his wrath for the sangliers, the wild pigs so beloved to France since Astérix and Obélix.

"I'd say this year those beasts ate ninety-five percent of the truffles." This requires a bit of translation. In Haut Var peasantspeak, fifty percent means "some," and "ninety-five percent" means a lot. Yet he was far from alone in his judgment.

In the past, sangliers seldom made much of a dent on truffles. The backwoods were more heavily settled with people, keeping them at bay. More wild berries and fruits curbed their appetite. And your basic French sanglier was not a particular fan of truffles.

A decade or so ago, however, sanglier numbers dropped sharply. Hunters crossbred native wild pigs with exotic species and even some domestic porkers. The result was enough to stagger Doctor Frankenstein: a truffle-loving wild pig.

Of course, this was France. I mentioned the problem to Florence Ferte, a Parisian mother of three who loves to cook game almost as much as she loves to hunt it. "It's not so terrible," she said. "That gives sanglier sausage a delicate flavor of truffle."

Nonetheless, the potential of this menace was evident in the Aups Truffle Fair's main event.

Chalk on the dirt marked out a grid of eight squares, each with an upright oak branch to symbolize a tree. Men in folkloric whiskers, red scarves and black droop-brimmed hats paraded their champion truffle hounds.

The enthusiastic crowds were swollen that year because Aups was a stop on the newly established Black Diamond Rally, a two-day joyride of ancient cabriolets and roadsters along what Var authorities had laid out La Route de la Truffe.

One after another, dogs did their damnedest. Mostly, they romped around, excited by the crowds. A little frou-frou poodle, handled by a woman from the nearby hills, earned appreciative applause. A mangy cur did better than the rest, unearthing most of the hidden truffles in impressive time.

But, with major fanfare and stunned surprise from jaded townsfolk, the pig appeared. This was Pépette, a hippo-sized porker from Griot-les-Bains near the Gorges du Verdon. Guy Corriol, his handler, unleashed him and yelled, "Allez, zou!" Pépette cut straight to the chase. His quivering snout uncovered the first buried truffle in seconds.

As the black lump rolled into view, Corriol whacked it with a stick, and it skidded away before Pépette could gobble it down. In the same motion, he dropped an acorn in its original place. The pig ate his miserable substitute reward and, without a pause, rooted out the next truffle. In minutes, the square was cleaned out, and so were adjoining squares where dogs had left truffles behind. Pépette looked around hungrily, wondering where to look next. Pigs, among nature's most intelligent mammals, love truffles.

NOT SURPRISINGLY, the principle attraction at the Aups Truffle Fair is lunch. Every nearby restaurant offers a special menu and is packed solid. But that does not worry visitors equipped with their red bibles. Mostly, they drive twenty minutes south to Lorgues for a one-star lunch with Bruno the Truffle King.

Bruno Clément is not what you might call a modest man. In case you miss the huge green sign that says "Bruno" on the Taradeau road, you need only look up to a long, low building on the hill above his helipad. A giant mural shows a band of chef disciples seated at a table, as if assembled for the Last Lunch. And hovering above them is a huge Bruno, arms outstretched, with a halo above his luminous head.

Once inside, any lingering suspicion is quickly laid to rest. For instance, there was the morning I came by and mentioned the chapter title I had in mind.

"Hah! Bruno ze Trooffle Keeng," the chef bellowed in pleasure, striking a Roman-emperor pose as he savored the echo bouncing back from walls adorned with his image. In the kitchen and dining rooms, the staff took in the outburst with weary indulgence. The epithet might be new, but they had heard others.

This is, of course, an act. Not that Bruno is pretending to lack humility. But he is performing for effect. With the bulk and presence of an Alaskan grizzly, decked out in a crisp white chef's tunic embroidered "BC," his eyes glinting behind bottle-bottom lens with wire rims, and the fireplace catching highlights in his thick chestnut hair, he pulls it off well.

Bruno, at least, could laugh at himself. "Larger than life" hardly covered it.

"I do theater every day in my restaurant," he boomed when I asked him if he had been on the stage. This was not exactly news. I had posed the question in hopes of eliciting his version of all the stories local people love to tell about his checkered past. For a time in the mid-1980's, the popular impresario Chantal Goya put him into her revue for children. Bruno sang and danced as *"le petit marin,"* an unlikely six-foot-five, 280-pound little sailor boy. He did not bring this up.

Bruno mentioned he had taught himself to cook while in the real estate business. He volunteered nothing about what local authorities call "serious legal difficulties" related to his land sales in the area.

Writing about food, I realized, was no easier than my day job of reporting on world turmoil. How do you press a man about his rap sheet when you are halfway to heaven eating his sliced truffles on toast with olive oil, pepper, and Guerande salt?

For Bruno, the past begins in 1983 when he opened his restaurant in the stone-walled house where he spent his earliest years. He has been a smashing success, with new projects underway. He owes it all to *Tuber melanosporum.*

"My love for the truffle goes back to when I was five, living with my grandmother, who had come over from Italy in 1922," Bruno said. "We were very, very poor." Like many families now settled in the Var, his had left impoverished Piemonte to try their luck over the border. But his grandfather suffered from emphysema and died at fifty after five years on his back. Bruno's father left his mother when he was two months old, and she was forced to work all day as a maid. His grandmother raised young Bruno and his brother.

"She took me with her to hunt for truffles in the hills, *à la mouche,*" he said. This was how people did it when they had patience and no pig; a particular fly hovers over buried truffles in search of a place to lay eggs. "She dug up two beautiful truffles and took them home to make in *brouillade* [scrambled eggs]. I was hooked."

I was getting hooked myself. Bruno told his story with practiced pathos, but the taste of his truffled toast was mesmerizing.

"We didn't have a refrigerator, so my grandmother would always put the remains of our brouillade in a Pyrex dish on a windowsill, covered with a cloth," he said. "When I came home from school, she fed me that with bread. All the other kids had chocolate to put in their bread, but I had only truffles. It was not until I grew up that I realized how lucky I was."

I knew this story, which picked up occasional embellishments to suit the occasion. A year before, I heard it in Ampus. "Bruno de Lorgues" spoke as honored guest at a ceremony to induct new members to the Order of the Truffle. Speaker and inductees wore black robes and their truffleheads, great furry black helmets in the rough shape of the beloved black diamond.

"I was born under a truffle oak," he said. As the laughter subsided, he added with a dramatic flourish, "It's true." Then he told how he was deprived of pain au chocolat and forced to eat truffles, making the poignant point with the same careful pauses.

Altogether, it was a memorable speech. He then went into an off-color oration on what a matched pair of shriveled truffles can resemble, a clear sign that they amount to a natural Viagra that should be subsidized with other medicines by Social Security.

In the circumstances he describes, I would have thought Bruno would grow up to be a chocolate maker. It was hard to imagine abject poverty in that large, lovely farmhouse, with its carved stone fireplaces and elaborate walls, ceiling, and floors. The comfortable home seemed a better spot to give birth than the woods out back. Anyway, records show his birthplace as Toulon.

But the story is basically true. Mame, his devoted grandmother, came at the start of the same Piemontese wave that brought my neighbors, the Romanas. Few of those early immigrants had much wealth. Most of their descendants still work the land in the same villages where families sunk their roots, as much for nostalgia as necessity. For anyone who grows up gathering wild asparagus and forest berries or digging up truffles, fruits of the earth has a whole different meaning.

In any case, Bruno tells a good story, and nothing rings phony about his great love for food.

Every day, Bruno feeds the world twenty-five pounds of truffles—that approaches eight tons each year—in dishes not soon forgotten. He layers them with foie gras, shaves them into tender potatoes, folds them into his grandmother's scrambled eggs. They flavor pigeon and add delicate depths to sauces. One speciality is shoulder of Pyrenées suckling lamb baked five hours in its own juices and stuffed with truffled potatoes. Another is lentils with truffles, foie gras, and cumin. Chez Bruno's repertoire runs to a soufflé-sorbet dessert with apples and truffles.

An attentive wait staff instructs novices in how to best savor the items on the fixed menu. Chez Bruno is no place to give orders to the chef. Once Jeannette brought a tour group for lunch, and a young woman balked at the runny scrambled eggs. When she asked that they be cooked more, the stricken waiter resisted gamely. Finally, Jeannette took him aside and explained, "Look, she lives in England." He nodded in sympathy and brought the eggs back a golden brown.

"Cooking is all love and tenderness and old memories," Bruno said. "It is intensely personal. I can eat a meal and without seeing the chef, I can tell you whether he is homosexual or a great lover of women, whether he is stingy or generous, whether or not he appreciates life. If he's a brute, I'll know it. If he's fat or skinny. It is all in how he handles the food, how he cuts and spices, the proportions and combinations. Cooking well is just like making love to a woman. You touch each ingredient, feel its textures, sniff its aromas and only then do you know precisely what you will do with it."

Warming to his theme, he recalled a sous-chef who once worked for him. "One day I told him, 'Look, if you make love like you cook, your girlfriend is going to leave you.' He laughed, but two weeks later he came to work in tears. She had gone, and he was surprised. I knew it would happen. He lacked passion, warmth, sensuality, and you could see it in his cooking."

By now, Bruno's shoulders and fingertips had entered the conversation, and his big voice filled the large vaulted room behind his kitchen. He recalled how his grandmother took him often to eat with a neighbor named Simone.

"She was a wonderful cook, but I hated to go there because I always thought her dishes were dirty," he said. "They were perfectly clean, in fact, but they were all worn at the edges with years of use, and I had never seen that as a kid. One day here I decided to serve what I called *salade assiette sale de Simone*—Simone's dirty-dish salad. It was local greens, olive oil, and salt, and we used spices to dirty up the edges of the dish. At one table, a group of distinguished men was disgusted at the name. One was president of one of the biggest companies in France. But then I told them the story. One began to weep. Soon, all of them were crying. Each had been taken back to his own childhood kitchen memories."

At that point, someone rushed up with a crisis, and Bruno was off like a shot. Moments later, he was back, his thread unbroken and his nostalgic mood instantly restored.

"My own cooking changes with my mood," he said. "It can be ebullient and happy. It can be austere. If I'm angry, someone else can cook. There is no better way to show love, respect. And always, it starts from the ingredients. When I am making lunch for friends, I go early to the market. I carefully find the best of everything: the freshest greenery, the plumpest fruit, the choicest meat. I never count my money. I want only the best. Then I take it all home and savor each item another time. I handle it, turn it over, smell it. Only then I decide how I will prepare it all."

With an enormous sigh, he leaned back to savor the images he had evoked. It was an impressive performance considering, as the regional food review De Bouche en Oreille often points out, Bruno is not a chef.

"And the truffle?" I asked.

"And the truffle," he replied. "It is the most sensual ingredient of all. It stirs the imagination, fires the flames, suggests passion and pleasure like nothing else can."

. . .

BRUNO, NATURALLY ENOUGH, has an answer to McDonald's in France: the McTruffle. "I'm not joking," he said, not joking. "I wrote to the head of McDonald's in Paris to suggest it. We worked it out perfectly."

He stopped and bellowed, "Dominique!!" For the third time in ten minutes Dominique Saugnac, his harried head chef, rushed out of the kitchen to join the conversation. "What was our proposal for the Mc-Truffe."

"Very simple. You take the standard sesame bun and put on a little olive oil. Then you spread *fromage blanc* and on top of that thin slices of truffle. You add a little bit of salt and pepper. It's wonderful."

Bruno was excited by the concept. "That's how you keep young people interested in our culinary heritage, how French people can stay in touch with their cuisine, even while trying something new. It is delicious, and it would not cost that much to make."

When I last checked, McDonald's had not taken him up on the idea.

Another idea remained on hold, looking for funds. Bruno wants to erect a giant sculpted grass truffle on a low mountain peak in the Var. Along with that, there would be a truffle museum.

Bruno had plenty more to keep him occupied. His restaurant seats one hundred diners—and more, when pushed to its limits—which makes it hard to assure the personal, flawless service required for a second Michelin star. He may reduce the number of tables and add a touch of class. Besides the restaurant, he has a shop that offers packaged truffles, truffle oils, local olive oil, books, and such kitschy items as ceramic plates with grotesque black lumps on them.

Peripheral activities are vital to a chef-propriétaire, Bruno said, launching into what was getting to be a familiar theme. "How else do you survive?" he asked, voice booming. "With all the laws, taxes, crazy economics, you have to have some kind of religious calling to keep at it. Pretty soon, we'll all be outlaws or in the *merde* up to our shoulders in debt. At this rate, the future for France is small family auberges. There is no other way out."

At the end of 1999, Bruno opened a new restaurant in a restored Cistercian abbey. It was too much for him to handle alone, so he called in his friend Alain Ducasse as a partner. Ducasse already had six Michelin stars to worry about, separate restaurants in Paris and Monte Carlo;

along with other culinary enterprises. But, like Bruno, he was a sucker for truffles.

In his book *Rencontres Savoureuses*, published in 1999, Ducasse rhapsodized for pages about his favorite fungus. "The truffle has always evoked mystery and legends," he wrote. "One pretends that it made its first appearance under the Libyan sands, thanks to the curiosity of holy men. One says the Greeks and the Romans did not deprive themselves of tasting it to further the drunkness of their orgies. One easily imagines their pleasure, lying at the feet of muses, as they bit into the mushroom of vertiginous perfume."

If its real secrets are still unknown, he adds, "the truffle seems like a gem from somewhere beyond that has ripened in the entrails of the earth. When one discovers it under a tree, one has the sense of exhuming an ancient treasure. It is miraculous. The subtle force of its scent rests on a question: Are we breathing an offering of nature or the deep heart of a woman? Voilá, that's it. All the charm of the truffle links spirituality with the eroticism of the senses."

Finally, Ducasse says, the divine flirts with animal instincts, "and a blinding flash surges in us for a brief instant to light the darker parts of our human affections."

With a bit more elegance, that was Bruno to perfection. My fevered imagination pushed its limits trying to picture the two partners, in their kitchen late on a February night, enlightening their darkest parts with the flash of ripe truffles.

Bruno the Truffle King is very good, and Ducasse the poet of the palate is clearly a master. But my favorite truffle dish, in fact, is by Paul Bajade, at the one-star Les Chênes Verts near Tourtour. It is a whole truffle inside a flaky crust, warmed and softened slightly in a savory light cream sauce but still with its natural crunch.

While Bruno serves truffles all year around, buying huge quantities from Spain and Italy and freezing them to serve during the long months out of season, Bajade uses only fresh local black diamonds from December to March. He is diffident, hardly the type to paint himself under a halo on the wall of his country inn tucked away under sheltering oaks. But love, tenderness, and sensuality emanate from his kitchen.

The French like the phrase "to die for," and they use it lightly to describe things that arrive on a dinner plate. If that phrase ever had to be taken literally, I think I'd pick that *truffe en croûte*.

FRANCE'S TRUFFLE PASSION went wild in the late 1880's when phylloxera destroyed grapes all across the Southwest. Farmers ripped out vines to plant truffle oaks. After an agonizing wait of up to fifteen years, the fungus made them fortunes. At the turn of the century, yearly production was a thousand tons. For four months a year, French families ate truffles with everything.

Truffle oaks have a lifespan of less than a century, however, and those old trees are mostly gone. With perfect rains and a minimum of marauding by sangliers, France is hard-pressed to turn out a tenth of those old record levels. Italy and Spain produce about the same as France.

"We are doing everything we can to encourage produce and to rewaken people's love for the truffle," explained Jean-Claude Savignac, a charming man of many hats. During the week, he wears a silk tie as social affairs director for a large Parisian public works enterprise. Weekends, he commutes home to his truffle plantation in the Périgord village of Sorges, where he is mayor. And for ten years, Savignac has been president of the Fédération des Trufficulteurs Français.

This last job is serious business. Perhaps 20,000 French families make a living from truffles, and the number is growing. Any number of crises affect their lives. There was, for example, the great Chinese truffle scare of 1994.

"All of a sudden, importers started bringing in huge quantities of black truffles from China," Savignac explained. "During one year, they brought in twenty-four tons, almost as much as our entire production. They looked just like ours. They even had a promising aroma. And they cost half as much as ours. The difference was that they had absolutely no taste."

The federation got a court to order that the foreign fungus be labeled "*truffes de Chine*." That was enough for French consumers, who know when taste is missing. Some Chinese imposters are bought in bulk by industrial packagers of prepared dishes with truffles in the recipe. That is legal, since botanically the Chinese variety passes muster. It is hard to legislate flavor.

Then there is the thorny issue of poached truffles. It is not easy to lock up a forest plantation, and thieves take full advantage. This runs from the occasional raid into a neighbor's oaks to wholesale destruction.

"The worst is when people take pickaxes and dig huge holes around someone's trees," Savignac said. "Usually this is done in September or

October, when the truffles are formed but long before they are ripe. Not many people are out watching then. Commercial packers buy up these tasteless truffles, often the same people who buy truffes de Chine. It is a cheap way to comply with a list of ingredients."

Savignac, a dapper man of elaborate courtesy, spoke on and on, reeling off figures, facts, and Latin names with a consuming passion. He stopped short when I asked him what words he uses to describe the aroma and taste of black truffles.

"Incomparable is what we usually say," he replied finally, clearly not satisfied.

Nope, I said. Try again.

"Earthy. Mushroomy, but with a slightly sugared overtone. Like Pommerol wine."

Since I could do no better, I let him off the hook. Some things simply escape language.

Savignac found his old rhythm again when I asked about his dog. He has a King Charles terrier that grew up in Paris but flipped at the first scent of truffle.

"He is amazing, almost as good as a pig," Savignac said. "If I leave him in Paris and come back with truffles, I have to fight him off before he can rip open the sack. Mostly, truffle hunters like labradors. They can pick up a molecule of scent at fifty meters."

Late in 1999, Savignac's federation invited specialists from around the world to meet in Aix-en-Provence. The 120 papers they produced filled three volumes that weighed in at twenty pounds. An American scientist reported progress on growing diamonds in North Carolina and California. Every other aspect from health to marketing came under careful scrutiny.

We were meeting in Savignac's office, and the buzzing telephones grew more insistent. Assistants repeatedly poked their heads through the door with the look of someone waiting too long in line for an airplane lavatory. I tried to leave out of courtesy, but he kept on going.

"Truffles are a very passionate subject," he said, unnecessarily.

As we finally stood to go, Savignac recalled a last bit of lore. The high-speed TGV train tracks through the Drôme were supposed to have sliced through a stand of truffle oaks owned by a national assemblyman. But a quick call to his friend, then-President François Mitterrand, shifted them a kilometer away. Truffles, Mitterrand knew, are a very passionate subject.

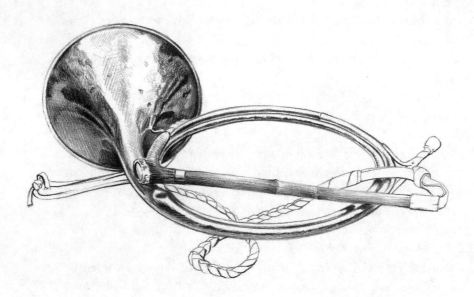

—◁◇▷—

THIRTEEN

Killers' Corner

THERE ARE DECIDED drawbacks to gangs of wine-warmed lunatics spraying your property with twelve-gauge shotgun loads for months on end. Sanglier hunters are a particular nuisance if you're in the habit of scruffling in the underbrush around your olive trees. But there is nothing like a crater scooped out by pig paws where truffles used to be to make a hunting fan out of you.

Of all French male instincts, few are as basic as the urge to kill and consume wildlife. Before the Revolution, only aristocrats were allowed to hunt. Harsh penalties for poaching were one reason that rural peasants supported Parisians who stormed the Bastille. France, in fact, may be the only country where the reign was called on account of the game.

On a continent that once fed itself by hunting, no nation still goes after game like the French. Each year, a million and a half hunters take out licenses for everything from starlings to the stags which descend from the wild herds that kings once stalked in royal reserves. Mostly, they use rifles and shotguns and the occasional bow.

French hunters manage to kill at least forty people a year, and they injure hundreds more. But opinion polls show that about half the country defends their right to blast away.

Among the strongest fringe parties in France is a hunters' rights group, Chasse, Pêche, Nature et Traditions. CPNT polled 6.7 percent of the vote in 1999 European Parliament elections. That was better than the splintered far right or the once-numerous Communists. Its leader, a firebrand young mayor from southwestern France named Jean Saint-Josse, draws lines in the sand and holds fast.

Of all their quarry, something about the wild boar inflames the hunter's soul. *Sanglier Passion*, one of several magazines of its specific genre, even runs a monthly centerfold of a naked pig.

A decade ago, too much hunting caused the sanglier population to crash. Several exotic species were brought in to help restore the numbers. In some cases, domestic pigs were bred with sangliers. Suddenly, the problem was reversed.

"They're destroying everything, those beasts," my neighbor Jeannot Romana remarked one morning. A farmer and olive grower, he much prefers his sanglier as chops, sausage, or in a terrine. "Wheat fields, fences, everything gets trampled. It's a plague of pigs."

This was not news. Late one night, Jeannette looked out the window to see a family of wild pigs headed for a moonlight dip in our hot tub. Similarly, Saint-Tropez families report porcine guests lounging by their pools.

The National Hunting Office estimates the French sanglier population at 700,000, nine times greater than it was in 1975. This is in spite of annual kills surpassing 325,000.

Near Montpellier, 250 miles west of us, a vintner named Yvon Creissac echoed Jeannot's ire. He blames hunters for destroying a natural balance. A pure sanglier female had one litter a year of perhaps three piglets, he said, but hybrids can reproduce twice, with up to twenty babies in all.

"It's been a disaster, and it's getting worse," Creissac said. "These animals look just like sangliers, but they're different, much bolder, much less fearful of man. They tear up vineyards, gardens, crops, and you can't keep them out. They charge an electric fence and knock it over before it stops them."

Hunters agree the number is up but are not happy to shoulder all the blame. Yves Merino, whose Grand Café du Cours at Aups displays a prize boar wearing Elton John glasses and Christmas bulbs, reports mounting kills. His club shot 125 sangliers in 1998, easily beating the previous record of eighty from the year before.

If anyone messed with genes or mating habits, Merino insists, it was not him or his buddies. Farmers are compensated for damage with money paid to the state for licenses, he said, so why are they complaining? And anyway, he adds, they exaggerate.

"They claim boars kill their sheep," he said. "Please. Wolves, maybe. Not boars."

Sangliers are not known to be carniverous. They just look like it. Brawnier and meaner looking than their southwestern U.S. cousins, javelinas, they attack humans only when threatened. Éric Tournier of the National Hunting Office says no one has convinced him sangliers kill sheep. But, he confirmed, they wreak major havoc.

Boar hunting can be almost poetic when serious devotees follow spoor through thick bush and bring down a beast with bow and arrow. It can also be a massacre by men in grimy green coats.

Hunters organize in teams, called *battues*, with strict rules and practices. They chart out a pig-inhabited area, and post sentries within sight of one another across roadways or paths that fleeing pigs might cross. Point men go deep into the bush to roust out their quarry.

From fall to late winter, country roads are lined with armed men peering into the bush. As dusk falls, they cluster around their muddy jeeps in places like Killers' Corner at Aups. As their dogs whimper toward relaxation after a charged-up day, they extract corks and lie about the hunt. When wine washes away the excess testosterone, they go home to their families.

"We love hunting," Merino told me one night. "We have always hunted. We will always hunt. As long as there are sangliers, we'll be out there."

Most likely. As long as sangliers do annual damage in the tens of millions of dollars, even anti-hunters are likely to be cheering them on.

IT WAS IN Paris that I first realized the extent of French hunters' passion. One June morning in 1998, nearly a quarter million people crowded the Champs de Mars, the vast open park that spreads from the base of the Eiffel Tower.

The European Union had drafted new rules for hunting water fowl.

Shooting was banned during part of migratory periods. This, the hunters railed, was typical Brusselsthink. Did the Eurocrats expect them to shoot when there were no birds at which to aim?

Environment Minister Dominique Voynet supported some of the limits, which made her as reviled an enemy as the Brussels people.

The protest march was huge and noisy. Contingents had come from every corner of France, representing stalkers of all manners of game. Duck calls blasted. Hunting horns blared. Mostly, marchers chanted vulgar slogans having to do with Madame Voynet.

Several families, with tots in strollers, made a picnic of it. I collected a few recipes from housewives who regarded game as an essential part of the French diet. Gentlemen shooters explained to me their reasoned philosophy of nature. But the general mood was far more truculent.

"I wouldn't mind getting Voynet in my sights," observed one man in a field jacket with a huge decoy duck strapped to his head. The problem, he said, was that government functionaries who made rules had no idea about wild game populations. They worked on the basis of emotion, not science.

"There are no better conservationists than hunters," Duckhead told me. "We are careful to maintain populations so that we will always have something to hunt. Many of us grew up in families where the men, even the women, have hunted for as many generations as they can remember. It is a natural state of things, and it is a basic right."

If hunters don't maintain the ecological balance, he added, species will overbreed and cause serious problems.

Some of this was true. National research teams found that an eightfold increase in deer over twenty-five years caused major damage to forests and crops. Similar imbalances among other species caused problems in different parts of France.

But, with passions running so high, findings tended to clash. Opposing sides accuse each other of skewing data to make a case.

And then there are the more basic human issues. Hunters, for instance, are outraged by a new law imposed by Brussels. They may no longer be permitted to charge onto anyone's land, without permission, in hot pursuit of their quarry.

During 2000, a government commission studied the problems and sought compromise. No one was particularly hopeful. Saint-Josse and his CPNT party insisted that Voynet resign. And the minister, in a stiff response carried in the daily *Le Monde*, replied, in essence: Hunters ought to realize they are hardly alone in the world.

Meanwhile, as usual in France, the sound and fury over a larger issue masked respectable status quo at a more noble extreme.

FROGGY RANG EARLY on a wet and freezing November morning. "We're going deer hunting," he announced. "Bring a suit and tie."

I was in Paris, after a long stint in Provence, with the intention of observing how the rest of France lived. And Jérôme had found an unusual point of view. It was Saint Hubert's Day, he explained. The patron saint of hunters was being called upon to bless the hounds and horses, thus formally initiating yet another season of *chasse à courre*.

The English hunted foxes, I knew, but I had no idea the French pursued stag in a similar manner, with less pomp but much more circumstance. After tagging along on three hunts over a month, I finally saw what it was all about.

Peering through thick brush in the old royal forest near Villers-Cotteréts, north of Paris, I watched a Louis XIV painting come to life. Riders in blue velvet reined in their lathered horses behind sixty howling hounds and the magnificent old stag they held at bay.

For five hours, there had been furious crashing through the undergrowth, trumpet tattoos and booming shouts of *"Taiaut,"* an ancient French hunting cry the English borrowed as "Tally ho." But now it was the end. For a long moment, nothing moved. Forest mists blurred rich colors into soft focus. The exhausted buck eyed the waiting dogs, its five-point antlers cocked in a noble pose. And then the hunt master dismounted, strode forward, and put a single bullet into its heart.

A few things have changed since the glory days of Versailles. The Sun King's quarry never leaped over a Porsche 911 Turbo parked in the woods. Commoners by the score did not follow with their kids in the family Renault. Otherwise, the French sport of riding to hounds—known as *"la venerie"*—is much the same as it was before the Revolution or, for that matter, a thousand years before that.

With all the modern technology added to hunting by rifle, ten thousand Frenchmen still ride to the hounds, in the old way.

The rules and traditions are set in stone. Once the quarry is singled out, the dogs follow it alone. If a wily old buck spooks a younger stag out of hiding to take its place, the pack doubles back to pick up the original scent. Villages are sacrosanct. A stag hiding among sugar beets or in a wheatfield risks a farmer's fury, but he is safe from the dogs.

Dress is immaculate, from the velvet crash helmets to the blunt silver spurs on high black boots buffed to a dull matte finish. Long swallowtail coats might be royal blue, forest green, scarlet, or black, depending on the club. Embroidered leather vests cover scarves in white silk or fine linen. Veterans favor a stickpin made from two stag teeth. Each carved button has a meaning. Riders carry a scabbard knife and crop.

And no one is without a sixteenth-century cell phone worn around the neck and under one arm: *la trompe*, a trumpet's mouth at the end of three and a half loops of shiny brass. It talks to the dogs and directs the pack. It signals the lost and the laggards, whether canine or human. Before and after, it stirs the air in ceremonious concert.

In England, protesters and saboteurs make every fox hunt an ordeal, a crisis of conscience accessible only to those who are comfortable in their class. Germans must content themselves with chasing fox droppings in a leather box hauled by a horseman at high speed through the woods to the amusement of anyone who happens to catch a glimpse. Their hounds follow, like racetrack greyhounds pursuing a fake rabbit. Belgians, too, are denied the kill.

But in France, an average of five enthusiastic spectators turn out for every mounted hunter. Called *suiveurs*, or followers, they bounce down forest lanes in their cars, clustering at likely vantage points in hopes of seeing the stag burst from the foliage with hounds in hot pursuit. With no bullets flying, they can take their infants and the house mutt for a day in the country.

Hard-core suiveurs learn to recognize distinct blasts of la trompe, which tracks the progress of the hunt. If the stag crosses a road or a railroad track or a stream, there is a separate call. At each flat-out charge, a stirring chorus notes direction. A few suiveurs keep pace on mountain bikes. Some even try it on foot, logging up to fifty miles as the buck streaks forward, zigzags, and doubles back to lose the pack.

The anti-hunting lobby is confounded by this population of common-folk fans who could not dream of keeping a horse but still regard la venerie as part of their birthright. Any one of these followers will explain that they love the thrill of the chase, the fresh outdoors, the ancient traditions brought back to life.

And these are Frenchmen. When the hunt is over, most are there with plastic sacks awaiting their customary chunk of fresh venison. If any meat is left over, it is given to charity. The hunters, who keep only a hoof and the antlers for the person who merits the day's honors, head off for a Champagne apéritif and a proper banquet.

ALTOGETHER, NEARLY FOUR hundred French clubs keep dog packs to hunt stag, deer, wild boar, fox, badger, or rabbit. Many of them started after World War II, as soon as German occupiers had fled France's beloved forests, and the number has been growing steadily since.

Froggy had good friends among the Équipage de Longvesne, so later on that Saint Hubert's Day morning we showed up for mass outside of François I's hunting lodge-castle at Villers-Cotteréts.

At 10:00 A.M. sharp, everyone was in place under the freezing, gray drizzle. Instead of the customary church organ, a dozen trompes blasted away in harmony. The *sonneurs*, in red velvet, brass buttons, and leather trim, stood with their backs to the congregation so their circular trumpets projected to the front. The priest wore a thin white hassock that barely disguised thick underwear against the chill.

Spectators formed a ragged crescent around the serious participants: ranks of hunters, powdered and polished, each standing ramrod straight with a gleaming horn under one arm. One tall young man with a luxuriant Guardsman's mustache whom I'd seen smoking a weathered pipe seemed to have fallen from the pages of an early P. G. Wodehouse. Several others, silver-haired and stolid, might have been in recess from the House of Lords—or the Reichstag. A blonde woman with amused eyes and delicate features looked nonetheless equipped to ruin the morning of any stag within range.

I kept noticing an older gentleman, short and slightly toad-shaped in a noble sort of way, with an impressive patina of age on his leather fittings and battered horn. His eyes crackled with electricity behind gold-rimmed glasses. His well-shaved jaw and upper lips formed upswept parallel lines like an amused crocodile.

This, I learned, was Didier Heilbronn, the retired head of a French trading conglomerate, whose sons ran Chanel in New York. At seventy-three, he had been riding to hounds ever since the defeated Germans gave back the royal forests north of Paris in 1945. Every Tuesday and Saturday,

Heilbronn is at it again. An easy hunt takes two hours of hard work. Tougher ones run to six, as horses slide in the snow and branches slash at faces.

Partly paralyzed on one side and slightly stiff of limb, Heilbronn laughed when asked about a trip into space by the septuagenarian senator John Glenn. "I would have liked to have gone to the moon," he said, "but this is good enough."

He had just become the senior Villers-Cotteréts member. Solange Fenwick, heiress to a forklift fortune, had just given up the hunt at eighty-two, still able to ride all day, then dance on the dinner table in the evening.

"Some go for the forest, some for the dogs or for the horses, some for the atmosphere and the hunt itself," Heilbronn explained. His eyes glistened as he ran down the list. "Everyone has their own reasons. I love it all."

Next to him, Maurice Velge nodded grave agreement. A Belgian who owns much of the port of Antwerp, is hunt master. He first rode to the hounds at the age of twelve, a half century earlier. Now the sport is banned at home and, like many Belgians, he drives down once or twice a week.

The main thing, Heilbronn and Velge agreed, is to get it right. "We have ancient and strict traditions to follow," Velge said, "and it is important to respect them. When you do, when you are there in the open forest, man pursuing beast and each has a fighting chance, there is nothing on earth to compare with it."

Jean-Luc Corroyer, better known by his nickname, Pic Avant (Point Man), handles the club's hundred hounds. He feeds them their 220 pounds of meat a day and listens to their troubles.

Short, stocky, gruffly pleasant, he might be well cast as a sergeant for Napoléon. At full tilt, bellowing at the dogs and herding human stragglers in his ranks, he could be Napoléon himself.

Pic Avant is a national champion horn blower, a virtuoso of the complex calls that signal a quarry's progress and identify different animals. Each fanfare is distinctive and authoritative. Before the hunt, I asked him to play the lilting yet stirring badger melody. His dogs nearly turned themselves inside out looking for the badger.

On that first Saint Hubert's Day, it was a very long hunt. Froggy and I climbed into a little Suzuki with Jean-Pierre Baudin and Julien Seigne, the sixteen-year-old son of his good friend. Jean-Pierre, a suiveur for years, rocketed down forest lanes ahead of the pack. With an ear finely tuned to the horns, he noted when hunters deep in the trees found their stag. Sometimes we got out and chased on foot, scrambling to keep up with Julien's deer-like gait. Other times, we waited by the road for the quarry to burst forth.

Either way, it was stirring. Old noble trees were planted in rows among the natural forest where French kings hunted in the same way. Mists rose off thick undergrowth. Shouts and hoofbeats approached, then receded. It was cold as hell, wet, and windy. We loved it.

At lunchtime, no one had to blow a signal on the trompe. Every French suiveur knew the exact moment, and car trunks flew open in perfect unison. A few items were basic kit, and they varied little from trunk to trunk: a wicker hamper with linen napkins and weighty forks and knives; charcuterie ranging from thinly sliced raw ham to elaborate pigeon pâtés; cheeses of all sorts; fresh crisp-crusted baguettes; red wine from some little-known vintner in Bordeaux; fruit tarts and mixed pastries; chilled Champagne.

José Baudin, Jean-Pierre's wife, had some lightly salted smoked salmon of admirable tenderness. But the hands-down winner was a lady lawyer from Vannes, on the Brittany coast, who produced half a bushel of fresh oysters.

It was a total surprise, this seafood feed in a forest clearing, but nothing a reasonably prepared Frenchman couldn't handle. Without missing a beat, Jean-Pierre reached into his hunting jacket, extracted an oyster knife, and began shucking.

Didier trotted up and, in the saddle, slurped down a few fines de claire as if he were at La Coupole. I don't think a truffle-stuffed Bresse capon would have fazed him.

Most of the riders missed lunch, plugging on after the wily stag. Velge decided not to give up on Saint Hubert's Day, the rain-soaked, mud-spattered band was still at it, six hours after the start, until it was too dark to see the hounds. In any case, it was dinnertime. The stag got away.

THE NEXT TIME we went out, it was over fast. Pic Avant and his dogs quickly picked up the scent. The stag tried a few tricks and shook the pack. He doubled back sharply, then set off at full speed in a straight line. José, nearly as crafty as her husband, found a vantage point. The animal leapt from the trees, across the road, in a single graceful arch. No photographic evidence exists, however. Jérôme and Jean-Pierre, who decided to follow on all-terrain bikes, were somewhere else.

The stag sought refuge in a village, a trick he likely learned from past hunts. Pic Avant held back his dogs, and the mounted hunters circled in frustration on the outskirts. But then the quarry bolted into open country and found himself trapped by a pond. The dogs cornered him, and it was over. José and I got there late. Jérôme and Jean-Pierre got there very late.

But our last chasse à courre was something else entirely. Guests had come from Germany, Britain, and elsewhere in France. A magnificent five-point buck had been sighted in the section the club planned to hunt. The weather was crisp and dry. Car trunks were stuffed to breaking point with lunch and liquid.

I noticed a dashing black-bearded Irishman, comfortable atop a handsome horse that seemed as eager as its rider to get underway. The man, Gary Timbrell, studied bugs for a living.

"This is the best hunting anywhere," Timbrell told me. "It's fairly unknown, but I'm afraid the secret is getting out. The French do it the old way, preserving a noble tradition in a way that's open to normal people. It takes you completely away, as the kings did it, with much less of an entry requirement."

We were all back in Jean-Pierre's jeep this time, with a better notion of what to look for. Julien came along, proud of a new battle scar. He had ridden in a hunt for the first time the previous week and performed admirably. But he had to ignore his mother's wails when a branch tore his lip, pouring blood onto his white ascot.

A particularly genial band of suiveurs had gathered for the hunt. Since the only shot fired is a carefully aimed coup de grâce, on the off chance that dogs corner the quarry, parents feel safe enough to take kids along on a family outing.

"With rifles, hunters go out alone, and each tries to get a deer," Jean-Pierre said. "Here, two dozen people take one animal, and a hundred others get enjoyment from the hunt."

It all went as promised. The stag employed its full repertoire of subterfuge, but the dogs were at their best. Long sprints across open fields were broken by quick-step threading through dense forest. For hours on end, hunters, hounds, and quarry worked themselves to exhaustion.

Several times, we watched the animal run, half flying, as it guided its broad antlers under low branches. Once we saw it jump, as smoothly as a gamboling gazelle. Finally, it had had enough.

Jean-Pierre veered around a forest-lane corner and stopped behind several cars already parked by the road. In dappled light filtered through the trees, we saw the stag at bay. Dogs stood around it in a circle, oddly silent after a long afternoon of howling without letup.

The stag watched the dogs with antlers lowered, ready for a last defense. The pack remained in place. After a long moment, the standoff was over. The stag cocked its head in a final noble pose. Velge dismounted and shot him once with a rifle.

A successful hunt ends with a ceremony known as *la curée*. The carcass is hauled to an open spot, where hunters and suiveurs gather. A butcher skins it and distributes meat to the followers. The head and hide are draped over the remaining innards, and a huntsman moves the antlers from side to side to excite the hounds awaiting their reward.

To the blast of horns, he steps back. Then, as hunters play a farewell concert, the snapping and snarling dogs work over what is left like piranhas in a pond.

An honored guest receives the stag's foot, as well as the right to buy Champagne back at the clubhouse.

"This goes back in time, and it used to be a noble sport, but it's not only for the rich," Florence Ferte explained. If comfortably situated, she is not in any dizzying tax bracket. Her husband works for the government. With their two daughters to help, the Fertes have filled an entire living room with trophies over the decades.

Still, *la venerie* is not exactly cheap. A good horse costs two thousand dollars to buy and about as much per year to keep. Many riders keep several. Annual club dues can run to four thousand dollars. Nor has it gone totally to commoners. The previous Villers-Cotteréts hunt master was Viscount Philippe le Hardy de Beaulieu, descendant of the dukes of Burgundy.

—◁◇◇◇▷—

FOURTEEN

The Belly of Paris

JUST GLANCING AROUND, it is easy enough to panic over the state of things in the world capital of food. Take, for instance, la Place de la République. Great boulevards and bustling little streets converge onto a vast open space, around a soaring statue of Marianne, the female embodiment of France. This is a crossroads of real-life Paris, where plumbers in faded blues jostle insurance adjusters in silk ties and natty shoes on their way to meet friends for dinner.

A few years ago, fourteen bistros and brasseries around la Place de la République served tasty traditional meals to full houses. Now four remain. Along the old restaurant row, today's choices are different: Between the Quick and the McDonald's, a franchise El Rancho offers what it misrepresents as "Tex-Mex" cuisine. Past the Bistro Romain, a chain outlet of Italianish food endorsed by Marc Veyrat, there is a Buffalo Grill. And that is just a start.

One evening, gritting my teeth, I headed into El Rancho. The menu was not promising. "Mexican paella"? "Gaspacho Old Taos"? At the bottom, a helpful glossary defined "jalapeños" as *très doux*—very mild, or sweet—green peppers that came in melted cheddar cheese and batter.

Other Tex-Mex specialities included baked salmon, hot chèvre salad, and crème brûlée.

In decor and menu descriptions, corporate minds had jumbled together the Deep South, odd bits of Spain, and passing notions of Mexico. A western saddle was flung over a bannister amid neon ads for Miller and Bud. The plastic-plaster walls were a sickly shade of adobe.

I had seen a French television feature on El Rancho that focused on its turbospeed time-management computers meant to ensure that servers rushed through diners in minimum time. The staff, apparently, had missed that program. Although waiters outnumbered customers two to one, dinner took forty minutes to arrive.

Not that I was anxious for it. My margarita was sticky sweet and algae green. The guacamole had the consistency and flavor of library paste. (That TV story had reported that sixty tons a year were imported frozen from the United States.) Tacos came as a salad: marinated beef, grated cheese, and lettuce in a bowl made from deep-fried corn meal. This is the Paris way; French people do not eat things that drip through their fingers. The menu promised *pico de gallo* sauce, and I asked for some. The waitress pointed to some chopped tomato with green flecks hiding under a piece of meat. "That," she announced, sniffing slightly at my denseness, "is the pico de gallo."

Not even my noble purpose could drive me to order what was labeled as enchiladas. Instead, I had "entrecôte BBQ." Leaving aside the cup of dubious barbecue sauce, it was an acceptable version of what old-style French restaurants have served around La République for generations: steak frites.

Before dinner, I wandered past the ornate entrance to the Hôpital Saint-Antoine, not far away toward Nation, in a neighborhood I used to enjoy. The blue awning of the fishmonger was still there, but bins once stacked high with fresh bass and tuna on chopped ice had been carted away. Instead, a cheap housewares shop sold Korean batteries and plastic garbage pails.

Every few steps, someone offered a fast hit of indigestible calories. A Greek and Turk glared at one another from their side-by-side holes in the wall, each offering greasy national specialties. Tunisian joints sold canned tuna and olives on a bun. Chinese families displayed take-away steamed tidbits and overfried Vietnamese nems. Cold pizza awaited the microwave in one place. Falafel smoked in another.

A cluster of café-bars still thrive around the hospital's carved stone gate, full of patients working up courage and orderlies winding down from the day. I walked into L'Étoile d'Or and found it remodeled in formica and fake wood. On one wall, gaudy photos on glossy paper display the frozen, industrial items that might be ordered: a poisonous-looking pizza, a brick of lasagna, baguette sandwiches, red-dyed sausages in a bed of soggy frites.

Below them, a hand-scrawled sign on the wall warned, "Don't bring your own food to eat in here." It was policed by a woman with puffy, purple-lined eyes who paces behind the counter like a junkyard dog.

But you only have to look a little harder. The following night, on the rue de Bretagne not far from La République, I joined friends for oysters at a café-brasserie named Le Progrès. Oysters were on the menu, but we brought ours in on trays from an open-air stand down the street. Le Progrès cheerfully served only Sancerre and charcuterie, and it also provided platters for our carry-in shellfish.

"That's the whole idea of a café, for customers to feel at home however they're most comfortable," explained Didier Bouyssau, the owner. He apprenticed under the Troisgros clan in Roanne and then cooked for Joël Robuchon. But he decided he would rather be his own boss.

Bouyssau found Le Progrès languishing under a couple who served no meals and closed on weekends. He remodeled the place but was careful to keep the old mosaics and tiles behind the bar. Within three years, his business tripled.

"For me, a café is alive, and people should feel this," Bouyssau said, polishing a glass against the light as if auditioning for a bartender role. "I rent out my wall space to artists, which adds color and decor. A group of philosophers comes in one Sunday every month. My neighbors leave me their keys when they go on holiday. I help them out with buckets, ice, whatever, when they give parties. Everyone says hello and good-bye. It's that kind of place."

The boss's lean good looks and barside manner help. He is usually in a good mood and hides it when not. What attracts the customers, however, is fresh food. Eighty to ninety people drop in daily for lunch. Bouyssau offers a choice of two main courses, prepared by a chef who also learned from Robuchon.

Bouyssau has worked out the economics. Tiny three-table bistros of the old sort are doomed, a victim of the pace and cost of life. To survive, a café-brasserie needs at least eight tables that turn over at least once during the meal times.

All in all, there is nothing special about Le Progrès. It just feels like a Paris street-corner bistro ought to feel. Service is fast and efficient. Food is good and reasonable. And sometimes it's nice to find a place where everybody knows your name.

To no one's surprise, the range of Paris eateries is vast. Without even leaving the category of French food, you can taste spicy specialties from overseas states in the Caribbean, the Indian Ocean, and the South Pacific. And then there is all the rest.

A careful study conducted in 1997 by a consultancy named GIRA SIC quantified some important trends. True enough, people eat fast and poorly at lunch. It is a question of time. Chain outlets are opening at twice the rate of old-style restaurants. But Bernard Boutboul, who conducted the survey, is oddly upbeat about it.

"Three thousand restaurants a year close in France, but it is certainly not because of the value-added tax," he said. "They all have a point in common: They're lousy. No welcome. What you eat is no good, or too expensive, or both. No quality. In France, you can go to a restaurant with ten seats where they hardly say hello. And then they wonder why they had to close."

There will always be room for good French restaurants, he said. The competition is forcing the bad ones to get better.

Boutboul believes fast-food operators like McDonald's make only a minor dent in a large market. "Let's put things into perspective," he added, hauling out a fat report. "Eight baguette sandwiches are eaten in France for every hamburger. When you have fifteen minutes to eat, which is getting to be a frequent problem, your reflex is to eat a jambon beurre rather than a hamburger. It's in our genes."

Boutboul calculates that there are 160,000 places to eat in France—including snack stands and service stations—and 90,000 of them are restaurants where you sit down calmly to eat. If ethnic restaurants are making inroads, they do not amount to a revolution. He estimates their total at somewhere near three thousand; no doubt, he missed a few.

But, of course, there is ethnic, and there is ethnic. One Michelin starred restaurant in Paris specializes in Peking duck. Chen-Soleil de l'Est, a Chinese restaurant with attitude, is no noodle joint. Paris has always had wonderful Asian food, with fresh ingredients from all corners of its former empire and immigrant cooks trained by old masters at home. But Chen goes a step further. Young French chefs enliven dishes by borrowing from Asia; he returns the favor.

Although the style is all French, Madame Chen takes orders like the Dowager Empress. I inquired about a menu item that looked interesting to start. She shook her hand vigorously. "No," she declared, "you want *xxx*. It is light, delicious." The x's are because I had no idea what she said. Her low-volume, rapid-fire French, flavored with native Shanghainese, went straight past me. But, of course, she was right.

That first course turned out to be delicately fried courgette flowers with bits of lobster in a sauce, carefully arranged on a bed of thinly slivered squash.

We had far more than enough time to look around before the duck appeared. Recoiling at the wine prices, I had ordered something simple. It was nonetheless decanted with great ceremony and placed on a silver pedestal. Elegant table settings offered knives and forks. Chopsticks were added, for the diehards, but they were those short, splintery jobs you break apart at cheap take-away places.

After a first round of crispy duck skin, in the finest tradition, Madame Chen carved pieces of nearly raw breast: an undeclared *magret de canard à la Chinoise*. Then came a tasty duck soup.

I'd seen an article on Chen, who came to Paris from Shanghai with a dream of opening a classy place that towered above sweet and sour pork. He had obviously worked hard at it. On the way out, I spotted him flying about the kitchen among his white-clad sous-chefs. He would have stopped to talk, but I did not have the heart to ask him.

It was a bizarre dining experience. But according to the Patricia Wells test—would I want to go back?—it was a very good restaurant.

A HALF DOZEN three-star restaurants make up the top rank in Paris, from Alain Passard's intimate Arpège to the venerable Taillevent. Alain Ducasse is among them, but his empire is a whole separate phenomenon.

Putting together separate three-star restaurants a thousand miles apart, in Paris and Monte Carlo, took some doing. He has put his name on more books than many full-time authors. He feeds Air France Concorde passengers, among whom he often numbers; new projects are underway in New York. He already has so many filials and franchises scattered about, from remote villages in France to the Indian Ocean island of Mauritius, by way of Tokyo and New York that the French may soon call him McDu.

Ducasse manages to bring quality to everything he touches. But the man is stretched thin. When I asked for an interview, his handlers said he would be happy to see me. Would I mind showing up at such and such a place on the strong chance that he might be there and have a moment to stop and talk? No, I was told later, the Concorde was leaving earlier than they had thought. Could I catch him at the new place he was opening in a restored abbey in the Var with Bruno Clément?

I eventually found him.

"One is limited only by the ability to find good people, to train them, to encourage them, to listen to their ideas, to inspire them further," Ducasse explained, in the matter-of-fact manner of any decent Director of Human Resources. But he was talking about the elusive spark that creates culinary excellence.

"I don't even train people anymore, except to supervise programs once in a while," he said. "My role is to design the grand scheme, make sure it is working, and bring in new people. I do it just like I would run any other big business. I interview, I listen, I watch, I look for that undefinable quality that shows great promise."

Ducasse sees himself as the father of a very large family. His enterprises, like his 350 employees, count as offspring. For each new project, he makes sure he is around at the moment of conception. He is there to bring it successfully into the world. Then he drops in when he can to make sure it is growing properly.

In a nation short of superstars, Ducasse falls somewhere between Mick Jagger and Martha Stewart. At l'Hostellerie de l'Abbaye de la Celle, he was hanging pictures when I arrived. We were introduced, and he gave me a curt nod. His head was elsewhere. But when my turn came, we were shut together in the tiny *fumoir*, a smoking room given over largely to humidors of Cuban cigars, and I was all that existed in his world. Half an hour later, an assistant tapped on the door with a problem. Ducasse threw himself fully into that, and we separated without a word of good-bye.

It was a fascinating half hour. Ducasse can afford to be blunt.

"I don't believe in all that industrial vacuum-pack and canned stuff that Loiseau and the others put their faces on," he said. "When I think of food, I like to imagine something cooked at the last minute, actually prepared, rather than fashioned in some factory."

Frozen and packaged food are essential in any modern society, Ducasse allowed. Yet if France heads off too far in that direction, he added, a great deal could be lost.

"There is no shortage of top-end good eating in this country," Ducasse said. "My three-star restaurants are always jammed, and they are extremely expensive. So are the others in their category. Plenty of people with money want to eat well. But what France needs badly is to encourage young people to rediscover the profession of aubergiste. We need young restaurateurs who can deliver a good, fresh product at a reasonable price, with help from the society not to go broke doing it."

My ears perked up at that lovely old word aubergiste. I mentioned my first culinary adventures in France to see Raymond Thuilier at Les Baux and Alain Chapel in Mionnay. Ducasse, I knew, worked for Chapel at the time. And Thuilier was his hero.

"Exactly," he said. "That tradition. It is where good French cooking started, and it will be the salvation of it. The point is not expensive food but rather good food at honest prices, served with style by someone whose heart is in the business."

Ducasse himself, meanwhile, was headed off in a half dozen other experimental directions. At his Paris food laboratory, De Gustibus, high-tech digital cameras are able to zero in on a chef's own digits as he—or more likely someone else—works ingredients into a complex dish. The running images could be reflected electronically to any of Ducasse's kitchens. Or eventually, for that matter, to any e-gourmet who was willing to pay for the privilege of logging on to McDu magic.

His Spoon Food and Wine restaurant off the Champs-Élysées offers such eccentricities as iceberg lettuce and Philadelphia cream cheese. The world's only six-star French chef also runs an Italian restaurant in Paris.

"World terroir," Ducasse replied when I asked how he came down in the debate between world food and terroir. Borders were essentially obsolete. Why should cuisine be limited? In an age of airfreight, why should stupid regulations keep soft-shelled crabs out of France or runny Epoisses out of America?

"We French will always have an edge, our savoir faire, le French touch," he said. "True, we have some wonderful ingredients, some artisanal products you can find nowhere else. But other countries also have wonderful products of their own. What we have is mastery of the process, and we can guide others."

Before my moment in the master's presence expired, I asked a final question, my usual. Did he feel that the standard of cooking, and of food in general, was declining in France?

"No," Ducasse replied, in a word. "It was a few years back, I believe, but we saved ourselves. We started to decline dangerously." He did not specify, but his time frame coincidenced with the sudden advent of fast food, chain restaurants, and that state of industrial nourishment known as malbouffe.

"Once people saw how far we had dropped in our standards, what we were up against, the curve changed," Ducasse concluded. "The levels began to rise again. I see growing new demands for good products that are cooked well. And now that we've realized this, as a nation, I don't think we'll slip again."

THINGS DO NOT look quite so optimistic in the average Paris supermarket.

When talking about French grocery stores, vocabulary is important. An *épicerie* remains a little family-run place with specialty items and personal concern over quality of the stock. Increasingly, these are owned by North Africans, like Koreans in New York, who stay open late and cut down on supplies of ham. In rude Parisian French, a place like this is known as *"l'Arabe du coin"*: the Arab on the corner.

The outlying communities around Paris feature a new style of huge emporiums, les hypermarchés, or *les grandes surfaces*. These range in quality from very good to food hell. Under one roof, they offer everything from onions and garlic to heavy-duty freezers and tractors.

But les supermarchés are the backbone of modern family shopping. They are bigger, cheaper, and, generally, far seedier than épiceries. Most offer their own house brands of packaged foods, canned goods, household products, and assorted staples. For more money, you can usually find something better. Meat comes in pressed plastic containers, suspiciously inexpensive. Vegetables and fruits are purchased in bulk with an eye toward shelf life.

One lunch hour I dropped in at a Franprix supermarket near my office to watch what was going out the door. At each of three registers, long lines of workmen in blue coveralls were lined up with handfuls of items that would make up their lunch. It was a desperate sight.

Not so long ago in Paris, work was what a guy did to afford the delicious meals his wife packed into layered buckets known as *gamelles,* which he ate at leisure on lunch breaks among pals. Food was washed down with enough red wine to slur speech and slow movement until quitting time. If not all that productive, it was sacred.

These Franprix customers clearly had a different sort of boss. Most had packages of boiled ham—the North Africans preferred turkey breast—shot with enough chemicals to stay fresh until their retirement. Likewise, industrial cheese and bread. A daring fringe leaned to canned tuna and corn salad laced with sweet peppers, or tins of Spam-like corned beef.

Women office workers chose small tubs of yogurt or ready-made salads in plastic. But, like the men, each seemed in a hurry to get outside, absorb the mass-market food-substance hit, and get back to work.

Among the most popular items was a parody of what used to be called jambon de Paris, originally a flavorful cooked ham that, at its best, was cut close to the bone. Now, figures show, ninety percent of ham sold in France is water-filled, processed, plastic-wrapped supermarket replica.

On a grand scale, the numbers are unsettling. Nervous about encroachment by Wal-Mart, two huge French chains—Carrefour and Promodès—decided to merge during 1999. Between them, they account for thirty percent of grandes surfaces distribution. Around Paris, the total approaches thirty-five percent.

In the United States, better supermarkets compete to offer quality products, at least as an option to cheaper alternatives. In France, shoppers who seek quality go to small shops or real markets. The driving force at hypermarchés is trimmed corners and low prices.

But that is changing. Carrefour, among others, has substantial fancy food sections. Shoppers in a hurry can buy portions of freshly cooked classic French dishes. Appetizing fish and well-aged meat are on offer, for a price.

The overall balance could go either way.

For people who worry about these trends, the key is teaching children about taste. If they demand quality and flavor as they grow up, the thinking goes, they will get it. A Paris-based group called the Conseil National des Arts Culinaires heads a crusade to let school kids know what they might end up missing.

One morning I decided on another outing and followed Laurent Jizard, an CNAC crusader, to the Rue Arsène elementary school near Montparnasse. I found a class full of eager eight-year-olds.

"The idea is to expose kids to tastes, smells, textures at an early age so they can recognize things as they grow up," Laurent said. "Once they get a notion about this, they are more interested in what their mothers cook, how they do it, what they have to eat."

I happened to catch the third lesson, all about smelling. There were ten lessons, including a visit to the market, making a simple meal, and learning which regions of France were known for what foods. Emphasis was not only on taste and touch but also color and the sounds of cooking.

Each pupil had a colorful workbook for following the classes. Lesson three began with a diagram of how the olfactory system worked, complete with relevant parts of the brain. Laurent passed around thirty-six vials of scented essence—this is not easy with third-graders—and each kid matched the aroma to a list. Cherry scored higher than clove or bitter almond, but they all got the idea.

Afterward, we poured each child four cups of syrup in water to see who could name them. Coconut and cassis did as well as lemon and strawberry.

A girl in black pigtails, Paula, took it all in with grave attention. She helped her partner, a small impish boy. When his attention wandered, she smacked him with her workbook.

"Oh, I adore this," Paula proclaimed after a polite sip, as her mother might comment on a 1996 Pauillac.

Before the class, Laurent had assured me that McDo had made only a passing impression on the hundreds of children he saw each week. Friends in other programs reported the same thing.

"I always ask their favorite food," he said. "It might be something simple, like frites or spaghetti, but it is never a hamburger."

When the class ended, I talked to Paula. She paused only seconds when I asked her mealtime preference.

"I adore gigot d'agneau," she said.

· · ·

FRENCH KIDS LEARN reverence for food by going to pet it at an early age. Foreigners may flock to Paris for fashion salons, the air, and auto shows, or grand art exhibitions. Parisians prefer the Salon d'Agriculture. Each year, more than 600,000 of them pack solid into vast hangars at the Porte de Versailles. You might say people jam in like cattle. Cows, however, suffer none of the elbow-to-armpit jostling of their human visitors.

Long rows of fluffy, white Charolais munch on selected hay in spacious splendor, each more than a ton of uncooked steak on the hoof. Tiny children worm through bars in the pens for a loving pat. Parents and security guards ignore signs warning, "Do not touch the animals."

Bulls are led to the judging pens with as much fanfare as a Chicago basketball team dribbling onto the court. A few weigh in at over two tons. Sheep attract the biggest petting mobs, with their woolly coats brushed to high sheen, but visitors to the fair can also fondle giant mutant rabbits, dwarf goats, monster pigs, killer geese, and fancy chickens that might have been designed by Paco Rabanne.

Altogether, there are 580 cattle of twenty-five races, and thirty sorts of horse, not counting a hundred varieties of donkey and pony. Then there are all those fish, down the half-mythical silure from the depths of the Seine.

The thirty-seventh Salon d'Agriculture, two months into a new millennium, came as José Bové and his Confédération Paysanne rose to folk hero status for resisting malbouffe. President Jacques Chirac and Prime Minister Lionel Jospin both showed up. Each feigned jocularity with Bové.

But, as every year, the real action was in the outlying hangars. People from every region of France brought their specialities to sample.

Farmers from the Pyrenées offered mountains of sausages, from wild pig to donkey and flavored in any of several ways: with cèpes, high-country herbs, blueberries, garlic, extra grease. Nearby, a young man in climbing gear scaled a huge vertical relief map of the Rhône, hauling himself from truffle country near Froggy's place past the blood-sausage haven of Lyon up to Bresse chicken territory.

At the far end, around the corner, black and brown Frenchmen served fiery hot deep-fried delicacies from bits of France scattered around the Caribbean, the Indian Ocean, and the South Pacific. Normans put apples in their sausage. Savoyards made theirs with onions and hot mustard. Bretons had fresh oysters and mussels.

I stopped for a breakfast baguette smeared thickly with foie gras from a goose in Toulouse. It was early, and Lydia Romana had a moment to chat as she stacked up columns of tinned delicacies from the Gers.

"Sure, sure, everyone wants to buy duck now," she said. "It's cheaper. It is easier to work with. Geese can be a real pain to handle. But, really, ask anyone who knows what they prefer, and they'll tell you goose. It is much finer."

A few of her coworkers listened with half an ear as they bustled around getting ready for the crowds. Lydia turned and hollered out, "What do you all think?"

"Goose!" came the answer, in perfect unison. It was hardly scientific, but it was good enough for me.

ONE COLD PRE-CHRISTMAS morning at 5:00 A.M., I went to Rungis to see what had become of Victor Hugo's "belly of Paris." If Les Halles had moved from the center of town, its ancient purpose had not changed. What France boasts is the "world's biggest fresh-food market" looks from the outside like a gigantic truck park and munitions dump among linked freeway interchanges. Inside any of those countless hangars, however, it might be old Lutèce on a market morning.

The roots of Rungis go back to the twelfth century when King Louis the Fat decreed Paris should have a central market. Shopowners, innkeepers, and housewives pawed among products strewn on the ground, haggling for the best prices they could get. Over the years, the market grew bigger, noisier, and more chaotic.

During hard times, scarcities sent the population to the edge of panic. Gradually, royal administrations began to regulate the food supply. Finally, in 1811, Napoléon imposed order on Les Halles. He ruled that its prices would establish official rates in France. His planners designed the market's first modern structures. But it was Napoléon III, a half century later, who created Les Halles as Parisians loved it.

An architect named Baltard used wrought iron and glass to create rows of ornate pavillions. By the 1920's, all-night restaurants and pre-dawn bars sprang up, all within tsk-tsking distance from Saint-Eustache church. In those happy years between wars, Les Halles was functional, funky, and fun.

Paris took time to restore itself after 1945. And in 1953, French authorities decided that what with unpredictable weather and Germans living next door, they needed a system of Marchés d'Intérêt National. France did not do well on an empty stomach. The mother of all MINs would be built at the southern approaches to Paris, hard by Orly Airport. Early in the 1960's, Les Halles began shifting to Rungis. The whole process took a decade, until the butchers and fowl wholesalers finally made the move.

Rungis today covers more than a thousand acres, with twenty miles of roadway linking its 1,500 different enterprises. Color-coded markings help the visitor get hopelessly lost on the way, say, from the flower zone to the tripe and animal innards sector. Thirty restaurants are scattered about, along with twenty banks, assorted laboratories, railway yards, administration buildings, and a clinic.

The meat section alone handles a quarter million tons a year. More than two-thirds of that is produced in France. Trucks and railcars bring the rest from abroad. Between fruits and vegetables, the annual tonnage tops a million. More fruits are imported than are grown in France.

I thought about visiting the salad greens or the cheeses but instead went straight for the game. It was, after all, hunting and holiday season.

"Allez, oooh!" someone screamed at me, not unkindly. "Coming through!" I dodged in time to avoid being trampled by a dozen wild turkeys on a handtruck. Narrow aisles in the cavernous hangar, lined with everything from boxes of bunny rabbits and songbirds to whole sanglier carcasses on hooks, were not meant for half-asleep gawkers.

Each year, 80,000 tons of fowl and game pass along those corridors. In December, the pace is frantic. Exotic fowl from the Gers were trussed in bright red ribbons and bows. Capons from Bresse were done up in blue. Turkeys in Christmas decor were emblazoned with Arabic labels declaring them fit for strict Muslim consumption. Each of the big birds was packaged the way French buyers like them: fans of tail feathers left intact; heads craning over the sides of crates.

Vacuum-packaged deer haunches were stacked next to wild boar sausages. Skinned piglets hung in rows. All manner of waterfowl, from garden-variety ducks to wild geese that looked like Stealth bombers, fought for attention with barnyard birds. The foie gras and assorted organs were some-where else on the vast Rungis plain. This section was only meat.

Health laws require everyone in the meat section, visitors included, to wear a clean white coverall and white headgear. But this is France. I bought a throwaway plastic coat and a white cotton visored cap from a store out-side the door. A few veterans wore tailored whites, some with tweed sports coats over them. One young man had a "Redskins" cap, inexplicably in dark blue.

Only authorized buyers, the retailers and restaurateurs, are allowed to do business at Rungis. They order, and high-speed helpers load up the small trucks they park among the wholesalers' big rigs. Being a sucker for nos-talgia, I could see how this all might have been a colorful sight in the heart of Paris. But in a city where traffic is already a nightmare, Rungis was probably a pretty good idea.

"My God, it was impossible," Jean-Jacques Coquet recalled. He was twenty when he started lugging meat at Les Halles, and that was after most of the market had already gone. "Trucks were lined up halfway across Paris. It was a madhouse. Out here, everything works pretty smoothly."

Coquet, looking happy behind thick round glasses and a cheery red mustache, was in his element. He knew his customers and was proud of his meat. His hired hand, Mohammed, flung an arm around his shoul-ders and asked me to take a picture. Amused insults flew about from old pals and competitors. No one put words to it, but these guys seemed to know they had chosen the noblest of callings. They were feeding France.

And, of course, France was feeding them. "I don't really miss Les Hal-les," Coquet said. "Out here it's more industrial, but we still have some pretty decent cafés and restaurants."

Le Saint Hubert, for instance, sits square in the center of the great hangar as though it has been beamed intact from a Paris street corner. It is perfect, down to its name: Saint Hubert is the patron of hunters. Its decorative metal exterior and old wood sashes are painted in dark forest green. The picture windows are beveled glass. The lettering is gold leaf. The beer taps are brass, and the bar is zinc.

Inside, it might have been any bar-café in a city full of such establish-ments. Old friends chatted over shot glasses full of fiery marc. A few solitary drinkers hovered over their petit coup of red. Beer slopped over the side of half-pint glasses as bartenders in white shirts and black aprons scrambled to keep up their shouted orders.

Here in the transplanted belly of Paris, it hardly made any difference that the time was 6:00 A.M., and the patrons all wore red-smeared white coats like emergency room doctors knocking off after a firefight. A café is a café.

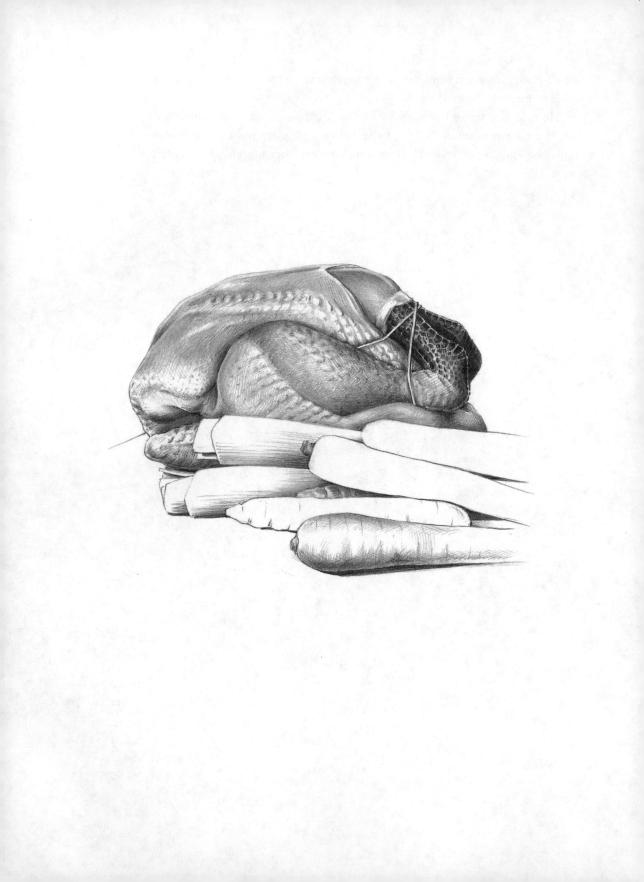

———◁◇◇◇▷———

FIFTEEN

Star Wars on Calorie Alley

IN A HURRY, you can drive from Paris to Lyon in three hours. If you take your time and mortgage your house, however, you can rack up fifty Michelin stars without straying more than a short way on either side of the A6 autoroute. This is Calorie Alley.

The first high spot is the third-generation Côte Saint-Jacques at Joigny, where Michel Lorain and his son, Jean-Michel, perform nightly miracles with Brittany oysters a long way from the sea. Loiseau's La Côte d'Or is at Saulieu. Down the road in Chagny, Jacques Lameloise serves Burgundy snails but puts them in a delicate ravioli with sweet garlic bouillon. Then, with a jog to Vonnas, there is Georges Blanc. That is a dozen stars already. Closer to Lyon, Paul Bocuse and the Troisgros clan, stalwarts in the firmament, add another six.

Until the heavens mysteriously shifted, there was yet another three-star auberge, between Joigny and Saulieu. Marc Meneau of L'Ésperance near Vézelay was anointed in 1984, before Loiseau or Lorain. For me, he had always been the Burgundy master. He taught himself to cook in the café-grocery his mother ran while his father mended shoes. Then, acquiring urbane polish but staying rooted in his village of Saint-Père, he created a hotel-restaurant that drew regulars from halfway around the world. When the century-special 1999 Michelin Guide came out, Meneau was stunned. His third star had blinked out.

French food writers noted the change with gravity normally reserved for the shifting of the earth's tectonic plates. Most recalled the de rigueur reference for such cases, the Parisian chef who shot himself, years ago, on losing his third star. Meneau was mystified. He told a reporter, "This came like a sledge hammer blow, a total surprise."

No one seemed to have an explanation. In Paris, I put the question to André Daguin, the retired duke of duck whose new role was to keep track of the industry.

"It could be anything," he replied. "The real definition of a three-star restaurant is a two-star restaurant that never, ever makes a mistake."

The celestial incident sent shivers down Calorie Alley. Lameloise had been a three-star chef since 1979. Was he next? Loiseau had sunk his fortune into La Côte d'Or and then launched it onto the Paris stock market. Economics aside, egos hung in the balance.

When I visited l'Ésperance six months later, however, I found Meneau comfortably unperturbed. Solidly built and graying at fifty-six, with the chiseled features of an Italian matinée idol, he displayed no signs of insecurity. He was hardly clamoring for allies to help right a perceived wrong.

Meneau showed up an hour and a half late for our appointment. His wife had forgotten to tell him about it. "Alas, one's days don't always go as one plans," he said mildly and sat down to talk about what he loves. Unbriefed, he did not know why I was there, and he did not seem to care what my purpose was. I wanted to know about his cooking, and that was enough.

"My focus is not on the loss of a star but rather on the reconquest of it," Meneau said, when I finally asked the question. "I hope to get it back, and we're doing all we can, but that is what we would do anyway."

Michelin made no comment when the new rating appeared; it never does. Eventually Meneau was given the customary brief annual audience with Bernard Naegellan, who told him obliquely that there had been complaints of irregular quality but indicated that this was not without remedy. There was always another year.

"Look," Meneau said, "you can't take this as some God-given right.

When Michelin awards you a third star, you don't stop to wonder whether maybe they made a mistake. It is the same thing if they take it away."

Not long before, a food writer for *Le Monde* had described his own view of Meneau's dilemma. The new stars seemed to be going to innovators, the Passards and Gagnaires who brought exotic flavors to their tables, casting aside the old notions about traditional French cooking. Meneau was known as a master of the classic Burgundy style, the writer said, and—even if he wanted to—he was too old to change.

When I asked Meneau about this, he replied with a wordless intake of air, a poignant pause, and a barely perceptible tightening of the jaw muscles. He then followed with an hour-long off-and-on discourse that put to rest convincingly the whole nondebate about tradition versus world cuisine.

"The point is to take things from wherever you can in the world and put them to use in French cooking," he said. "That is what virtually every good chef does, whatever words they use to describe their particular philosophy. We're fortunate enough to live in an age where that is possible. You can't cling to the past. You can never go backward. Instead, you keep what is good, and you add what is better."

Some products have been lost, but there are new ones. Practices change. What is important is not individual aspects of classic cooking, he said, but rather an underlying philosophy of terroir.

"Three hundred years ago, it took three to four hours to cook an onion," Meneau said. "Now it takes half an hour because the species have improved. Were things so much better before? Would I still like those acidy apples that I loved so much when I was an eight-year-old kid? I wonder."

Meneau preaches an open mind. McDonald's is a blessing, he said, because it has forced the French to realize what they have and are in danger of losing.

"Look at the age range of McDonald's customers," he said. "At first, curious adults went to see what it was about. Now it is mostly parents with their children, or schoolkids and students. When people get a little older, they make an effort to get to a good brasserie for the sort of decent meal the French appreciate."

Frozen food and prepackaged meals do not scare him. "The state of the art is so much better now than compared to, say, thirty years ago that there is no comparison," he said. "The wiser industrial producers understand the need for quality and taste. They hire good people to advise them. Competition is fierce."

Meneau was among the most upbeat and optimistic chefs I had yet found. He thought that globalization, with its challenges, could lift French cooking to higher levels than ever.

"This is our great chance to capture new currents, find different ways, seek better products, and evolve them into our own philosophy of terroir," he said. "If we can find a more flavorful flour in South America, a superior pepper in the Seychelles, why not? Change is also an advantage, not just a threat. Things evolve. Do you still want to go to Paris on horseback?"

The menace, he said, comes from today's economics. Food management on a big scale makes it hard for small independent producers to compete. This I had seen everywhere in France, again and again. People are willing to pay more for a better piece of meat, a superior cucumber, a sausage of uncommon flavor. But only up to a point.

Even worse, Meneau continued, is government by bureaucrats who like large units with no untidy edges. At the extreme, they can tax excellence out of existence. He calculates that for every franc he spends on salaries, he pays more than an additional franc on social security charges and other levies.

"It can kill a restaurateur who tries to maintain quality," Meneau said. "Something has to give. For instance, I think that sauces are going to all but disappear." He did not mean ketchup and A-1 but rather those centuries-old recipes that can take days to prepare properly. "We will see on menus maybe one or two, possibly three dishes in sauce, and the rest will be simply seasoned."

I asked Meneau how long it takes to make his signature braised beef marrow in caviar, steeped in the stewed juice of shallots. "Altogether, enough for four people requires about two hours' work," he said. "Lobster takes three minutes."

He lamented the decline of *gibier* in French restaurants, especially game birds that were no longer hunted because of what he called bad decisions by people who thought they were preserving a species.

"If you respect the laws of nature, you can continue to produce wonderful, healthy food, with ingredients from the wild as well as what you can domesticate," Meneau argued. "But that takes sense and understanding by the people who make the rules."

French legislation was bad enough, he said. But European Union regulations added a series of needless steps designed to thwart any possible risk. This, again, had gotten to be a familiar theme. Eurocrats in Brussels with a thin command of reality seemed intent on squeezing all the juices out of life.

"Now, for instance, if you serve kidneys, they have to be hung first to see if they are somehow bad, even though chefs have been safely preparing kidneys forever," Meneau said, with an outraged snort. "In the name of hygiene, they are creating aseptic environments that destroy something fundamental."

With a laugh, he added, "Personally, I like to see a lot of germs in my kitchen. They keep us in touch with natural order, and they make the body function like it is supposed to. Careful cooks do not make people sick."

Meneau waved off questions that looked too far forward. But in the near term, he saw France's better chefs concentrating on the best possible basic ingredients, raised or prepared for taste rather than industrial convenience. But he came back to his point about quality being crushed by economies of scale. The value structures are skewed.

"Everything is turned upside down," Meneau said. "It is ridiculous. Who is this American computer man, Gatt, Gutt?" I asked if he meant Bill Gates. "Right, Gates. Why should he earn more than the local farmer who produces a good potato? He provides a product, and so does the farmer. Why such a difference?"

The argument had a certain appeal. My potato-growing neighbors could certainly use a few extra billion dollars, I knew. Meneau was not joking. To him, a computer was just another item that helps him run his business, like a broom to sweep the kitchen. But a good potato?

By then, lunch was upon us, and I happily turned my attention to the table. Meneau's wife brought out a single perfect oyster *en gelée*, a house specialty. By coincidence, I had eaten nearly two dozen oysters the night before, but none was like that one. It was meaty, crisply chilled, with a slight peppery tang.

I guessed it might be a special fine de claire from Marennes-Oléron, but Meneau shook his head.

"My oysters come from the Bay of Cancale," he said, "which is the biggest inlet on the French coast. The tides move the farthest there so the oysters have to work harder. They are more muscular."

I rolled my eyes, and he smiled, as we both conjured up the image of legions of little bivalves doing their twice daily push-ups against the current. But Meneau was serious. That mattered. Everything is in the extra subtleties. The lovely green leaves atop the fresh oyster under chilled aspic were not decor. Watercress added the hint of pepper.

"I wanted to serve oysters," he explained, "so I sat down and asked myself how would someone living in Saint-Père, so far from the sea, best appreciate a plate of seafood. Cooked, they would end up like mussels, so that was out. They had to be fresh. I couldn't drain off the water, because people here don't waste anything. So I made the liquid into gelée."

Next came a dozen small pitted green olives, warm and softened but still crunchy, with flakes of truffles in a froth of cream. No word fits but unbelievable; I could not remember ever tasting anything that good. It was October, a good two months before the first new black truffles would appear.

When I asked where he got them, Meneau just smiled and resumed his disquisition.

"I got the idea because olives and truffles grow in the same places together, and they ripen at the same time, and both are the rich fruits of the earth," he said. "If that isn't terroir, what is?"

The combination was typical Meneau masterworks. To a bit of cream, he added port and cognac. "That takes just enough bitterness from the olives," he said. "In every dish I make, there is always a balance: a trace of sweet and bitter, salt and sugar. Sometimes there is a fifth element, a hint of hot pepper."

I consumed the first two dishes esconced in a deep leather armchair. At l'Ésperance, diners sip their apéritifs and muse over the menus in a plush salon, under the barman's gentle gaze. When the first real course is ready, they take their places among the hanging ferns and flowers of the glassed-in terrace. Tablecloths are pink, not white. China is elegant but not fancy. Each perfect rose and orchid is placed in a discreet silver vase. The effect is meant to be homey, in case you're lucky enough to have a home like that.

A waitress brought a plate of Meneau's legendary *cromesquis de foie gras*. These are bite-sized little bomblets, cube-shaped crisp croquettes breaded on the outside. They require a lesson. The waitress began, but I was too impatient to listen. Before she warned me to use my fingers and pop them whole into my mouth, I pierced one with a fork. An aromatic geyser spewed halfway across the table. She laughed, and so did I.

Somehow, Meneau has managed to liquify foie gras inside the shells, a sublime blend of texture and taste. When I'd popped the last one, I got up and found the chef.

"How do you do that?" I asked.

"With love," Meneau replied.

A longer answer would have involved gelatin, cream, and pepper, an overnight stay in the refrigerator, breading, and pop-frying in hot oil. But the short version was good enough for me.

Afterward came the *moelle de boeuf au caviar, jus d'échalotes*. As with his other dishes, Meneau had taken separate flavors and produced something the imagination is not equipped to handle. The familiar salty rush of caviar enlivens the rich braised marrow onto which it is generously spooned. Both are perfumed by the delicate essence of shallot.

The main course was yet another Meneau creation: a *darne de turbot* in lobster butter baked in a salty, flaky, thick crust. When presented at the table for admiration, it is an oversized mystery tart. After deft knifework at the adjoining serving table, a handsome cut of fish emerges, and escaping aromas turn heads across the room. The skin is lifted off carefully, leaving only white, tender steaks. Each bite is infused with the trace of herbs and lobster.

The sommelier had steered me to a lovely Chassagne-Montrachet. Madame Meneau, by way of unspoken apology for the late appointment, had started me off with a glass of exquisite Champagne. In a pleasantly buzzed state, I watched the staff move around the large room as if choreographed, watching for slight gestures that signified an empty glass or bare bread plate.

It was Sunday lunch in a rainy October. The tourists had gone, and Frenchmen on vacation were back at home. Mostly, the other diners were regulars who knew what they liked. An old couple across the way savored a single course. Others sped from amuse-gueules to petit fours at astounding speed. At the next table over, a hefty man among friends slowly worked through a lobster salad, a substantial fish course, and an enormous piece of rare Charolais beef.

I finished every scrap of my turbot. Then there were the cheeses, desserts, the little pastries and homemade candies, the coffee, the Armagnac and cigar. The usual.

Returning to the salon, I settled back in my leather armchair and watched Meneau visit briefly with every guest, soliticious in the grand aubergiste tradition. When the bill came, I did not flinch. Some things are beyond price.

After four hours at lunch, I found l'Ésperance even better than I had remembered. I eased myself toward the car and wondered if it wasn't, in fact, Michelin that ought to lose a star.

As it happened at the time, the fat and friendly Michelin man was catching hell from one end of France to the other. Edouard Michelin, at thirty-six a dead ringer for a balding Peewee Herman, inherited the position of chief executive officer of the giant tire company from his namesake grandfather.

He took over in June 1999 and three months later announced that profits for the first six months of the year had increased by twenty percent. At the same time, he said he was eliminating 7,500 jobs, ten percent of the European work force.

In the past, young Michelin told reporters, the family that owned a third of the company was happy for any profit, even if it was only 0.3 percent of sales. "That's so French!" he added.

As part of his cost-cutting package, Michelin claimed a package of state subsidies to offset the expense of early retirements and retraining. That, too, was pretty French.

Politicians from the Communists to the hidebound right wing howled in protest. "Cynical" was the term most often employed, but other epithets were far worse. Socialist Prime Minister Lionel Jospin, in New York at the time, was furious. "We didn't renounce the dictatorship of the proletariat just to replace it with dictatorship of the shareholders," he said.

Public outcry was intense. Michelin was hardly the first big French company to attempt the popular new global practice of downsizing. But somehow this was different. Maybe it was because so many Frenchmen had latent feelings for Bibendum, the doughy tireman. Or perhaps they felt the people who wrote their red bible had joined the forces of evil.

"La maison," headquartered in the provinces and run in a secretive fashion by a single family, was among the few French companies to lead the world in its domain. It was a symbol of old-style French capitalist paternalism, anti-union but eager to regard workers as part of an extended family. When others followed the American trend toward departments of human resources, Michelin insisted on keeping a personnel department.

In Clermont-Ferrand, the dreary company town, workers on a brief strike renamed Edouard Michelin Avenue the Avenue of Full Employment. Weeks later, union firebrands were still bringing down the house with speeches like the one that began, "Thank you, Edouard, for this perfect cynicism, without nuance, which marks the date of awareness of citizens' consciousness."

But, as usually happens, the mood calmed. French captains of industry argued that while young Edouard might need a public-relations adviser, he had sensed the way of the world, whether it was pleasant or not. The languishing stock did rise. *Business Week* summed it up: "Michelin may not win any popularity contests in France these days, but one day he could be remembered as the CEO who saved his grandfather's company."

The layoffs stung so painfully because France was struggling to reduce the unemployment that hovered for years near twelve percent. Jospin had just decreed a thirty-five-hour week to help spread work around. An upturn in economic growth was creating new jobs. Every poll taken showed that, by far, the Frenchman's greatest concern was job security and reducing unemployment.

And here, suddenly, lovable Bibendum was shoving market-driven global reality right into their faces. The next step might be some conservative party trying to trim the cradle-to-crypt benefits that provide health, education, and the minimum essentials of a decent life to everyone, job or not.

Against this background, and curious to learn what I could about star wars, I went to the stately Avenue de Breteuil headquarters of Michelin in Paris to see the Godfather himself, the man who can make the haughtiest superstar chef tremble like a schoolkid.

THE SENSATION OF meeting Bernard Naegellen must be akin to Dorothy's reaction when she yanked back the curtain to confront the Wizard of Oz. No ogre, he is a friendly man with a gray buzz cut, a professor's tweed jacket, and the comfortable pear shape of a man who forces down haute cuisine to earn his daily bread.

Naegellen fetched me from the lobby with solicitous politesse and an apology for the mess of remodeling. As we passed the union's notice board and its printed insults at management, he said the publishing branch of Michelin remained unaffected. With brisk sales of nearly 500 guides and maps in a dozen languages, his domain was what accountants call a profit center. We ended up in the bare-walled visitor's cubicle, empty but for a few chairs, a table, ourselves, and the thick red breviary that Naegellen clutched in his hands.

For a man with more durable power than the elected monarchs who sit for seven-year terms in the Élysée Palace, my host seemed remarkably modest. Like the other Bible, the red guide is anonymous. Naegellen's name appears nowhere in its 1,500 pages. Nor does anyone else's, except for an artist acknowledged in minuscule type inside the back cover. The interview was unusual; he shuns reporters. He is likely over sixty-five, but no one knows that from him. A nod from Naegellen puts a chef into Who's Who, but each year he refuses to fill out paperwork for his own inclusion.

And yet each time I mentioned the reverence his guide evoked among Frenchmen and foreigners, a look very much like pride played across his face. He had a product to sell, he explained, and continued success amounted to another year of three-star status.

"It is not enough for us to be the leading guide," he said. "We have to progress, to evolve with the times. As well as restaurant critiques, we're engaged in commerce. People can't do without tires, but they can do without a guide."

For all the fuss about stars, Naegellen stressed, the latest Michelin guide listed 9,226 restaurants, about half of them in hotels, and 84 percent of them were in the lowest two categories. Unstarred entries are ranked by crossed forks and spoons. The maximum five black sets of flatware signifies "*grand luxe et tradition.*" A single set means "*assez confortable,*" or good enough. Red letters denote an especially pleasant ambiance.

Naegellen laughed when I asked how many inspectors toured France each year. Rumor puts the number at sixty, but one is likelier to worm nuclear launch codes out of the Defense Ministry than to get that confirmed officially. "It is a state secret," he explained, without elaboration.

When I asked why, he chuckled again. "I like secrets." There are enough to do the job, he said, and enough to form an effective team.

Much later, he laughed harder when I tried to convince him to let me tag along with one of his undercover agents. This time, he gave reasons. "The ways we sample and make judgments amount to proprietary trade secrets that are valuable to us," he said. "If you wrote anything, you would have to describe this process. If not, what would be the point? Besides, you'd certainly be bored. It's all very normal. Just someone eating."

Inspectors' visits, and revisits, are linked to mail from readers. Editors receive 23,000 letters a year, mostly offering praise. If a particular place inspires unusual negative comment, red flags are waved. Each letter goes into a file. At the end of the year, an evaluation panel makes decisions. The impassive Buddha did not tell me exactly how.

All this secrecy is a little unsettling. Under such circumstances, Michelin could get by with a half-dozen tasters and a few clerks to handle the anonymous denunciations. For the half-million devotees who buy a fresh red guide each year, however, such doubts border on blasphemy. One must take it on faith.

We covered the Meneau question quickly. Naegellan had been over that ground before.

"We ask these people to be consistent, extremely consistent," he said. "At three-star levels, a meal is extremely expensive, whether diners pay for it themselves or charge it to their companies. It is often a special occasion. They do not want to be disappointed, in any aspect of the meal. A top chef must never let his quality slip."

I pushed for details on how l'Espérance had slipped in quality. Was it a dud foie gras bomblet? An oyster that failed to quiver in its gelée? An errant dribble of sauce on a plate? Naegellen replied only with a well-practiced evasive smile. At least, he allowed, the failings were observed by official inspectors rather than customers. "In this category," he said, "we watch each place very carefully."

From all I could determine elsewhere, the problem at l'Espérance was about staff and service. Meneau had mentioned that good people are hard to find and harder to keep. *Le Guide Bottin*, a Michelin competitor with a more complex rating system, had given Meneau's kitchen its highest marks.

Naegellan had no comment on this. But, he insisted, even though atmosphere and physical surroundings have a certain importance in ratings, Naegellan said, stars are about food.

"We look at what is in the plate," he said. "The proof is Alain Passard. He started out with a tiny place that was, let's admit it, pretty ugly. But his cuisine was exciting. The real difference between two stars and three is the potential of the chef. Is he capable of producing something truly exceptional, and is he prepared to do it again and again, at each meal? There are other French chefs capable of earning three stars, but they are not interested in the grinding routine of absolute consistency."

At the mention of Passard, I brought up the Band of Eight. Had he any thoughts on the debate over tradition versus le world cuisine?

"We're not up on all that," he said, dismissing the whole idea with a wave. "One chef might be a pal of someone else, and they get together, and suddenly they are in opposing circles. Discourse changes. All we care about is how their food tastes. We look for personality, distinct style. We don't care what that style is, as long as it works. Chefs don't agree on a lot of things, thank God. That's what makes cooking in France so rich and varied."

That touch of arching pride crossed Naegellan's bland features when I mused at how powerful an impact the guide made on chef-propriétaires' lives. Was it true, I asked, that each chef was granted an annual fifteen minutes of audience in the spartan holy chamber? No, he said, laughing yet again. It was not.

"We simply try to be as responsive as we can," he explained. "Sometimes chefs come around sniffing, trying to find out how things are going. We receive them but, of course, don't tell them very much. After the guide appears, a large number want to register their unhappiness, or find out what went wrong."

The post-edition deluge is handled mostly by a trio of assistants. If a chef insists on seeing Naegellen himself, he will usually get that chance. But the red bible is firm. It never explains. It never rescinds.

Happily, Naegellen was expansive on the general subject of French restaurants in general. After ten years of directing his team of spies, and a lifetime of thinking about Sunday lunch, his judgment mattered.

"The state of French food is not declining," he pronounced. "On the contrary, it is improving. Twenty-five years ago in the small villages, we had a lot of cooks who did the same thing every day, and they took it seriously. They gradually disappeared with population movements and retirements, and nothing replaced them. Now, new people are coming back. We see an enormous amount of talent and imagination among young people who work well in limited circumstances."

If a small restaurant can't afford turbot, Naegellen said, it serves something cheaper. "The test is what the cook does with what he has. We start to notice when he takes his mackerel and does something new and interesting with it."

The future seems to be in this broad middle range. The fast-food menace is overrated, Naegellen said. McDonald's fills a niche but will hardly replace serious chefs. Its impact is felt most by incompetent cooks who cut corners more readily than prices. A greater threat, Naegellen concluded, was at the other extreme.

Here again was the theme I had heard in top-quality kitchens from one end of France to the other. Haute cuisine is a devilishly expensive business. With three stars, chefs can draw wealthy clientele from far away and rent their name for extra income. With a mere two stars—particularly if they have made the investment to hold on to a third—a cleaver of Damocles hangs over their heads.

THE LARGER ISSUES that affect France in general have a particular impact on Calorie Alley. First, there is geography.

Before World War II, the Hostellerie de la Poste at Avallon had three stars for an obvious reason. At 120 miles from Paris, it was as far as southbound motorists could get in a day before their radiator blew. These days, the twenty-seven room auberge is still there, a charming eighteenth-century stagecoach stop. But its kitchen has no stars at all.

The well-heeled flash past Avallon on the A6, their Citroëns barely out of first gear from the tollbooth at the autoroute entrance. But now Avallon is the perfect distance for a romantic weekend escape from Paris. If it had a three-star auberge, it would draw a substantial clientele. Michelin defines its highest rating as "worth a journey," and food lovers take it seriously enough to keep a chef in business. This is what keeps Marc Meneau up at night. His place at Saint-Père is just a few miles west of Avallon.

The geography won't change, and neither will the other factor that plagues Calorie Alley: the labor situation. If Meneau, or someone like him, can't fill the chairs in his high-overhead dining room, he will not be able to meet a payroll that grows fatter with every new twist from Paris and Brussels.

"No one wants to work anymore," Meneau had told me, as we delved into the subject. "Today, most of the grapes out there still have to be picked, but no one showed up. Maybe four out of twenty. It's sunny, and it's Sunday. They'd rather do something else."

What he did not have to add is that harvesting grapes is damned hard work, which pays little. And most labor related to producing and processing food is the same.

In an orderly world, double-digit unemployment would suggest an army of people, young and old, desperate to make a few francs at whatever activity they can find. But in the European Union, and especially in France, that does not necessarily follow. Certainly in a restaurant where work is constant from early to late, with moments of seething tension in between, only the committed future restaurateurs stick to it for long. The others soon catch on to the drawbacks of slave labor.

Nearly every great chef has spent time sitting at the knees of a master. Apprenticeships are still highly prized. A young hopeful might dice and slice for years before ever applying fire to a pan. But the pay for such grunt work is no longer mostly skill and confidence. Apart from minimum wages and maximum shifts, social security taxes add a fifty percent cost to each salary. If a faltering restaurant lays off workers, officially decreed severance pay is impressive.

France's workweek was cut to thirty-five hours in 1999, a fresh blow to restaurants. Employees can log that much time on a busy two-day weekend.

Besides workers, restaurants need customers. For people who fear losing the job they have, or who get by on a relatively generous but hardly extravagant dole, haute cuisine is beyond reach.

Families with reasonable incomes may splurge at a fancy table if they have something rare to celebrate. But their ordinary Sunday lunch takes place in more modest circumstances.

Altogether, three dozen starred restaurants lie in the narrow galaxy between Paris and Lyon. Most are small one-stars, with charming but simple overheads. A few little-known but ambitious chefs are investing enough to court an extra star or two, risking an eventual demotion that is tantamount to doom. Some are underrated. Others struggle against difficult odds to keep what they have. And nearly every one is run by a chef who wakes with the roosters and beds down long after the last customer has wobbled out his front door.

Besides good food, the main attraction a country restaurant can offer is the charisma of its host.

The quality of the cuisine need not, in fact, be dependent on the boss's presence. Bocuse rose to prominence by stirring the black truffle soup and whipping up lobster mousse with his own hand. When he began gallivanting from Tokyo to San Francisco, someone asked him who cooks when he is not at his restaurant. He had a simple enough answer: The same people who cook when he is there.

With separate three-star restaurants 800 miles apart, not to speak of all the other enterprises he oversees, Ducasse can't even make a pretense of minding the store.

Naegellen insists that Michelin is pragmatic on the subject. Any sizeable restaurant must have help, and if a chef can produce superlative food by delegating to assistants, that is good enough.

But ever since the early days of Dumaine, Pic, and the elder Troisgros, people eating their way south have made a practice of hobnobbing with the master. The loss of a chef-propriétaire can count heavily. When Alain Chapel died, his widow and his sous-chef took over his restaurant at Mionnay with no discernible drop in quality. But a star was removed.

Meneau has always stuck close to his kitchen and the dining room. "At restaurants like ours, people don't come because they are hungry," he explained. "They want a pleasure experience, and they want a certain sense of theater. We provide a good meal, plus an ambiance they do not easily find elsewhere."

He has the host role down to perfection. Mostly, he is in the kitchen, but he makes no fetish of avoiding the dining room. For honored guests, or if he is in an ebullient mood, he will discuss the day's menu and take the order. As is the style, his wife shares this role. Unless some pressing reason prevents him, Meneau always makes his rounds at the end.

Down the road in Saulieu, Loiseau works hard at the same tradition. Calorie Alley geography applies to him as well. When cars improved after the war, Dumaine's La Côte d'Or was the preferred first night's stop. After an ignoble hiatus, Loiseau restored old glory. He made the place "worth a journey" by the force of his own personality.

These days, Loiseau is happy to say he has not touched a pot in years. "I have trained my people well," he boomed, as he introduced his chef de cuisine. "This man eats Loiseau, sleeps Loiseau, pisses Loiseau." But the real Loiseau watches. If he leaves the dining room strictly to Hubert, he is in the kitchen, hovering over the piano with an eye peeled for the unruly rivulets of sauce. He directs, cajoles, praises, and berates. Then, with the coffee service, he floats through his salon to exchange pleasantries with customers before they reach for their credit cards.

For all of his branching out into other culinary pursuits, Loiseau breaks into a sweat when he spends more than a day away from home. Once when I visited him, he spent fifteen minutes talking about his fight for that third star. It was a personal quest, a dream ever since he watched as a galley slave when the Troisgros broke out the Champagne to celebrate their ascendancy. But also, three stars were the difference between success and sinking under a load of overdue bills.

"But once you get it, you don't automatically keep it," Loiseau said. "Every day, I wake up wondering if something might go wrong, if some mistake might be made, and they will take it away."

Hardly a modest man, Loiseau explained at length the personal sentiments attached to his Michelin honors. More important, there was his balance sheet. He had spent millions on adding new rooms and a shop for Loiseau-endorsed items. He was about to list his hotel-restaurant on the Paris stock exchange, the only chef-propriétaire to attempt such a gamble, and that move would raise five million dollars in working capital from investors.

That was late in 1998. The following spring, the 1999 bible appeared with its sobering surprise. By then, Loiseau's worst nightmare happened, to someone else. Anonymous accusers with unexplained complaints had done their damage.

When I went to ask Loiseau about Meneau, he was strangely unsympathetic. "Look, they don't give these things away lightly, and they don't take them away lightly, either," he said. "You have to keep your staff happy and loyal. Your people have to love you, the way mine love me."

Loiseau said that neither he nor other three-star chefs had noticed an immediate influx of customers who had abandoned Meneau. But he expected one in the coming seasons.

My lunch at La Côte d'Or was every bit as good as the one before it. But I left with a strange taste in my mouth. As a foreign correspondent, I knew a war when I saw one. Loiseau's ebullient confidence seemed forced to me. Very few chefs, I was convinced, slept easily on Calorie Alley.

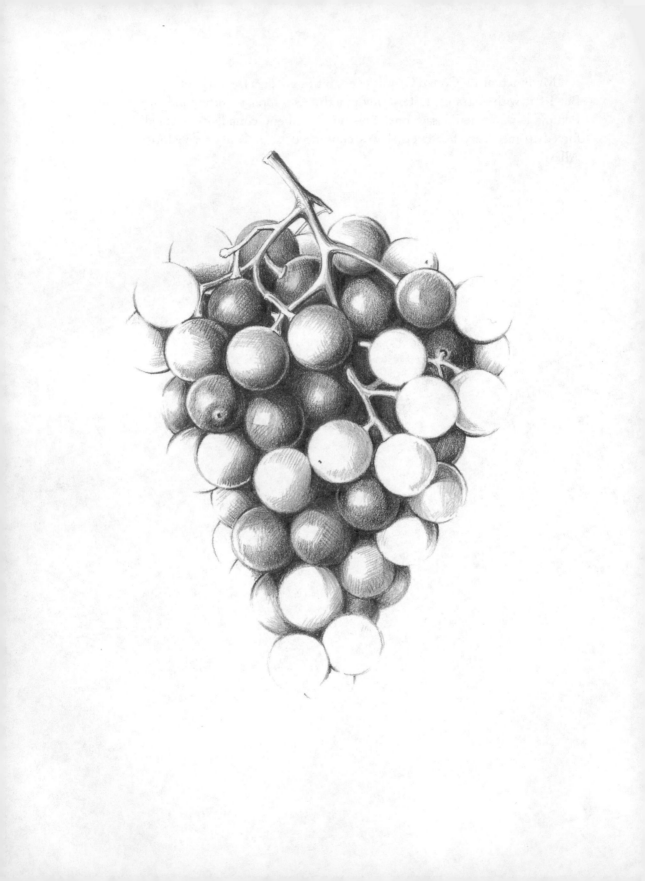

———⟨⟨⟨⟩⟩⟩———

SIXTEEN

Joan of Arc Slept Around Here

FROM MILES AWAY, the towers of Reims Cathedral rise above Champagne vineyards as though God had something particular in mind for those acidic cold-weather grapes. Closer up, the masterwork church overwhelms, and thoughts turn to holier wine. A dart thrown anywhere at the map hits a spot with a reason to be called the heart of France. But if there is one place where pride pumps hardest in the French bloodstream, it is Reims.

Ancient Franks passed through Champagne down the Marne toward the Seine, the first of later Germanic hordes who would come to France with more than lunch in mind. Gauls and Gallo-Romans moved in to stay, displacing original Roman settlers. They built village strongholds with chalk blocks carved deep under topsoil that now pushes forth those blessed chardonnay and pinot noir grapes.

The lines of history were never broken over the millennia. The original chalk quarries now extend like upside down cathedrals, ten stories deep, from narrow holes in the surface. Today those underground galleries, along with miles more dug under Reims and Épernay over the last few centuries, shelter 1.2 billion bottles of Champagne. But sparkling wine is merely an extra added attraction in old Reims.

Of all their many kings, the French regard Clovis as their nation's founding father. Born in 481, Clovis was a Frankish gang leader who rose quickly to tribal chieftain. With skillful use of manipulation and murder, he emerged as head of the Franks. He conquered Gaul by fighting off Romans, Visigoths, Burgundians, and assorted German tribes. Clotilde, eventually Saint Clotilde, married Clovis and led him full-tilt into Christianity. When it came time to be crowned king, only the cathedral at Reims would do.

At the last moment, the coronation was nearly canceled. Priests discovered they had no olive oil to anoint the king. But, legend attests, a dove appeared from heaven with a flask in its beak. The tear-shaped vial was placed for safekeeping in the nearby Basilica of Saint-Remi. With regular changes of oil, it was used to sanctify thirty-four successive monarchs.

Fire razed the cathedral in 1210, and a new one was begun two years later. It took nearly a century, during which townspeople attacked the archbishop's palace in an uprising over how much it all cost for the great church to be finished.

The new structure was hardly unique. During those three centuries from 1050 to 1350, masons in France quarried several million tons of stone to build eighty grand cathedrals and tens of thousands of other churches. The Egyptians used less stone for all of their ancient work.

But if Notre-Dame in Paris was certainly grander, the Reims Cathedral had a singular sacred purpose. To rule France, a king had to receive his crown under its soaring Gothic arches and magnificent rose windows. That was what all the fuss was about in the early fifteenth century, during the Hundred Years' War.

France desperately needed a king to unite its squabbling duchies and districts against England. The dauphin Charles VII waited in limbo by the Loire because the English held Reims, Orléans, and everything in between. It would take a field marshal, a mysterious young woman who listened only to God, to get him the cathedral.

JOAN OF ARC, I would guess, was a lousy cook. Back then, the French thought little about suppertime. Joan spent her time musing about God and slaving away on the family farm. By age sixteen, she was already wearing leather armor and leading gritty male soldiers in battle. In any case, as an immigrant from Rhine country, she wasn't even French.

But I was fascinated. Chaste yet romantic, first wronged then worshiped, falling somewhere between improbable myth and inexplicable reality, Jeanne d'Arc makes a perfect patron saint of France.

During most of the 1990's, Joan had slipped mostly into disuse as a French icon. The far-right National Front seized upon her as a symbol to such an extent that she bordered on the politically incorrect. When Jean-Marie Le Pen and Bruno Mégret took their extreme nationalism in separate directions, each claimed the right to have Joan waving blue, white, and red over their heads.

But then Luc Besson made his epic film, *Jeanne d'Arc*. Just as she had been rehabilitated and sainted nearly five centuries after being burned as a witch, she was suddenly alive again.

All of the ironies reflected the state of France's modern-day angst. Though a paean to French national spirit, the French director made his film in English. Charles VII managed to be John Malkovich; his duplicitous mother was Faye Dunaway with something like a pie plate on her head.

Ads in the United States for *The Messenger*, as the English version was called, said: "God ordered her to deliver France from her enemies." To many Frenchmen, of course, that seemed bogus: God would know better. The enemies France most needed saving from, as has often been the case over two millennia, were themselves French.

The king, once crowned, cuts her loose and leaves her twisting in the wind. Burgundians capture her for ransom. The highest bidders, naturally, are the hated English, who then deliver her to French clerics in Normandy. With much highly skilled low intrigue, Joan ends up yet again in the blasphemous men's garments she swore under duress to forsake. And she is burned at the stake in Rouen, in the shadow of a cathedral every bit as beautiful as the one in Reims.

Most people agree that Joan was born in Domrémy, which back around 1412 was part of German Lorraine. I skipped a visit to her hometown, assuming no one would still remember the plain-looking little girl who heard voices in the back pasture. With my tattered map, I plotted Joan's travels during the brief course of her life. She managed to crisscross through the most essential arteries of the bloodstream of France. She rode from the Rhine to the Loire, passing headwaters of the Rhône and Saône, and then following the Marne.

Joan's military campaigns stretched from the Touraine through Burgundy, until she met her final fate deep in Normandy, on the banks of the Seine. For reasons that should require little explanation, however, I decided to focus on only one of her stops: Reims and the surrounding Champagne.

Just about everyone knows Dom Pérignon, the eighteenth-century monk who discovered how to put bubbles in a bottle. But who knows about his Benedictine friend, Dom Ruinart, who figured out how to sell it?

Ruinart, a young man with a bald head and impish grin, acted quickly when Louis XV decreed that the sparkling wine of Champagne could be packaged and sold by any respectable business that elected to do it. He helped his nephew, Nicolas Ruinart, to establish the first Champagne house in Reims in 1729.

Successive generations added to the winery's prestige. It remained small and selective, pressing good grapes into wonderful Champagne.

Nearly three centuries later, Moët et Chandon's vintage Dom Pérignon outsells every other premium champagne in world markets. Among Americans, the ratio approaches four to one over Louis Roederer Cristal. The French, meanwhile, keep their secret. Two-thirds of Dom Ruinart never crosses the border.

"We would like to be a bit better known," allowed Guy de Rivoire, the marketing director, looking relaxed on a couch at the ornate stone headquarters.

When I called on de Rivoire, the millennium was much on his mind. Celebrating the turnover of three zeros around the world drained Champagne bottles like nothing ever had. Every house, big and little, was doing something about it.

Ruinart's creation sat on an end table next to the worn leather couch. Vintage wines from six different grand cru vineyards were blended to produce 14,000 magnums of L'Exclusive. Each bottle was clear to show off the pale-gold Champagne, but each came entwined in silver filigree designed by Cristofle of Paris.

L'Exclusive came nestled in a hand-crafted box of aged walnut fitted with a humidifying capsule and a thermometer. It would keep cigars long after the bottle was drained. The whole package cost about a thousand dollars, and people bought them up fast.

I was struck by the contrast between the slick, ultramodern packaging and the musty old feel of the visitors' salon. From stone walls, the only Ruinarts left gazed down solemnly from dark-hued paintings. Family pride is no longer an issue.

The old house passed without much of a fight into the hands of Bernard Arnault's LVMH, which owns the birthright not only of Dom Ruinart but also Dom Pérignon. The M in LVMH stands for Moët. Arnault also owns the house brought to glory by Nicole Barbe Ponsardin, widowed (became a *veuve*) at twenty-seven in 1805, who is now remembered as La Veuve Clicquot. And, along with other major Champagne properties, he also owns Krug, still run by Krugs who descend from the German who founded it in 1843, six generations ago.

Champagne vintners do not make much of an issue out of conglomerate ownership. The grapes are grown, picked, pressed, blended, and bubbled as they always were. Arnault, who realizes the value of soul—even if purchased—tries hard to preserve the mystique. If Christian Dior can spiff up its cousin, Pommery, with an isothermic carrying sack, so much the better. Champagne is for parties.

What Champagne makers really care about is their geographic name. It refers to terroir, not bubbles. Good Californian or Australian sparkling wine may be far more drinkable than poor-quality Champagne, but that does not change the appellation.

Beyond that, there is what the American food expert Edward Behr calls the logic of a brand. Each house has a style. Champagne is always blended, with only the rarest of exceptions, even when it has a vintage date. And, almost as invariably, it is assembled from grapes of several different vineyards.

Champagne grapes grow only in two enclaves a long hour by autoroute northeast of Paris. The only more northerly vineyards are in Germany, but they receive warmer summer sun. Cool-ripened Champagne grapes, like those in Chablis, produce aromas and acidity strong enough to push flavor past the bubbles.

Altogether, 15,000 growers tend to vines, and 5,000 of them have their own labels. Two dozen houses dominate, however, led by Moët et Chandon. They are either clustered in Reims or spread out along the avenue de Champagne in nearby Épernay.

As everywhere else in France when fine wine or comestibles are involved, the parameters are strict. Regulations on all stage of the process are set forth in *La Statue viti-vinicole de la Champagne*. As Behr points out, it is as fat as a phone book. The parcels it officially describes add up to 34,000 hectares. In 1970, only 19,000 of them were planted. Thirty years later, all but 3,000 were in grapes.

With each harvest, vintners blend a new batch of Champagne according to their own distintive style. They mix different varieties of grape from vines that might be at opposite ends of Champagne. Then they adjust the assemblage with reserve wine, superior stuff from past years held back for such occasions.

When a year is better than average, bottles are labeled as vintage. Remarkably, 1988, 1989, and 1990 all were superb. But even then, the Champagne was blended with wine from other years. This is not a forced compromise but rather a highly prized skill. The approach is different from Bordeaux or Burgundy, but it is the nature of Champagne.

Mostly, Champagne is a white wine from red grapes. Pinot Noir and an old mutation known as Meunier together make up three-quarters of the vineyard. Grapes are pressed gently while still on their stalks so pigment from their skins does not color the juice. The exception is rosé, or pink Champagne. Too often laughed off, rosé has a pleasant astringency from tannin in Pinot Noir skins.

The third Champagne variety is Chardonnay, a white grape that is mixed in almost all blends. Sometimes Chardonnay is used exclusively, and the wine is *blanc des blancs*.

The bubbles develop from a mix of sugar, yeasts, and wine added at bottling. This extra fermentation distributes fizz throughout the liquid as wine ages on the lees, the yeasty sediment. Aging lasts at least several years for good Champagne; excellent Champagne might take more than six. Over time, the yeast flavors mature from bready to a richer nutty.

For two centuries now, winemakers have used a technique devised by the Veuve Clicquot to clear sediment from the bottles. Over a month's time at the end, a skilled cellarman gives each bottle a twist and alters its angle on the wooden rack. Eventually, the bottles are upended, and all the sediment collects on the cork. This process is called riddling. The one that follows is disgorging.

To remove the sediment, bottle necks are plunged into freezing brine. When the cork is removed, the sentiment is poured out as slush. At this stage, the acidy Champagne is flinty and dry as a stone. To top up the bottles, vintners add enough sugar to give the character they want. Tastes, obviously, vary widely.

"Extra brut" means only a hint of sugar, if any at all. "Brut," by far the most popular, has up to fifteen grams of sugar per liter but tastes dry, nonetheless. Although "Extra-sec" means extra dry, it has a distinct sweetness. "Demi-sec" is sweet.

JÉRÔME HAD COME along to Ruinart, and together we went down into the caves. The hostess, an eager student from Reims, was still learning her lines. I made a tentative remark about Jeanne d'Arc, but she seemed not to have heard of the woman. Still, there was not much to be said. I knew how the wine was made. I was busy looking.

Thousands of years before, skilled hands had chiseled away huge blocks of underground limestone. With neither earth-moving equipment nor the souls of strip miners, the ancients had planned carefully. Crews dug downward from a small hole and then opened galleries wider as they went deeper. Cut stone was hauled up on pulleys through a narrow opening that provided access and ventilation.

The endless caves I had seen at Épernay were tunneled into the soft chalky rock, some only recently, for the single purpose of aging Champagne at cool steady temperatures. Ruinart simply made use of what had come down from the past. The original family would have stuck torches into the same niches the Gallo-Romans had used.

Our young escort, it turned out, excelled at her most important task. She produced a bottle of Dom Ruinart 1990 and opened it deftly.

However much the onomatopoeic Pop! may be associated with opening Champagne bottles, the act is best done gently. Rapid expulsion of trapped gas carries off a lot of those bubbles that took years to form. Foam may be fun, but it is wasted wine.

The best way is to remove the wire and cover the cork with a towel to prevent any cuts from the metal capsule. Hold the cork in one hand and twist the bottle with the other. Turning the bottle, not the cork, makes it easier to hold the cork in place for just enough gas to escape without foam.

The sound, Champagne makers say, should resemble the sigh of a contented woman.

To make a show of it, go the whole way: *sabrer* the cork. This is usually done with a sword, but a sturdy kitchen knife will do it. With foil and wire still in place, hold the bottle in one hand and slide the back of the blade (the dull part) smartly along the neck toward the glass ring under the cork.

With luck, the force of the knife makes a clean circular break of the glass neck, and the gas inside propels the cork assembly across the room. Then foam Champagne into the nearest glasses. It is easier than it sounds. Until you get it down, however, be ready for some dirty looks and glass splinters.

At this tasting, no one expected visitors to spit out the product. Fine tiny bubbles rose evenly through the pale gold liquid, a sign of well-made Champagne. A subtle veil of fruit covered the basic stony crispness.

Among the formal trappings and the original hand-drawn logs of the oldest house in Reims, I made a happy discovery. For years, I had thought that I was allergic to Champagne. In fact, I learned that morning, I was only allergic to bad Champagne.

AN HOUR LATER, Krug went down just as well. Krug makes a half-million bottles a year, not much compared to a big house, but it is all high quality and among the highest priced. Foreign customers each year snap up eighty percent of the production.

For reasons of taste and tradition, Krug alone still ferments all of its wine in wood. But Henri Krug, who considers Champagne to be too delicate for an oaky overtone, seasons each barrel with lesser wine for two years before filling it with Champagne. Even then, the blend is moved to stainless-steel vats after several months in barrels.

Krug's assemblage averages about forty percent reserve wine, an impressive figure. It remains on its lees for six years at least and sometimes ten. Bottles are partly riddled by hand, but machines are beginning to take over this old task. Krug's own grapes make up a third of the total.

Remi Krug, who runs the house with his brother, Henri, does not like to hear "nonvintage" in connection with his prestigious Grande Cuvée. That seems to disparage the idea of a blend. The brothers were gone when I visited. But in his newsletter, *The Art of Eating,* Behr noted Remi's sensitivity:

"I blundered [Behr wrote] by asking him how much variation from year to year was aesthetically desirable and how much customers might tolerate. His answer was firm. 'We blend to avoid variation and make sure every blend tastes the same. . . . If there is a difference, we have failed.' To achieve absolute consistency, 'there is no recipe, no formula. Each year you have to reinvent.' "

It seems to work. As the millennium approached, I talked to Olivier Krug, Henri's son, and his sister Caroline. They handle marketing. A flood of orders had come from people who wanted the Krug taste.

There is plenty of Champagne, Olivier said, but only so much of the best of it. And millennium celebrations made a dent in the stocks of all the better houses.

"You can't drink more, but you can drink better," Olivier said. "We would like to sell more, but we can't empty our caves. We made allotments and gave preference to loyal Kruggies who buy every year. We had to disappoint some others."

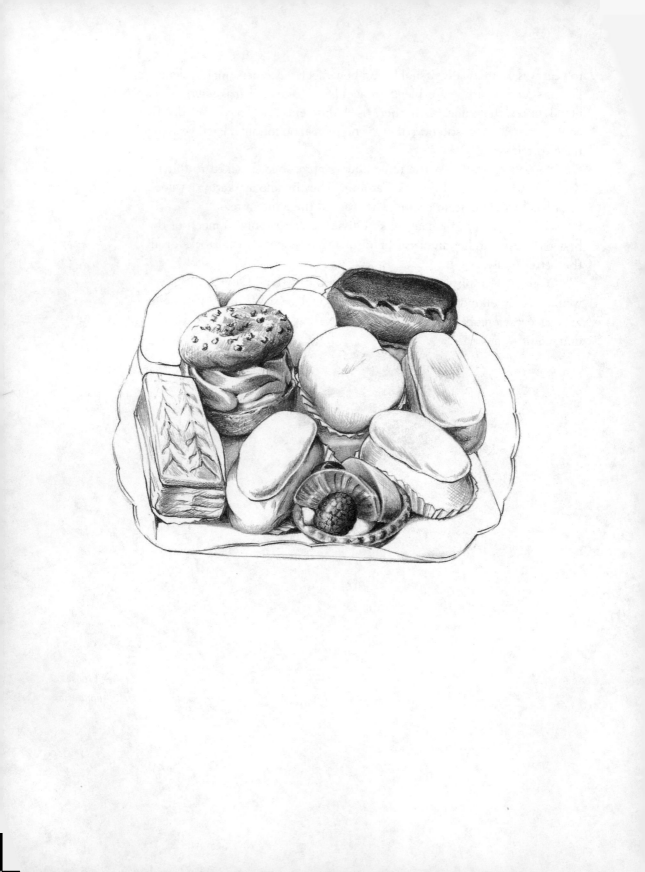

SEVENTEEN

Butter Country

I FOUND PIERRE ANDROUËT, at eighty-five with an injured knee and a scratchy wool vest over his tightly knotted tie, wandering lost somewhere between Iran and Afghanistan. He was deep into the *World Atlas of Cheese*, researching the masterwork he hoped soon to finish that would dwarf his own 1971 classic, *Guide du Fromage*. Each morning, he hobbled into his paneled den overlooking the lovely Risle river, off the Seine, to delve further into a passion passed on by an already famous father.

Madame Thieullent, *la grande fromagère* of Périgueux, had told me about Androuët with reverence. In France, every domain having to do with food has its hierachy of nobility. He is the big cheese.

A man of immense courtly charm, whose white mustache bristles and eyes quite literally twinkle, Androuët is thrilled to share his knowledge. "I believe that all this study I've done is not for me but to pass on to others," he told me. The trouble, of course, is that it would take me three-quarters of a century to absorb it all.

Besides the Guide, which has sold 100,000 copies in France over the years, he has turned out another dozen volumes on everything from the guts to the glory of cheese. Until the age of eighty, he ran the best loved *fromageries* in Paris.

"Look," he said, showing me a mountain of giant index cards, the sort of hefty rag stock few people make anymore. "Each one of these is a cheese, and I've written entries on most of them." The cards covered nearly every country on earth. Not surprisingly, by far the most numerous were from France. And many of those were from the surrounding farms of Normandy.

Androuët grew up in his father's celebrated cheese shop on the rue d'Amsterdam in Paris. A photo in his study shows Henri Androuët at work, researching cheeses at a time when few people gave much thought to dairy science. By the thirties, young Pierre had made his own name. He identified and named a little-known cheese—Brillat-Savarin—from the Normandy backcountry.

He still works in elegant longhand, with file folders in old oak cabinets; he could not even remember the word, computer. "What is that thing called?" he asked me at one point. "With the keys and all?" But the occasional senior moment does nothing to dim his wit. Or his fire.

"The age of cheese freedom is over," he said, outraged at the idea. The whole mystery of cheese, Androuët explained, is in figuring out how different bacteria behave in changing circumstances. Cheese people have spent centuries at this, perfecting how to get consistency and taste without danger to health. And now catch-all laws against any eventuality, drafted by people with scant understanding, impose preventive death on all bacteria.

"We are at the end of an era, I'm afraid," he said. "Once the public powers interest themselves in some field, you know it is facing its finish. Now they have discovered cheese. These European Union regulations are designed to favor the far less skilled, who make bland cheese: the Dutch, the Danes, the others. France is greatly disadvantaged by all of this. In ten years, I suspect we'll be down to the thirty-six appelation d'origine contrôlée cheeses that France will have to protect for reasons of national pride."

Already, he said, cheeses are fast dropping off the map. "None of the well-known ones are gone yet, but certain wonderful farm cheeses just can't be found anymore. Once, there were thousands. Every farmer made his own cheese, with a slight variation, and sold it in the local market to help make ends meet. Now incomes are higher, and so much work is involved, this is simply no longer feasible for farmers."

Occasionally, something goes wrong, such as a limited outbreak of listeria during 1999 in the smelly Époisses cheese so beloved to Burgundy. Listeria, though nothing to shrug off, happens. So do traffic accidents, but driving is not banned even after a particularly nasty pile-up on a freeway.

If fresh raw milk is turned quickly to cheese, it is perfectly safe, Androuët explained. "Natural inhibitors in the milk prevent any pathogens from forming. This is nature's way of protecting calves when their mothers suckle them. Before, farmers made cheese from raw milk within three hours, and it was impossible to have problems. Impossible."

Modern times have changed the process. Most farmers store milk until someone collects it to take to a cooperative or a factory. It may wait longer there. This requires an unbroken cold chain to be maintained by different people. If controls are adequate, nothing goes wrong. But the possibility of bad bacteria exists. And governments take the safest course, which is to ban whole categories and processes.

"There is simply no relationship between the taste of cheeses with raw milk and with milk that has been sterilized," he said.

ONE PROMINENT VICTIM is the Normandy stalwart, Camembert. Without raw milk, it is an empty name—and not even legal, since the appellation d'origine contrôlée requires raw milk—with no taste.

Officials are only partly responsible for ruining cheese, Androuët said. The rigors of mass production do the rest. When milk is Duclauxized (here is another of his research treasures: Louis Pasteur did his work with wine; milk was done by a colleague named Emile Duclaux), it can be done at sixty-three degrees centigrade, which need not destroy all the flavor. But this takes too long. Industrial processors zap their bulk milk in seconds at temperatures above ninety degrees.

And now that so many people are getting used to tasteless cheese, fewer consumers demand anything better.

Pliny the Elder wrote about what was probably Roquefort, and cheese is as old as France. Brillat-Savarin called cheese the first dessert. But, Androuët remembers, the great days of cheese began only on the eve of World War II. When his father opened his shop early in the century, his wares were not easy to sell.

"Even in the 1930's, cheese was rare at fancy dinners," he said. "People served Camembert, but they served it rolled in bread crumbs and cornstarch, and no one ate it. It was not until the late 1930's that the bulk of Frenchmen developed their love of cheese."

And in the late 1940's, cheese was one of those delicacies that war-deprived Frenchmen devoured in a big way. It was in 1962, by the most popular accounts, that Charles de Gaulle observed, "How can you be expected to govern a country that has 246 kinds of cheese?"

Androuët chortled when I asked him about that.

"Actually, it was Churchill," he told me, "and what he really said was, 'France has three hundred cheeses and one religion, and England has three hundred religions and one cheese.' After that, people took what liberties they wanted with the remark."

Androuët, a life-long Parisian, "retired" at the age of eighty to the tiny old village of Conde-sur-Risle. His wife brought her hotel-sized collection of copper pots and pans, which she still keeps gleaming. They eat well but simply.

"Hmmm," Androuët answered when I asked if cheese had anything to do with his vitality despite advancing age. "I doubt it. You know, I've eaten a lot of cheese in tastings and competitions and experiments over the years. But on my own, I don't really consume so much that it is a danger to my health."

I had gone to Normandy in search of butter as well as cheese. For most of us, it is a simple choice between butter or the low-priced spread. The French have any number of varieties, often sold by the gram from huge tubs.

Brittany produced the most butter. The Vendée and the Beauce, among other regions, were known for excellent dairy products. But the lush pastures of Normandy had always seemed to make up France's butter heartland.

The first step in cooking almost anything *à la Normande* is to melt a grotesque amount of butter and then glug in fresh cream. I had visions of old women with powerful biceps at their grandmothers' churns. So I asked Androuët where I might find someone who still made butter the old way. He sighed heavily.

"Nowhere," he replied. Perhaps a few diehards with extra time on their hands made old-fashioned butter on remote farms. But he did not know of any.

"Churned butter exists only on labels," Androuët said. "This is a terrible tragedy. The process that industrial butter makers use is called a 'cannon.' Milk goes in one end and it is shot out of the other as butter. The process is so fast that milk has no time to release any of its subtle flavor elements, and the result is as insipid and tasteless as factory cheese."

A week earlier, he said, he bought some half-salted butter with a label that claimed it was made with a churn. "Then I tasted it," he said. "On the label I found an address printed in microscopic letters, in three languages. I wrote and asked them if they would please send me a photograph of their churn."

At this, both of Androuët's eyes flashed a major twinkle.

PONT L'ÉVÊQUE IS a cheese, but it is also one of those wonderful French towns where past and present suggest a very enjoyable future. I mused about this over lunch at the Aigle d'Or, which has been feeding travelers since 1520.

The restaurant was built as a post stop around two gigantic walk-in fireplaces, back-to-back in two different rooms but sharing the same chimney. Monster oak beams support low ceilings. Roughly hewn window sashes open in half-timbered walls. Diagonal and upright beams divide the main room into sections.

Anne-Marie Duhamel, a beautiful woman of perhaps forty, takes care of the dining room. Her husband, Thierry, is chef. They had run a restaurant in a troglodyte cave near Tours, their home country on the Loire, but wanted a new challenge. After three years, they had a Bib, a smiling red Michelin symbol that denotes exceptional, reasonable restaurants that choose not to be stuffy enough for stars.

The Duhamels are exactly the sort of aubergistes on whom the great chefs of France say the future depends. I thought of Alain Ducasse's criteria: wonderful food at honest prices, served in a setting that makes diners not want to go home.

Anne-Marie offered a house cocktail, a blend of calvados, peach, and ginger, to get my taste buds' attention. And she put down a plate of Thierry's appetizer olives. These were little black niçoises, pitted and cured to a perfect chewiness, flavored with caraway and his own bouquet of herbs. After years of scouting olives all around the Mediterranean, I had found some of the best in the depths of butter country, made by a Touraine chef who grew up with duck fat.

The menu was ample and ambitious. I pondered the local Pays d'Auge fixed lunch. It began with three sorts of smoked salmon, including a tartar, which I loved. The main course was a roasted wild duckling in a sauce of cider with grated potatoes. Dessert might have been a plate of three sorbets and ginger, or perhaps a *tarte tatin*—that rich Normandy upside down apple pie—with vanilla ice cream and a calvados cream sauce. Oh, and the cheese. The price of this lunch, 140 francs, was what my corner Paris brasserie charged for a modest piece of steak.

I noticed warm foie gras in cider vinegar and also some fish from nearby waters. But I settled on *homard poêlé sauce corail et estragon* with *risotto de petit épeautre*. When it arrived, I wasn't sure whether to eat it or have someone paint it as a still life worthy of the Musée d'Orsay.

Chunks of the lobster's meat were lightly poached in a pan and arranged on a palette of sauce colored with its own coral. Thierry had arranged the small scarlet lobster head to one side, looking upward. The center section of the shell, upright, was stuffed with a savory al dente grain I had been chasing for months.

Épeautre, which translates to German wheat, may be Europe's oldest grain. Its kernels are large, with several husks; it is a pain to prepare. For a long time, it all but disappeared. But farmers in the Vauclause and elsewhere in northern Provence were growing it again, giving it a new life. I had yet to taste it. Only chefs like Thierry, with patience and imagination, took the trouble.

"Risotto" was just a manner of speaking. It was all épeautre, cooked delicately with tiny bits of carrot and other tender vegetables the way Milanese do their finest grains of rice.

This single dish was by way of fast food. I was in a hurry, between appointments. I had dropped by only because my old pal Barbara Porter, who had a house nearby, told me the Aigle d'Or was not to be missed.

"It's just simple cooking, dishes that we like ourselves, which we think other people may also like," Anne-Marie explained. "We try to incorporate local products from Normandy, with more cream and butter than we might normally use. But we also use ingredients from where we came from, and other places."

She saw no particular crisis in French cuisine.

"Tastes are changing perhaps," she said. "People eat more fish and vegetables, less red meat, than they used to. I find it very hard to sell game when it is on the menu. Partly, it is the strong taste. Also, I think some people don't like to imagine those poor wild creatures on their dinner plate."

By now, I was seriously late for my next appointment. Still, there was that cider-scented green apple sorbet to try. And I had a cell phone in my pocket. What the hell.

CLAUDE CRÉTIEN PATTED his half-dismantled still with an affectionate hand, and he locked the door again. The scene seemed particularly touching because I was primed for high drama. I was also half ablaze and feeling a pleasant numbness. We had been sampling the twenty-year-old contents of a jug marked *"Le Calvados du Père Crétien."*

Crétien, at sixty-six, was shaped like a cider barrel, with a face as round and red as a Royal Gala. He retired from making calvados early in the 1990s, but I had heard about him for years. In fact, had we sampled any of Crétien's younger calvados, I might have picked some of the apples that went into it.

Long before the rest of us thought about the Dordogne or Provence, my friends Jim Bitterman and Pat Thompson were smart enough to move to Normandy. Both worked for NBC at the time, liable to go busting off to cover distant disorder at a moment's notice. They wanted a little peace in the meantime.

Pat and Jim bought a lovely old stone mill in the lovely old stone village of Gilles, far enough from Paris to be Normandy but close enough to reach before breakfast. Among other things, they grew apples. On those years when I was around for the harvest party, I helped pick. Until young Tess, their daughter, got old enough to displace me, I was designated tractor driver.

Ward Just, whose day job was writing novels, normally appeared each year to be cider master. Jon Randal, when not tracking Kurds for the *Washington Post*, kibitzed from the sidelines. All told, there was a large and happy crew. The day always ended in the basement, among old lovingly tended crocks.

"This is last year's," Jim would say, pouring out a clear liquid harsh enough to strip paint off a Lexus. Gradually we worked background until we reached the *hors-d'âge*. This was calvados at least fifteen years ago, strong but strangely smooth and pleasant, with a sweet backdrop taste of apple. I loved it.

Calva is meant to be a digestif, like cognac, and is reputed to have special stomach-aiding properties. Its devotees, however, seldom worry about whether they have a dinner to digest before indulging.

The mysterious element at Gilles was always a certain Monsieur Crétien, the alchemist behind it all. He appeared only days later, when all but Jim, Pat, and Tess had gone. He hefted the 200-pound cider barrel onto his truck, and weaved off into the distance.

Years after he retired, Pat found Crétien's telephone number for me. He answered on the first ring, but he was wary.

"You say you're a friend of Jaim?" he began. "You're writing a book about calvados? No? What then?" I explained. He demurred. Finally, he named a time and gave me his address. "I guess one has to have a little trust," he concluded, a little shakily.

Any misgivings Claude Crétien might have had were gone by the time I arrived. It would be hard to imagine a nicer man. I know he was not making moonshine calvado, because when he took me to his old half-dismantled still, I found it immobilized by the revenuers with a wire and a lead seal.

"I miss this old monster," Crétien said, giving the ancient contraption another pat on a copper vat. It was exactly the machine in that poignant old Fernandel film, l'Alambic. In the movie, the horsey-faced actor took his animal-powered still from village to village, having adventures while the machine distilled batches of various sorts of fruit. But Crétien's alambic stayed put on chocks dedicated solely to making calvados from Normandy cider.

The thing might have come straight out of the Kentucky hills. Cider or mashed fruit was poured into twin copper tubs at one end. Steam from a coal-fired boiler ran through Rube Goldberg circuitry of tubes and faucets. Evaporated fluids rose and condensed in coils deep inside. And liquid fire dripped out of a spout.

We had started the morning at his kitchen table, with nothing but coffee. He lived in a rambling old place in a placid village by the Eure River, just inside the Normandy line. The battered truck he had used to collect cider was rusting in a garage.

"The government has wrecked calvados," Crétien began, striking what had become a familiar chord. "Not this government. It was back in 1973, when they decided to abolish le privilège. Now you have to pay ninety-three francs tax for every liter you produce."

Since forever, Normandy farmers with apple trees on their land had been entitled to brew ten liters of pure calavados without paying taxes. It was a source of cultural pride. Even more, it was a major economy for families who scraped by close to the line.

"My father was in this business for fifty years," Crétien said. "That's all he did with his life, and he took great pride in it. He went from farm to farm, got to know the people, and he made calvados to remember from the apples they pressed. I did it myself for sixteen years, but then it was time to stop."

His nephew and a friend, relaxed types of the kind Frenchmen call marginals, make an attempt to carry on. His son is interested in other pursuits entirely.

After half an hour, Crétien winked. "Want to try some of the real stuff?" He produced a squat dusty bottle that looked as if it had survived the Hundred Years' War. A friend had handpainted the label: a sprig of apple blossoms on one side, with two juicy-looking apples, one red, one green, on the other. Only a few words observed that it was Père Crétien's calva.

"I thought you might like this," he said, when I admired the label. He rummaged around and found one that he had put aside on the chance that his uninvited Paris visitor passed muster. Just the same, he read my mind when I noticed the lack of any of the usual information about the bottle's contents.

"Make sure you don't say I'm selling this stuff, or the customs people will be after me," he said. For the record, in case any customs person is reading this, that is decidedly correct. Crétien has only a small personal stock remaining of his best-of calvados. And it is a damned shame.

Other old-timers are still out there, and a few young distillers study the ancient craft. Alain Passard gave me the name of his supplier, near Pont l'Évêque, whose still was in perfect working order. But they seemed to be a vanishing breed.

Calvados is available commercially, of course, including prestigious hors d'âge made by Magloire in Pont l'Évêque. But the old artisans are not impressed.

"Degree of alcohol changes over time until it stabilizes," Crétien explained. "If you want it to remain eventually at forty-three degrees, or fifty-two degrees, you have to adjust it at some point by adding water. What old-style distillers do is add the water at the beginning of the process, using our noses, so the final product comes out just the way we want it. The commercial guys just test the product at the end and dump in enough water to get the level they need."

Crétien shook his head, made a face, and repeated those words I had been hearing from Roquefort to Rouen: "It's just not the same."

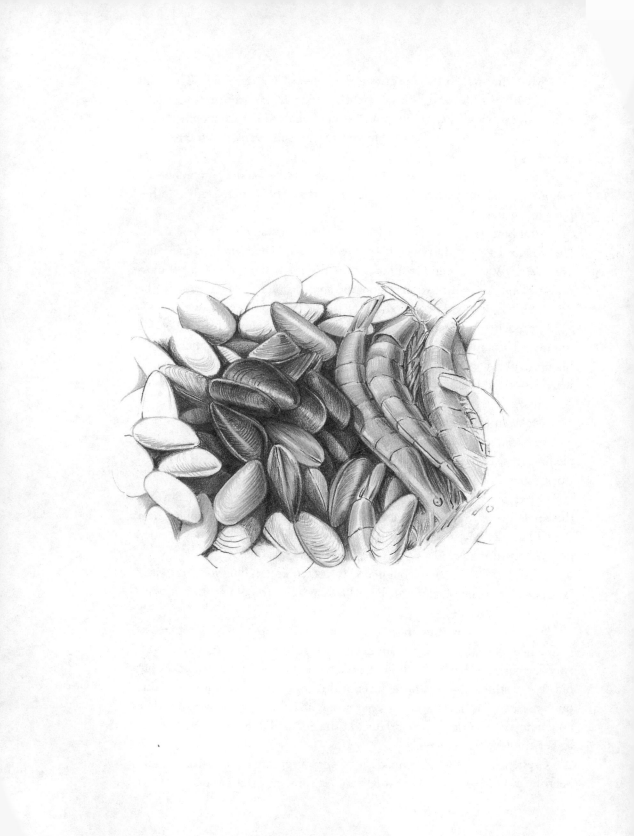

EIGHTEEN

Hard Times on the Half Shell

HEAVY SWELLS TOSSED around the Bugale Milbiz like a cork in a dishwasher, and the deck was slippery with halibut guts. Last night's bottle of Old Paddy was wreaking havoc with his frontal lobe, but Aurélien Masson was still grinning. He loves his work. And that is an encouraging sign of the times. If he didn't, France might have to get used to frozen fish.

The Massons' forty-foot boat, which roams from the fly-speck Île de Molène off the western tip of Brittany, is not exactly the main source of France's fresh fish. But Aurélien, with attractive other choices at twenty, typifies the last of an ancient breed. When they go, the future is trawlers. Fish sticks and catfood. On that particular morning, however, the future looked pretty good.

I was on board by a stroke of chance. On the daily passenger boat from Brest to Molène, I had run into Aurélien's father, Émile, much better known as Milo. With stern glasses and thinning hair, he might have been a retired tax inspector. I guessed his age at somewhere near seventy. As it turned out, he was fifty-five—Brittany winds and hard work had added an extra decade or so—and he had never spent a day of his life in an office.

"I am a lucky man," Milo pronounced. "I have a profession I love, and I have freedom."

A fisherman friend next to him nodded enthusiastic agreement. "We don't worry about a thirty-five-hour workweek," Milo added. "Maybe a thirty-five-hour day sometimes, but if we want to knock off for a while, no one says a thing."

The friend had already knocked off permanently, leaving Milo as the last captain of any sizeable boat based at Molène. Milo was also easing into retirement, but, as he said, he was a lucky man. His son Sébastien, at twenty-six, would take over the boat, helped by Aurélien and two young crew members. Sébastien's son, Damien, had not yet elected a career; he was five. A second kid was on the way. With some luck, yet another generation would go on fishing.

Milo wasn't quite sure what number generation that would be. His grandfather fished off Molène, he knew, and so did his father. But nearly half the population of the island is named Masson. What might have been a single family tree has split into mysterious branches so distinct that Massons marry Massons without fear of retribution from God or their gene pool.

No one knows when the first people—Masson or otherwise—came to Molène. The mayor, a man named Masson, who is Milo's friend if not distant cousin, replies simply: "It was always inhabited." In any case, a fifth-century fresco found near the church shows islanders welcoming visitors with lobsters. Obviously, the hosts had been fishing.

In its heyday, Molène supported a stable population of well over 700, and every able-bodied male was a fisherman. Today, there are barely 300 inhabitants, mostly retired people, including a lot of strangers from the continent. Tourists swell the number up toward 1,500 when it is warm, but many of them are day-trippers. Except for the mayor's grocery store, a small hotel and bar, Madame Caraven's tobacco and newspaper shop, the summers-only restaurant, and a tackle shop, there is no business. A half-dozen little boats still go out to fish from Molène. But the only serious operation left is Milo Masson & Sons' red-and-white Bugale Milbiz.

When we docked at Molène, Milo invited me home for a coffee and a snort. His wife, Jeannette, served butter-rich Brittany pastries and talked about life in a microcosm.

"We have everything we need," she said, in her tidy kitchen, which might have been in the seventh arrondissement of Paris. The television set was linked to a satellite dish tucked discreetly in the bushes out back. The freezer and larder were well-stocked. "Well, almost."

The island has only a dispensary and a nurse. When necessary, she describes symptoms to a doctor in Brest, who tells her what medicines to give. The doctor drops in personally every Friday. For emergencies, there is the rescue boat. These days, if weather permits, a helicopter can swoop in from the mainland.

"Sébastien was born on the island because my labor pains came on too quickly for me to be taken by boat to Brest," Jeannette said. "There are kids here who were born on the boat halfway across." She gave a little shrug. This was a small price to pay for paradise.

Meanwhile, Milo and the boys consulted the family bible, a small red timetable of the Brittany tides. If they left at noon on the dot, they would have two hours to haul in nets left the day before and lay out a new set for the following day. This was *lieu* season, which is only January and February, and they did not want to waste fishing time. Also, competitors from Le Conquet on the mainland snooped around to work their favorite grounds. If they did not keep claim to the territory with daily visits, it was up for grabs.

A MOTLEY CREW scrambled aboard the no-nonsense Bugale Mildiz. Sébastien and Aurélien were still recuperating from a postprandial conversation with friends that contributed substantially to the forty-five tons of glass garbage produced each year on the tiny island. Ludo and Nico, dressed like brothers in blue gum boots and nylon jackets, stepped even less lively.

The deck was stacked with nets in plastic bins and empty aluminum bins. I nosed around to see what I had gotten myself into. It was a reassuring sight. Though hardly fancy, the metal-hulled craft was built by Beneteau, fine French yachtmakers. The engine was a Belgian Baudouin, as good as exists anywhere.

Sébastien flicked a toggle on the wooden dash panel, and the heavy anchor hauled itself up onto the bow. He spun the small varnished wheel, heading us out in the same westward direction his Breton ancestors took to colonize Canada and a lot of the world beyond.

This was, however, a different age. If the dash panel looked homemade, it was flanked by a glowing sonar screen that depicted the ocean floor in coded colors. A separate radar screen showed schools of fish and algae patches. A large computer sat off to the left, its keys protected from salt-water by a plastic cowling. Its map program displayed every rock, shoal, and sandbank from Molène to Madagascar.

When I went back on deck, I found that the motley crew, now in yellow oilskins, had evolved into something closer to the accomplished cast of a ballet. Each moved with sure-footed grace, handling a specific task. Except for the occasional joke, no one talked. Everyone knew his own role, as well as the others'. When the boat pitched, and full nets were hauled up at high speed, even the jokes stopped.

The procedure was simple enough, in theory. Each net was about 250 yards long, plastic with large mesh to let smaller fish through. A row of cork floats held up the top end. Lead weights carried the bottom down toward the ocean floor. Bright orange buoys with black numbers marked the position. Ropes of carefully calculated lengths kept the nets in a position to spare the lobsters and crayfish. When it came time to go after crustaceans, or other sorts of fish, there were different nets to use.

Aurélien manned the big black drum that hauled up the nets. He directed the slimy mass into a plastic bin. Ludo extracted each fish, working its gills through the netting. If the fish was too big, he cut the plastic. The odd small shark got tossed on deck by the scuppers. An occasional flat sole, or plump bass, was flipped into a special bin. The lieu went onto Nico's black rubber operating table for disembowelment at lightning speed.

Nico rapidly examined each fish. If it was gnawed by crabs or somehow offensive to his discerning eye, it went over the side. Otherwise, it was tossed into the bin and kept fresh with seawater until it could be iced. Once, Nico inspected a fat lieu that seemed fine except for squid bites just below the gills. He whacked away the damaged part and put the rest in with the others. I wondered idly what would become of it.

Sébastien, meanwhile, maneuvered the boat. Against winds and waves, he had to keep the long trailing nets parallel to the hull so his brother could reel them aboard. A miscalculation, easy enough to make, was out of the question. At best, the propeller would chop the costly net into useless vermicelli. At worst, a rope would foul the prop and immobilize the boat. "No," he remarked, in his usual deadpan delivery, "it is not very easy."

On one recent voyage, Sébastien had to leave the wheel to help free a net. A lead-weighted float came loose and smacked him in the nose, knocking him nearly unconscious. He looked awful for a long time.

Aurélien could only help a little. He lost his balance during a violent pitch and sprained his wrist.

Above everything else, Sébastien has to find the fish. The fancy electronics help fine-tune the search, but he relies on the same basic instrument that had guided fishermen when Molène was first settled: the nose. He knows what each sort of fish does in every type of weather and current. Secrets have been passed along in the family forever, and each generation adds its own.

"These instruments are the last things we use, after following our own instinct," Sébastien said, in a rare loquacious moment.

Aurélien is the talker of the two. After one wild flurry of net-hauling, he relaxed on the stern with a cigarette. Clouds had blown off, leaving a cheery blue backdrop and, for January in the North Atlantic, a balmy breeze. He grinned even more than usual.

"Well, it's not always like this," he explained. "When freezing rain is pounding down, and it's black as hell at four in the morning, and the damned boat is pitching nearly sideways, and the net is caught, and you want to puke up your guts because you had too much wine at dinner, you might want to be doing something else. But even then . . ."

By his thirteenth birthday, Aurélien was a seasoned hand, working a full shift with his father and brother. Most of his friends, and all eligible wife prospects, have left the island. He gets away to see a girlfriend in Paris four or five times a year. Nights could be long, especially since he boycotts the only bar. The cantankerous owner, it seems, belted him in the chops once for no reason he could discern.

"I guess you could say sometimes this place drives me a little nuts," Aurélien allowed. "Still, I love this life. And I've got plans."

So far, the Masson brothers have done things Milo's way. Neither Mick Jagger nor Mozart helps them through long voyages because the salty old captain does not believe in loudspeakers on a fishing boat. But a new millennium is underway.

"We are setting up a system to sell directly via the Internet," Aurélien said. "It would be perfect. A chef anywhere in France could e-mail an order for so many lobsters, say, directly from us. We could dispatch them as soon as we got back to port. That way, we would know what orders we had even before we went out. They would get the freshest possible stuff, and we would make a lot more money."

Under the old system, he said, five or six middlemen got involved in the distribution process. And none of them had to go fishing in freezing rain.

"Why work your butt off for nothing?" Aurélien concluded, before heading back to the big black drum to work his butt off some more. "It makes no sense."

Like most fishing sorties, this was a mix of frenzied activity and idle hanging around. Once, a burly man in a speedboat approached, a good friend who had come to say hello, and left laughing under a hail of fish bladders.

"His job is to count seals for the natural reserve," Ludo explained. With money from the French government and the U.N. Educational, Scientific and Cultural Organization, gray seals and dolphins are protected in the waters around Molène. "There can't be that many seals," Ludo added, with a chuckle. "We only see one if it turns up dead in the nets."

When we got back to the jetty at 2:30 P.M., the plastic bins held 180 kilos of lieu, and another twenty of assorted smaller fish. During the summer, the Massons would sell the catch directly from its little boutique on the island. The rest of the year, fish on ice is sent to the market at Brest for auction.

Sébastien made a quick calculation. "This should come to about eight thousand francs," he said. "Not bad for two hours' work."

Not bad at all. But the boat cost two million francs. Nets run to 20,000 francs a month. Plus, there are social charges, insurance, taxes, fuel, and those days when the little crew catches nothing at all. There are easier ways to make a living.

THAT NIGHT, I learned the fate of that squid-damaged lieu Nico had put aside. Sébastien's wife, Magali, tossed it into a pot with water, salt, and laurel, and we ate it.

"Oh, you can mess around with court bouillon, or use some fancy recipe," Magali said, "but when fish is this fresh, all you have to do is eat it." After boiling for a half hour, the skin lifted off with a fork, leaving tender, succulent white flesh. She served buttered potatoes with it. It was magnificent.

The key word, Sébastien explained, is fresh. When the gills are still a deep pink, enough blood remains in the fish to give it its full flavor. "People say you should look to see if the eyes are clear," he said, "but you can have a blind fish who needs glasses that tastes perfectly good. The only real way to tell is to look at the color of the gills."

On ice, he said, you have a few days, maybe a week, after it is caught. After that, it goes fast. Fast-frozen fish stays edible, but it loses that fresh taste. That is only one of things independent fishermen have against trawlers.

"Des chalutiers," grumbled Aurélien, repeating the French word for trawlers. "They wreck everything."

With pen and paper, he made a quick sketch. Trawler nets are suspended from a long cable off the stern, with spreaders and fine-mesh net to scour the bottom. They scoop up fish and crustaceans of all species, sizes, and ages.

"The law says they have to toss back everything that is undersized or is a vulnerable species," he said, "but by then the thing is already dead. What's the point? Trawlers can ruin a fishing ground."

Molène fishermen know all about depleted waters. When the fish go, they're gone, and who knows when and if they will come back. Overfishing plays a role, but so do natural forces. Extended temperature changes, current shifts, or other phenomena have an impact. If bad luck is combined with poor resource management, it is tragedy. The lobster population crashed off Molène in the 1950's, sending many island families to the mainland for good. Between 1965 and 1970, a more general crash delivered a second blow.

Now there is fear that modern times, not only trawlers but also new European Union fishing rules, might deliver a coup de grâce. Under the Amsterdam Treaty, borders are all but dissolved. The twelve-mile international limit is preserved even among EU partners, but that is not a lot of water. Beyond that, French fishermen expect yet more competition from the English and Spanish, among others.

Complex new rules have been designed to limit the lengths of nets, the periods for fishing different species, and alter some other old practices. The good part is that this helps protect endangered grounds. The bad part is that the authors of the rules are functionaries sitting in Brussels.

"What the hell do they know about our waters?" Milo wondered. "True, you can't remain static and must progress with the times. In principle, it's good that someone is trying to do something. But if the result is a lot of silly rules that cost us more and earn us less, that will be the death of us."

The problem is that there is no organization to fight back. "The French fisherman is completely selfish," Milo said, "and he thinks of nothing beyond his own nets. That same spirit that makes us want to work on our own, free, is what keeps us from getting together. Sure, we have a lot of common interests. We just can't get together to express them."

Detailed studies by Ifremer monitor the state of affairs in the waters of Brittany, as well as all the other French coastal waters. But Masson & Sons don't need government scientists to draw them any graphs.

"In a word, less," Milo said, comparing today's technology-assisted catch with what he knew as a youngster. "Lobster, less. Crayfish, less. Lieu, less. Lotte, less. Saint Pierre, less. Skate, less. And everything else, less."

FISHING ASIDE, Molène is a useful bellwether for the mainland just barely visible from its eastern edge. If it can retain its distinct character, perhaps the rest of France can as well. So far, so good. Marcel Masson, the mayor, is extremely proud of his turf.

"I was born here, and left when I was sixteen to go see the world," Masson said. "When I got to be forty-two, I realized the world wasn't all that hot, and I came back here to stay."

That was in 1983. He spent five years fishing with Milo, his lifelong pal. Then he came ashore. Now he owns a grocery store, a franchise of a chain called "8-à-Huit." The name, like 7-Eleven, comes from the operating hours: 8:00 A.M. to 8:00 P.M. But Masson opens at 9:30 and closes for lunch. Afternoon hours are brief, if at all. On Tuesday and Thursday, the place is closed while he delivers groceries on his tractor.

"We make some money in summer, I guess, but otherwise this is more like a public service," Masson told me one morning. His son, Stéphane, sat behind one of the two checkout counters idly stroking his calico cat. Neither seemed disturbed by the lack of customers. Each knew exactly who would appear for their frozen bread—the closest the island came to having a bakery—and who was about to restock the coffee and sugar. Stéphane was about thinking about his upcoming nuptials to a woman named Masson.

Stress is not a Molène affliction. If topics of conversation are somewhat limited, time is not. No one fears being run over by any of the five trucklets and tiny cars. The few roads are hardly wider than a donkey, and none is longer than a mile. Motorbikes were banned because of the noise—and because they weren't necessary.

An hour later, I sat down with Masson at the town hall for a formal interview. His red parka was neatly arranged on a coat hook. Stocky and ruddy-faced, he nonetheless seemed comfortable elbow-deep in the papers necessary to do the people's business in modern France.

Running a normal municipality of Frenchmen was hard enough. But ever since Colbert decided to thank Molène for supplying Louis XIV's ships with skillful pilots 400 years ago, residents have paid no local taxes. Instead, the town council has to tap a dizzying array of subsidies, from Brest, Paris, and Brussels. Each requires budgeting and a bureaucratic fan dance.

"You cannot imagine how complicated and silly it can get," he said. I could, however, and did not make him explain it. Instead, I made a feeble joke: At least he didn't have to worry about car theft.

"That's happened," he replied, "but they didn't get very far."

The night that France won the World Cup, it seems, some over-oiled residents stole the town's ambulance-fire truck. Besides roaring around making noise, they managed to dent the roof. Someone repaired the vehicle with a sharp left hook. Masson decided to call it all a simple instance of borrowers neglecting to ask permission, since the titular owner—him—was not immediately available. Case closed.

That led to the obvious question: What about the gendarmes?

"That's me," he replied. "I used to be a gendarme on the continent, so I suppose I'm a logical choice. If there was ever any crime on Molène, I would deal with it."

The last incident that required a lawman's attention had happened a year and half earlier, he said. Four drunken youths from the continent chanced upon Nico Cariou at 1:00 A.M. down in the port. They beat him badly, for what Nico says was no particular reason. He was out of work for fourteen months with a broken wrist and battered nose.

"Nico is a big boy, all right, but he's not mean enough for a street fight," the sheriff of Molène explained. The four aggressors were still working their way through the mainland courts.

Except for building code matters, there are no longer many land disputes. Masson showed me an old aerial map of the island. Each square foot seemed to be planted in wheat, barley, or vegetables. Boundaries were so close, the joke went back then, that a cow standing still on one plot could graze on a second and fertilize a third.

Now no one plants. I saw rich fields overrun with brambles and ferns. A few sheep roamed the island, but the number was half as many as there had been a few weeks earlier before the night that Sébastien's Newfoundland retriever, Ido, got loose.

I must have passed some secret test, because the mayor shifted our conversation to the Council Chambers and opened the door to what is known to locals as *"le petit cabinet."* He poured a Brittany-sized pastis into a large glass and served himself. Soon after, Milo wandered in to join the conversation. On Molène time, we talked about the future of France.

When I asked if young families still ate well, the way families used to eat, the two Massons shook their heads in vigorous negatives. "No," each said, in impressive chorus. Nothing like McDonald's offered a siren song to the young, they said, but housewives seemed to be losing their passion for cooking.

"You should see all the frozen fish I sell in my store," the mayor said, shaking his head at the horror of it all. "Kids love it, and so do their parents. It's easy. There are no bones."

Milo nodded slowly, looking a little like he had been punched in the stomach.

This last thought stuck with me as I made a final stop on the island. I visited the kindergarten and primary school, where a total of fourteen pupils rattled around like BBs in the large old brick classrooms. The secondary school had even fewer students. After age sixteen, kids go to Brest to study.

Jacqueline Podeur, the teacher, had first come as a substitute in 1991 but was quickly wooed and won by an islander. It is a challenge to teach fourteen students at once when they range in age from two to eleven, she acknowledged. The hardest part, however, was trying to instill ambition.

"They just don't think beyond the island," she said. "I have one kid who is so smart, it is hard to believe. I told him he should be a surgeon, or anything he can dream of being. He wants to work for the Penn ar Bed, the company that runs the boats from here to Brest."

I asked Jacqueline about her pupils' diet, mentioning my chat with the two Massons. She gave a little shrug.

"Look, that's life," she said. "I have two kids of my own, and I work. I'm not going to get up at five to simmer something on the stove. When

I come back to make them lunch at midday, it's frozen food and the microwave. What else? There's no time."

No time? On the Île de Molène?

WHEN YOU DRIVE to Brittany on the main road from Paris, you don't have to watch for the sign. You only have to leave your window open. The polite term for what you smell is *lisier de porc*—that is, pig poo—and you cannot miss it.

The same time I was out fishing with the Massons, pork producers were working up to a serious protest over European competition and depressed prices. If fishermen in Brittany were not organized, farmers had no such problem. Any ministry official in Paris would far rather face a mountain of pig lisier than a pack of angry Breton farmers.

Occasionally, you can also hear Brittany. A tiny band of activists taps a wide vein of pro-autonomy sympathy. Breton separatists have been active, in one form or another, since the sixteenth century. These days, they sometimes make their point with explosives. And it was in the little town of Quévert, near Dinan in the heart of Brittany, where "Big Mac Attack" took on a grim new meaning.

On the morning of April 19, 2000, Laurence Turbec, twenty-eight, opened the back door of the McDonald's she managed. A bomb propelled her out into the McDrive lane, killing her instantly. Police traced the dynamite to l'Armée Revolutionnaire Bretonne. Apparently the fuse had malfunctioned; the bomb was supposed to go off at night when the place was empty. The only fatal victims of past ARB incidents were two terrorists who blew themselves up.

José Bové, the Roquefort peasant-intellectual, condemned the bombing and canceled plans to press his anti-McDo crusade in Brittany. McDonald's dropped its humorous "we're-French" ad campaign around the slogan, "Born in the USA, Made in France." Instead, new full-page newspaper ads declared: "*Assez!*" Enough.

Until then, the signature image of food fights in France had been Bove's manacled wrists held aloft in triumph, the martyr to *malbouffe* refusing bail to suffer for his society's sin. Suddenly, there was a real victim, a pretty young Frenchwoman caught in the crossfire. This was no longer amusing folklore.

Whatever anyone might think about McDonald's, eighty new locations were opening each year. The annual turnover, growing fast, approached two billion dollars. McDo, no longer solely the province of toddlers and teenagers, was as much a part of a new French culture as those millions of deliveries each year by Pizza Hut and Domino's.

Malbouffe was reality. The prestigious research institute INSEE reported in 1999 that eighty-seven percent of all Frenchmen enter a supermarket each year. Three-quarters of food budgets are spent in "*hypermarchés, supermarchés, et maxidiscounts.*"

But everywhere in France there were also the old specialities, produced by diehard devotees for plenty of people who still had the good taste to consume them. And Brittany had its oysters.

IN FACT, my oyster search took me to the Rue de Bretagne in Paris, and I ended up in the Charente-Maritime. It seems that it is possible to beat Brittany oysters.

"Here, see what you think," Philippe Privat said, knowing exactly what I would think. With a deft flick of his Laguiole oyster knife, he had popped the top shell off a *spéciale de claire*. It was large and firm, with a lovely green tint and a taste of hazelnut. And it was nearly a personal friend of Philippe's. In the three years between its appearance as an egg and its long ride in a bushel basket to his outdoor stand on the rue de Bretagne, he had handled it fifty times.

"Oysters," he declared, "are a damned lot of work." I accepted his invitation to come down and see how much. Not long after, standing hip-deep in a freezing offshore Atlantic tidepool, I decided he had understated it a bit.

France produces 145,000 tons of oysters in a good year, which is ninety-five percent of Europe's total and more than even the French can eat. Except for a small catch of the flat belons, or *Ostrea edulis*, they are all hatched and grown under controlled conditions. Philippe is known as a *paysan de mer*. Poetry aside, that is an apt description. He farms the sea.

French oyster farming starts in Normandy and the North Sea, about where pollution from the Seine Estuary tails off. It continues around the Brittany coasts, with a concentration in the south near the Gulf of Morbihan. More "*parcs à huîtres*" extend down the west-central coast, past the Île de Re. Oysters are also produced in the Mediterranean and in the waters of Arcachon-Aquitaine, off Bordeaux. But the prime oyster country is known as Marennes-Oléron. And Philippe's farm is in the heart of it, a half-hour boat ride from a tiny port on the Île d'Oléron.

I was first directed to Philippe Privat by the Saturday Afternoon Oyster and Sancerre Klatch, a group of friends who meet weekly to devastate shellfish. Their headquarters is a corner table at the Café du Progrès on the rue de Bretagne. Philippe's cheerful employee, José, normally shucks the oysters they shuttle into the Progrès by the platterful. But every other week the boss comes to Paris to make the rounds of his market stalls.

Philippe might have been a perfect Marlboro man except that he prefers small brown cigars. He is handsome in a weather-hammered way. A shock of hair, bleached by the sun, flies every which way in the wind. A great deal of laughter, and squinting into harsh light, has left crinkles around his eyes.

"Come down and work a while," Philippe told me, with an innocent grin worthy of Tom Sawyer. "You'll love it."

We postponed the first trip because Philippe hurt his back. On the phone, after a quick thumb through the tide tables, he suggested an upcoming Tuesday.

"I'll be all right by then," he assured me, basing the opinion on necessity rather than anything medical. A one-man show, he had nowhere to call in sick.

It was nightfall when I reached the Île d'Oléron, on the Atlantic coast south of La Rochelle, just in time for a briefing and a stuffing.

"How many oysters can you eat?" Philippe's wife, Marylou, asked. Any number up to four figures would not have surprised her, but I settled for a mere dozen. Philippe shucked an extra dozen for each of us, just in case. Neither he nor Marylou had any idea how far back their bivalve lineages went. Each knew their grandfathers were oystermen. Both attacked the mound of half shells as if it was their first taste of something wonderful.

Marennes-Oléron oysters are prized because they are refined—affinées— for at least several weeks as a last step in saltwater ponds known as claires. For taste and texture, that makes all the difference.

Raw is the recipe of choice on Oléron, wolfed down without so much as a squirt of lemon juice. But that is a tiny fraction of the possibilities. Just for starters, Marylou handed me a small brochure with twenty recipes.

Le Ratelier restaurant in Breuillet, for instance, offers *papillote d'huîtres au foie gras frais*. Oysters are sealed in aluminum foil with leeks, an escalope of foie gras, pepper, a lemon slice, a soup spoon of crème fraîche, and another of Sauternes. After twelve minutes in a medium oven, they're done.

Chefs' favorite ingredients include truffles with Champagne sabayon, reinette apples, Madras curry, sorrel, lobster and crab, bacon, aromatic herbs . . . The list goes on for a long time. Most recipes feature *fleur de sel*, the flavorful queen of salts scraped from the sea's edge on islands along the Charente coast. But that's another story altogether.

The oyster-raising process is complex. First the eggs are placed in tubes and arranged on steel-bar tables fixed to the sea floor within carefully delineated concessions. At high tide, the platforms disappear under water. When tides recede, the sea is shallow enough for oyster farmers to walk among their planted rows.

After the first year, young oysters are stitched into black plastic-mesh pouches about the size of cement sacks. These are laid side by side on the tables and tied down with rubber straps. When oysters are three years old, they are ready to be sorted and sold. In the Marennes-Oléron basin, however, first they must be affinées.

Pouches are stacked on the bow of the oyster men's narrow boats and brought to shore. Then they are forklifted or trucked to the claires, ponds lined with impermeable clay that are regularly emptied, cleaned, and resealed. For no particular reason, about half of the oysters immersed in claires take on a distinctive green, and the rest do not. All end up with a certain crunch and that delicate finish of hazelnut.

A normal fine de claire seldom spends more than two weeks in the pond. Red-label (label rouges) fines require at least a month of affinage under strict conditions. Their density cannot be more than twenty per square meter. Each shell must be handsomely rounded, with a green tint inside. Spéciales are selected for their larger size, finer texture, salinity, sweetness, and meatiness.

The prestige oyster is a *pousse en claire*. It spends four to eight months in the pond, sharing a square meter with no more than four others. The result is an almost audible crunchiness, with a strong flavor of terroir. It is harvested only until late fall and usually cannot be bought for any amount of money. The trick is to have an oysterman for a friend.

Compared to Île de Molène, the Île d'Oléron is a bustling metropolis. It extends twenty miles from an old fortress built by Vauban to rural vineyards at the far end. A year-round population up in the thousands zips back and forth to the mainland over a two-mile-long viaduct, the longest bridge in France. The communities of La Tremblade and Marenne, facing the island, are also pocked with refining ponds. Altogether, the region has 7,000 acres of sea farms and 7,500 acres of claires. It amounts to the largest oyster-producing center in the world.

Thousands of small independents work in whatever way serves them best. The Privats sell their own production. Each Thursday, Marylou drives five hours to Antony, in the outskirts of Paris, where she has a market stall. Philippe, or their twenty-four-year-old son, Peter, goes along to deliver the rest. A few long-time employees, Spaniards from the same family, sell oysters at several Paris locations. On Sunday night, the oystermobile comes home empty.

Oyster farming goes on without a pause. That business about months with an "R" in them was never much of a guide. Like kosher laws, that originated with practicality. In pre-refrigeration times, it was wise to avoid perishables. But oysters lay their eggs during the summer, and they are too milky for many people's taste. Then again, others prefer it that way.

PHILIPPE TOOK ME OUT in the dead of December, decidedly an R month. For a blustery winter morning, eight o'clock did not seem so early. We stopped first at his oyster shack to pick up some gear. Like the others, he works from a simple hangar with a dock on the narrow channel and a large room for sorting and packing oysters. A small room off to the side, with a stove and bottles of cheer, is for keeping the books or finishing off the day with friends. That morning, it was occupied by an oyster-loving black cat and a colleague who had come with news.

"Be careful, the government creeps are controlling like crazy this year," he said. "Some idiot taxman must be on a tear." Christmas was approaching, and labor inspectors were out. They knew what to expect. Most oystermen work alone; the economics do not allow for hired help. For the holidays, however, they need extra hands to meet the demand. If they employ someone legally, their cost is almost double, and they may be trapped by paperwork into providing a permanent job.

Philippe shrugged.

"I declare my help," he said. "What can I do? If I was trying to get rich, this is not what I would be doing. You work like an animal all day long, every day, for less than the minimum wage. This is smart? Hey, it's a life."

Our next stop was Chez Xav, a cluttered little café, magazine shop, and pool hall that oystermen regard as their clubhouse. Xav showed up from Paris four years ago and got himself accepted in record time. That morning was the usual. He unlocked his door a few minutes late, looking as bedraggled as the bedclothes he had just abandoned. With a friendly grunt, he ran a hand through his mane of prematurely silver hair. He slipped a Rolling Stones CD into a boombox tray. And the Île d'Oléron awoke to black coffee and Brown Sugar.

Eventually, we went to work. Philippe's boat, *Soccer*, is typical: twelve feet long, narrow, with a seventy-five-horse outboard motor and a tiny little wheelhouse. An old sock plugged up a hole in the shattered Plexiglas windscreen. A blue gas bottle served as a stove. A pair of Mylar glasses was stuck in a corner although the next scheduled solar eclipse was not for another eighty years. On deck, Philippe had stacked rows of black pouches to be placed in the water.

We put on rubber hip boots and headed into the channel. Suddenly, it all made sense. A flaming orange-red sun rose halfway on the horizon, at the end of the long mainland bridge. Pinks and purples reflected off gently rippled water. The air was frigid, but bracing, fresh with tiny droplets of rain from a few scattered clouds in a sky of dark blue. A buddy of Philippe's waved and grinned as he flashed past, unladen that morning. This was, as Philippe said, a life.

As A LIFE, it certainly had antecedents. Oyster peddling dates back somewhere into Antiquity. Greeks ate them with honey. They played a key role in the original democracy. When legislators banished someone, they wrote his name on an oyster shell; hence, ostracized. Romans preserved oysters in salt. Casanova ate them for breakfast, helping along their reputation for lifting the male spirit.

Parisians have eaten oysters for two thousand years, since the capital was called Lutèce. They were fished from the Seine estuary. By the Sun King's reign in the 1700's, Paris already had at least two thousand shellfish mongers, whose oysters were brought from the coast as fast as horses could haul them. This was not always fast enough.

Too much demand wiped out the Normandy oyster beds in the nineteenth century, and Paris waited a century until farming brought back enough stocks. The old habit is back. A recent study found that fifty-three percent of all French families start their Christmas meal with oysters along with the foie gras and smoked salmon.

Before long, Philippe was threading his way among hundreds of spindly, twisted tree trunks stuck in the sea floor in rows and rectangles. They marked carefully delineated beds.

"Each one of these concessions is leased from the government by the year, but the rights to it continue from father to son," Philippe explained. "You can cede your right to someone else, if you want. Not long ago, there were no concessions to be had. Now, sad to say, there are plenty."

It was the old story again. This sort of life, like that of cheese makers, snail ranchers, speciality farmers, and old-time chefs, was getting to be a calling only for the committed.

"The real problem is competition," he said. "Back in the early 1970's, the wholesale price per kilo was eight francs. Now it is eleven francs. That is a three-franc raise over twenty years. Compare that to how everything else has gone up. The demand for oysters continues, but too many big outfits are out there producing them in quantity."

Then there were specific problems, such as oyster rustlers.

"These SOBs steal from their own friends and neighbors," Philippe said. "Happens all the time. Guys come out at night when it is impossible to see them, and they just haul up pouches that someone else worked to produce."

Or oysterpeckers and killer snails.

"These birds, the *pic-huîtres*, just sweep out of the sky and crack the top shell so they can eat the oyster," Philippe explained. "But the real problem is the *bigorneau-perceur*, a sea snail that drills holes through the shell by secreting an acid. They can get to be a real plague, and there is nothing you can do about them except pick them up, one at a time."

All in all, the ecological balance is alarmingly fragile. No oysters were taken from the Marennes-Oléron basin until 1868 when Le Morlaisien ran aground. The little craft was bringing *huîtres creuses* from Portugal to Brittany, when storms in the Gascon Gulf pushed it off course. Sailors dumped the oysters overboard to lighten their load. The rest is history. In 1972,

however, an epizootic disease wiped out the population of [...]
ters in the basin. They were replaced by the Japanese varie[...]
today.

Philippe's sea fields are as carefully tended as Bordeaux vine[...]
of rubber inner tube move with the currents to sweep the san[...]
This makes it easy to take away the snails, mussels, and assorted [...]
[...] oysters from their business of growing.

One after the other, he heaved the pouches from the boat dec[...]
rows of steel-rod tables I helped him strap them down with metal [...]
on rubber strips, scrambling to keep up with his pace.

He leaned down and scooped up a flat, round oyster growing on [...]
own in the mud.

"This is a [...]" he said, tossing it in the bucket for a later sampling.
"These flat oysters are the best, but they're getting rare. They find them
growing naturally in Brittany but not here."

Philippe used to produce thirty tons of oysters a year, and he delivered
them to a wholesaler for eleven francs a kilo. Now he does twenty tons
which he trucks to Paris and sells in markets for thirty-three francs a kilo.
Adding it all up, there is not much difference in profit. But it is a little
less work.

"For every ton I produce, I have to handle fifty tons," Philippe said,
grimacing at the thought. He means that each oyster must be picked
up and moved fifty times, for one reason or another, during its three-
year life span. By that reckoning, he shifts a thousand tons of shellfish a
year.

Peter helps sometimes, but he would rather sell in the market than
slog in the mud. He prefers his computer screen to either. No family decisions have been made, but Philippe may be the last of the line.

"That's how it is going everywhere," Philippe said when we knocked
off for a chat with his friend Paul Vallade, hip deep in water. "In five years'
time, we'll see twenty-five percent fewer oystermen out here. In ten years,
no one."

Vallade nodded his downcast accord.

"It's not only us," he said. "The other day, some government man saw
Jean-Pierre's grandmother picking up loose wood around his vineyard. The
guy asked her what she was doing and she said, real proud, she was helping
her grandson. Clack, he took her name, all the details, and hit Jean-Pierre
with a fat fine. Undeclared labor."

Philippe shook his head.

"I tried marketing oysters to some supermarket chains," Vallade continued. "It's ridiculous. You've got to pay off the buyers, this agent, that agent . . ." The verb he used was *arroser*, a lovely French term used to mean watering plants, celebrating a happy moment with liquids, or greasing the wheels of a transaction. Bribe might be too crude. But the cost is the same.

Every season, the men agreed, some other problem seems to arise. Within weeks, in fact, Philippe and his friend would be facing drama neither one could have imagined as we stood out in the placid water.

First, a tanker spilled three million gallons of crude oil off the Brittany coast, fouling rich oyster beds to the north. The fringes of it would reach Oléron. Whatever was spoiled or saved, people would be afraid of oysters for a long time to come.

And then a storm hit the Charente-Maritime coast with such speed that no one had time to give it a name. Winds reaching 120 miles an hour smashed boats and tore roofs off sheds. Waves tore loose the rubber ties they had painstakingly affixed, carrying away whole pouches of oysters. Some of Philippe's friends would be nearly wiped out. He would lose many of his maturing oysters.

But that would come later.

"Now it's regulations from Brussels," Philippe said. "We're supposed to have refrigeration at all the markets. Pretty soon, I'll have to get rid of my stand on the rue de Bretagne. They don't want people selling out of doors."

He shook his head again. It was not as if oystermen had caused mass deaths by selling out of doors over the last two thousand years, under far less ideal circumstances than today's.

In fact, the only death noted in a thick booklet published by the Comité National de la Conchyliculture is a suicide: "King Louis XIV's chef, the celebrated Vatel, killed himself because a cart of oysters did not arrive in time for His Majesty's dinner."

We had to wait another half hour for the water to rise enough for boats to clear the mudbanks. Philippe and his pal talked on and on, along the same vein, and I listened with half an ear. By then two things were crystal clear: Small-scale oyster farming is a mug's game. And both of them would be back at it, happy in their way, with the next tide.

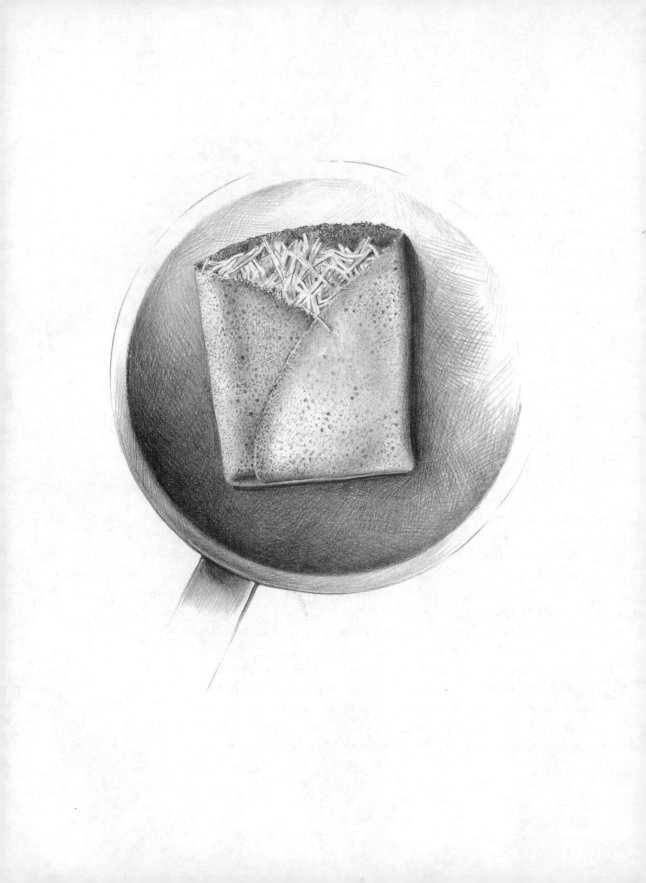

—◁◇◇▷—

NINETEEN

Sunday Lunch

FRANÇOIS VATEL DIED over more than oysters. He worked for the princes of Condé, not Louis XIV. He was maître d'hôtel, not chef. But the oystermen's pamphlet caught the spirit of that morning in April 1671. Vatel believed he was about to dishonor the French table in the eyes of the Sun King.

Two thousand guests at the Château de Chantilly expected a finale dinner to the weekend party of the decade. A foul-up had marred the first night's dinner. Two tables of unexpected hangers-on ran short of roast meat. No one else seemed to notice, but Vatel did. And now everything was on hand, but the seafood carts from Normandy were late. Vatel went to his room. When the crates of oysters and fish rattled up moments later, his staff went to seek his orders. They found Vatel in a pool of blood, impaled upon his sword.

The party, of course, continued as planned.

"Those who presided over the preparations of these grand feasts became men of consideration, and not without reason," Brillat-Savarin wrote long after the fact, describing Vatel's role at Chantilly. "They had to blend greatly diverse qualities, such as the genius to invent, the knowledge to achieve, the judgment to proportion, the sagacity to discover, the firmness to be obeyed, and the exactness to disappoint no one."

France loves the story of Vatel, however it is told. For people who revere "the long memory," it affirms a self-image, and it says as much about their present and future as their past.

Two letters from the Marquise de Sévigné to her daughter, Madame de Grignan, spell out the details. Condé princes had lost royal favor ever since their parents' wedding, arranged by King Henri IV, took a nasty turn. The king, it seems, lusted after the 15-year-old bride he chose for Henri II de Bourbon-Condé. But the prince was in love with her. The day of the marriage, the couple fled France before the king could exercise his *droit du seigneur* and join the honeymoon. Now a generation had changed. Louis XIV would attend a gala three-day weekend to honor Le Grand Condé at the family's magnificent château, with its gardens and forests laid out by Le Nôtre. Until two weeks before, however, the king did not fix a date.

Vatel was ordered to put it all together. He had to lodge, feed, and entertain several thousand nobles and their retinues, including a monarch who believed he ruled the world. He could only guess to the nearest several hundred who might appear.

Vatel did not sleep for eleven nights, at times personally fluffing up pillows in rooms created from hastily vacated barns. He sent orders to every reliable supplier of flesh, fowl, fruits, vegetables, spices, and wine. And fast runners went to every port within reach to secure the freshest possible catch.

His masters were thrilled. But he worried, the way three-star chef-propriétaires worry today. The goal was perfection, but surprise guests missed a course. Then the fireworks were a let-down, through no human failing. He had counted on a clear night-sky backdrop. But the moon shined too brightly in places and clouds fell too low in others. All he needed was a last straw.

A BOOK ENTITLED *Vatel and the Birth of Gastronomy* appeared on French shelves as the twentieth century ended, among many that obliquely searched the national soul. Another, however, went straight to the point.

"France," Alain Duhamel pronounced in his *fin-de-millénaire* essay, *Une Ambition Française*, "has become a melancholic nation. She doubts herself, her future, her identity, her weight, her capacity to be able to continue forging her destiny, and even to model a livable society. She remembers with bitter nostalgia the time when all of Europe called her the Great Nation, when she cut a figure of political power and military might, of incomparable cultural reference."

Duhamel, a durable journalist known equally for his trenchant analysis and his bug eyes, described a France "obsessed with decline." Borrowing the phrase of historian Pierre Nora, he said the French were now less of a nation than a *nation-mémoire.*

This would be a crushing indictment were it not meant as the preamble to a bigger point. If Duhamel starts his thesis with an eclipsed France slipping from the stage, he ends with yet a greater France, square in the floodlights of a bigger theater.

"Europe is a necessity," he concludes. "It also constitutes a unique opportunity for France. Far from putting in peril the national identity, it on the contrary offers a historic role, an ambition up to its measure, a prestigious project. France has always had the passion of influence, the right to recognition of its gifts to others, well beyond its frontiers. This essential dream, the flattering Utopia, this national design shaped to the twenty-first century, is Europe."

Maybe. Frenchmen may have thought up the idea of a European Union, but Germans, among others, have also made it their own. Communications are tearing down everyone's borders at the speed of light. The world speaks its languages, certainly French, with an increasingly American accent. Molière's old lexicon now includes such words as *bitoubi* and *bitoussi*, the "B2B" (business-to-business) and "B2C" (business-to-consumer) of the Internet.

The nation that over centuries brought its civilizing mission to every continent on earth reached 2000 with only a few scattered shards of empire. Even Africa, its last zone of influence, is slipping away.

In May 2000, the last *franc* notes rolled off the press. Years earlier, the French had abandoned those lovely pale yellow 500-franc notes, the size of bedsheets on which Blaise Pascal looked as if he were suffering a migraine. Now even the new no-nonsense green bills are to be replaced by the euro, common currency of a different kind of Europe. Unemployment had fallen back below ten percent, and growth rates were climbing. A new economy promised dramatic change. France has always changed dramatically. Fernand Braudel, the French century's great historian, traced hand wringing over national identity to the earliest foundations of the nation.

This time, though, the battle rages over the holiest ground, the family dinner table. In the midst of these broader themes, the moment calls out for a Brillat-Savarin: Yes, yes, but what about lunch?

As I suspected at the beginning, my questions had produced articulate and convincing nonanswers. I was left with that self-mocking phrase beloved to journalists expected to analyze events before they happen: The future lies ahead.

Putting my thoughts together, I went back to those essays of Edith Wharton's, from when she visited a France fighting for its life in World War One. Hardly a dewy romantic, she missed no French foible. And, eight decades ago in another time, she captured the essence of today's angst.

If a Frenchman amasses less money than an American might, Wharton wrote, his life is enriched by something worth much more: "Time, in the middle of the day, to sit down to an excellent luncheon, to eat it quietly with his family, and to read his paper afterward; time to go off on Sunday and holidays on long pleasant country rambles; time, almost any day, to feel fresh and free enough for an evening at the theater, after a dinner as good as his luncheon."

And this is possible, Wharton observed, because French civilization is based upon an innate taste and sense of proportion, intangible values that have always outweighed what might be more efficient in commercial terms. This sense of suitability is not a skill you can acquire, like learning to play the flute, she added. It comes in your genes and your upbringing.

"It is the reason, for instance, why the French have beautiful stone quays along the great rivers on which their cities are built," Wharton wrote in *French Ways and Their Meaning*. "Any American with eyes to see, who compares the architectural use to which Paris has put the Seine with the wasteful degradation of the unrivaled twin river-fronts of New York, may draw his own conclusion as to the sheer material advantage of taste in the creation of a great city."

That, of course, is the heart of it. Food may be the metaphor, but the picture is larger. A new mentality focused on the narrow short term threatens what was always the grand French view. Once even a Napoléon had difficulty moving things around. Now it is far easier for small men with power problems to change the face of France.

On New Year's Eve 1999, I watched lights blaze around the glorious creation of a nineteenth-century French engineer. On the Seine banks, the Eiffel Tower spewed symbolic bubbles over a planet in need of cheer, radiating the image that everyone would remember as the dawn of a millennium. France trembled with pride. *Rayonnement*—radiance to a benighted world—has been at the root of French grandeur forever. Here it was again.

Yet less than a week later, a few faceless French engineers took from the Seine, and the world beyond, perhaps its most beautiful and stirring piece of quai.

The idea, noble enough by itself, was to make another stop for the boat-bus that plies the Seine. This stop might also be used for tour boats, which already cluster at a half-dozen commercial docks. Several perfectly good, and harmless, sites were proposed. Instead, the engineers insisted on tearing out the heart of the last floating village on a river which has had floating villages for two thousand years.

I knew the facts well because I had been forced to send the letter that sealed the village's fate.

IN THE 1980's, I moved onto an old wooden boat by the Alexandre III Bridge, with its gilt cherubs and bronze lamp posts. To hurried passersby, our small community looked like nothing more than a bunch of houseboats. To anyone with the romantic spirit to notice, it was a living village of compelling charm, a gem in a country hardly short on splendor.

Soon I saw how the 150 people in the old port maintained a link back to the first boat-dwelling Parisii who founded the city. I wrote a book, *The Secret Life of the Seine*, and saw from reaction to it how much this beloved bit of Paris belonged to the rest of the world as well.

I was always surprised by Parisians' looks from the quai at *dimanche midi*, when boat people had their Sunday lunch. Envy might be expected, but there seemed to be none. We were enjoying life, and people felt a vicarious pleasure. The boats amounted to a floating museum: century-old French canal barges, Dutch tjalks with varnished leeboards, English gigs that helped save Frenchmen at Dunkirk.

Tourists had a similar reaction. My friend Barbara Smolian said it best: "Every time I see that village, with real people living real life on the river in the center of Paris, it makes me smile. Anywhere else, they would pass a law against it, make some big ugly dock, or floating monstrosity. But this is France."

The port's thirty-year concession expired, and a government agency called Voies Navigables de France assumed control. VNF engineers wanted to put a dock in the heart of the village. The idea was first to make a stop for boat-buses and then bring in other large new craft which would likely block the view of pedestrians who frequented the quai.

We resisted, pointing out two alternative sites where the boat-buses could dock without destroying the village. The quai was protected by Unesco as a world heritage site, we pointed out. The engineers insisted. When we asked for mediation, one sneered, "With who, the Dalai Lama? The Pope?"

Soon enough, our small affair grew to a blinding example of how France is still run in the twenty-first century. The mayor of Paris said he wanted to save the port, but under a holdover royalist system, he could not. He had the fanciest office in Paris, but very limited power.

A French senator on the Cultural Affairs Committee asked Prime Minister Lionel Jospin to intervene, citing "a unique living patrimony." Jospin directed his transportation minister to make a study. The minister's office wrote to confirm a study was underway.

The petty functionary who had sneered before laughed off this latest development. This was political stroking, he told one boat owner. By the time any study is done, the dock will be in place. For good measure, he noted that if they towed us away, we would be taken to a punishment pound far up the Marne, banned from returning to Paris.

I went to see the regional director of VNF, the engineers' boss. He had read my book, he said, and wanted to meet me. In his office, I noticed the VNF magazine, just published. Meant to show the Seine at its best, he had put on the cover the very port he had ordered destroyed.

A few days before Christmas 1999, my neighbors and I received a formal order to leave immediately. On the deadline date, the Seine was in flood, and we needed several more days to move without grave danger to the boats. "That's not my problem," the legal officer said. "You're costing us money."

The legal officer spewed abuse at boat owners for questioning his power. When I mentioned the process of appeal and the prime minister, he laughed. "You think I need to ask the Pope when I want to move a boat?"

I was back in Conques, where a tiny band of petty bureaucrats changed the face of France by simple default in the structures of power.

We had a trump card, I knew, according to the French way. Someone on our side had political leverage over somebody who could have overruled VNF. When I mentioned this to a reporter friend, he laughed. "You've spent so much time reporting on the system," he said, "that now you're going to work it."

I wasn't. Joan of Arc heard voices from God, but I didn't. French neighbors who might have persisted chose not to fight on the presumption that today the small people always win. We moved, and the ugly dock was built. Edith Wharton would have had a seizure.

All was not lost, however. The regional director of Voies Navigables de France had fed me a very nice lunch.

AMONG MY FRENCH FRIENDS, no one seemed surprised at such a clear case of official dysfunction. A cynical disregard for the state seeped in from all sides.

Newspapers played on a popular new restaurant term, *le self-service*, when referring to the giant quasi-official oil company, Elf Aquitaine, linked to unending scandal. "L'Elf service" implicated Roland Dumas, who as Chief Justice was the fifth-ranking man in power. As judges gathered evidence to bring him to trial, his mistress described financial foibles in a self-mocking book called *The Whore of the Republic*. Next a successful finance minister resigned under an Elf-related cloud. Then evidence showed that François Mitterrand, as France's Socialist president, had funneled money via Elf to the campaign of Helmut Kohl, the conservative German chancellor. That is only part of it.

In the end, with all of the evidence on the table, one is tempted toward pessimism. France is not what it used to be, and neither is the world it once sought to civilize. The people who at one time put human worth and passion ahead of blind function seem to be fading into history. A seamless global economy of single currencies and negotiated compromise has no room for that hoary concept, *l'exception française*.

But France, most likely, will always be different. Take, for instance, the Paris truck driver who blocks traffic for forty minutes while he unloads at a leisurely pace and then flips the finger at anyone who objects. This is a country with a special number to call to find out the day's strikes and protest disturbances.

Remember the Air France pilots who struck just as teams and spectators headed to a World Cup the French had courted for decades? They rebelled again in 2000. Air France executives decided that if their crews spoke English to the tower at Paris airports, there would be less chance that pilots from every other country might get confused and crash in mid-air. Air France pilots insisted on French.

In sum, any society in which *égoïste* is a compliment will be with us forever. And this may be good news. Edith Wharton had it exactly right. In a nation of extremes, it also works the other way. What other people, anywhere, are as rich in the things they hold dear to their own hearts?

I HAD MADE no prior plan for a last foray to close out my research. As it happened, I dropped in to see Aubert de Villaine of Romanée-Conti, near Nuits-Saint-Georges.

His sixty-three acres of vineyards, the world's most fabled grapes, had performed yet another miracle. Disastrous spring rains had seemed a curse until summer, when the sun blazed without letup. Grapes grew fat and full of juice, thanks to water trapped in the hardscrabble soil. And 1999 promised to be a fabulous vintage. God had not left France.

"It makes you want to light a candle in church," de Villaine said. He would not have to go far to do it. The Vosne-Romanée village church steeple towers over his old offices. Oaken barrels of his finest wines rest in vaults under a nearby chapel built by the monks who tended the vineyards a millennium ago.

The vines, in neat rows headed by weathered stone crosses at the edge of the village, were first planted in Roman times. De Villaine's family, along with the Leroys, whom his grandfather brought in on a fifty-fifty basis, is only the fourth set of owners of the domain since the original Saint-Vivant monks. The first owners were the princes of Conti and Condé, the same nobles Vatel served at Chantilly.

Internal troubles had caused bad blood among owners, but de Villaine steered the domain toward peace. A friend of Alexandre de Lur Saluces at Château d'Yquem, he breathed in sharply when I asked if Arnault or someone similar had come to call. "I think these big investors are a little afraid of the system in Burgundy, thank God," he replied.

"We are very sensitive to the roots of Romanée-Conti," de Villaine said. He was speaking literally as well as figuratively. He knows about each gram of manure that is applied every three years to replenish the ancient soil.

This soft-spoken man with bald head and gentle manner also knows exactly where human values and passion fit into the scheme of things. Deep in another cave under Vosne-Romanée, he showed me the last dusty bottles of Romanée-Conti left in his racks, and we surveyed dwindling stocks of other vintages. Millennium celebrations drank deeply of the domain's great wines already on the market or in private stocks, and he had to turn down pleas to release additional bottles.

But the miracle vines on what must be the world's costliest fragment of real estate have been around for a long time. There will be more.

The good news is sometimes bittersweet. One night I noticed a television program listing I could hardly pass up: "L'Oie de Toulouse." It was a half-hour documentary on a goose in Toulouse. That beloved traditional variety of fowl is endangered by modern times. Males are too faithful to their mates. Some prefer the company of other male geese. As a result, females do not lay enough eggs. Hybrid varieties make much more money.

Yet farmers in the Gers protect their Toulouse geese, even at a loss. "We grew up with beauties like this one, and they are part of our lives," one said, fondling an impressive wattle and pointing with pride at the fatty folds that reached to her feet.

And plenty of good news is buoyed by fortuitous economics. Lyon, for instance, thrives with the sort of eatcries that long ago made its reputation as the heartland of family-style cooking. Philippe Delorme, the 34-year-old chef at L'Amphitryon, feeds a full house every night with a three-course meal. The price is fifteen dollars. L'Amphitryon's style is "bouchon lyonnais," although to qualify as the real thing it would need a huge table covered in a checkered cloth, where people share local specialties from huge bowls.

Delorme is a master at *bavette a l'échalôte*, a juicy steak aged to purple and smothered in shallots cooked in butter, caramelized with sugar and flavored with juice from the beef.

No amount of alarming numbers dim the view in the village of Vonnas, not far from Lyon. Jean-Louis Blanc and his wife set up an inn there in 1872, serving soup to poultrymen who came to the Thursday market. La Mère Blanc was soon a legend. Their son, Adolph, and his wife, Elisa

A Goose
in Toulouse

——

283

Gervais, took over the place. In 1933, Curnonsky, the prince of gastronomes, declared Elisa Blanc the finest cook in the world. Two generations later, Georges Blanc has turned the whole center of Vonnas into an haute cuisine pilgrimage site.

One large Blanc shop sells gourmet take-away and tinned delicacies. Another offers every manner of utensil, from simple whisks to restaurant-sized cast iron stoves. The old lemonade factory is a Blanc café. But the centerpiece is a makeover of the original inn. Signed photos of obscure singers and great statesmen line the walls, each effusive in praise of dinner. The library has all the Michelin Guides back to 1900—none was published between 1939 and 1945—and Blanc's three stars are in the last twenty.

The menu makes for wonderful reading, but I got no farther than *"poulet de Bresse comme au G7."* This was the dish Blanc created in 1996 for a summit meeting at Lyon. One of his incomparably tender chickens is roasted with garlic and served in a creamy sauce of foie gras.

Food apart, my favorite feature was a picture window opening onto the kitchen. As you walk to your table, you see all the feverish order that goes into a large roomful of perfect meals. And at the heart of it, you can spot two young Blancs—Frédéric and Alexandre—ready to take over for yet another generation.

MY LAST MEAL on the road was a Saturday lunch, on Christmas Day. Alain Ducasse had just opened L'Hostellerie de l'Abbaye de la Celle, and my sister, Jane, was visiting for the holidays. It was the natural choice.

We ate like nobles, from the first course to the tenth. We had tender chicken breast molded with foie gras on a bed of crisp winter greens laced with truffles. A rich risotto, perfectly done, blended truffles with violet artichokes and a suggestion of onions. As yet another starter, there was a ragoût of tender sea scallops and plump warm oysters with spinach shoots and finely cut vegetables.

The young milk-fed veal, roasted in a sautoir to outside crispness and juicy pink center, was sown with bits of black truffle to achieve a taste only over-colored hyperbole could begin to approach.

Cheese followed, of course, along with three lush desserts and baskets of the pastry chef's nougat, chocolates, and cookies.

The waiters, smooth and eager, made no effort to whip up reverent mystique. This was only lunch. "I think we'll be eating like this for a long time to come," observed a young waiter named Michel with ambitions in the food trade. "But there'll be room for everything else. When we drove here the first time, my four-year-old daughter had a tough time in the car, wondering what was to become of her life. Then when we rounded a corner, she spotted the McDonald's up the road and yelled, 'Saved!' "

Thierry Blanc, the Ducasse deputy assigned to assure perfection at La Celle, hovered discreetly to the side. At one point between courses, he took me down to the twelfth-century crypt which is being fitted out as a reception room. We ended up in the fumoir, the smoking lounge he had stocked with long, fat Cohibas and a full range of Monte Cristos.

Sitting there puffing happily and sipping a pousse-café for the road, I thought back to Brillat-Savarin. The old savant-gourmand had linked the destiny of nations to their feeding habits, and concluded: "The pleasure of the table reigns among other pleasures, and it is the last to console when others are lost."

And I caught a whiff of Vatel among the old stones at La Celle. This was no Chantilly. Yet the aim was programmed grandeur. Ducasse was not a chef, but rather one of those considerable men that Brillat-Savarin described. With six Michelin stars and adulation swirling about him, he personified, as Vatel once did, honor to the French table.

It all worked, exactly right. But I wonder what would have happened had the truffles not shown up that morning.